Cotton Mather.

TO

WINSLOW LEWIS, M.D.

THE EFFICIENT AND JUSTLY POPULAR

PRESIDENT OF THE NEW ENGLAND HISTORIC-
GENEALOGICAL SOCIETY,

THIS WORK IS INSCRIBED BY

THE EDITOR.

THE HISTORY

OF

𝕶ing 𝕻hilip's 𝖂ar,

By the Rev. INCREASE MATHER, D.D.

ALSO, A

HISTORY OF THE SAME WAR,

By the Rev. COTTON MATHER, D.D.

TO WHICH ARE ADDED

An Introduction and Notes,

By SAMUEL G. DRAKE,

Late Prefident of the New England Hiftoric-Genealogical Society.

ALBANY:
PRINTED FOR THE EDITOR, BY J. MUNSELL.

1862.

HERITAGE BOOKS
2019

HERITAGE BOOKS
AN IMPRINT OF HERITAGE BOOKS, INC.

Books, CDs, and more—Worldwide

For our listing of thousands of titles see our website
at
www.HeritageBooks.com

A Facsimile Reprint
Published 2019 by
HERITAGE BOOKS, INC.
Publishing Division
5810 Ruatan Street
Berwyn Heights, Md. 20740

Originally printed for the editor
by J. Munsell
Albany
1862

— Publisher's Notice —
In reprints such as this, it is often not possible to remove blemishes from the original. We feel the contents of this book warrant its reissue despite these blemishes and hope you will agree and read it with pleasure.

International Standard Book Numbers
Paperbound: 978-1-55613-417-3
Clothbound: 978-0-7884-8996-9

PREFATORY BY THE EDITOR.

THE very great Scarcity of the *Brief History* of Philip's War, by the REV. INCREASE MATHER, D. D., has long been experienced, and a Defire has often been expreffed by Many that it fhould be reprinted. So great indeed was its Scarcity, that even hiftorical Students could feldom obtain even the Sight of a Copy; it exifted in fo few Libraries, public or private. Small Editions were probably publifhed, and thefe only in pamphlet Form; very Few had the Fortune to pafs into other than frail paper Covers. Thefe Circumftances will principally account for the very great Rarity of the Work. So that for many Years Copies have not been for fale, excepting in a few Inftances, and thefe have commanded Prices far beyond the Means of ordinary Students. When Copies have at any Time appeared in the Market they have been purchafed by the opulent Clafs of Collectors, or by Inftitutions, and are thus out of the Reach of the Majority of working Students in Hiftory. Hence we hear of *twenty-five* and even *fifty Dollars* having been offered for a Copy without obtaining One.

The Work was a hurried Performance; written out as the News arrived at the Capital from the Foreft in which the War Operations were performed. This muft be apparent to every Reader when it is confidered that the War was not ended until the Autumn of 1676; that the Work went through the neceffarily flow firft Printing-prefs of Bofton the fame Year; and that before the End of the Year a Copy croffed the wide Atlantic in a flow failing Craft of thofe Days, and was reprinted in London before the End of the fame Year.

That the Author was a little hurried in the Matter of getting out his Work is quite apparent, from his Knowledge of the Fact that the Reverend Mr. Hubbard of Ipfwich was diligently employed in a Work upon the fame Subject. There was then but one printer in Bofton—JOHN FOSTER by name—and he muft print both Works. Dr. Mather's was firft in the Hands of the Printer, and confequently appeared firft before the Public.

Prefatory by the Editor.

It is not propofed by the reproduction of this Work of Dr. Mather to fupply its Deficiencies in the Occurrences of Philip's War. To attempt that would be entirely inexpedient. A complete Hiftory of that War has never been written, much lefs publifhed. To attempt it by attaching Notes to any one or to all of the early Tracts and Chronicles would be a Failure. Even were it poffible to bring all the Facts belonging to the War into Notes, the amount of Notes thus required would render the Work awkward for Confultation, immethodical, out of chronological Order, and not unlike a Ship rendered valuelefs becaufe irrecoverably ftranded under the Weight of a valuable Cargo. And I may add further, that the impracticability of fupplying all Deficiencies in fuch Works by Notes, arifes in fome Degree from the many Errors and Omiffions in them. Thefe Errors and Omiffions were unavoidable at the Time, becaufe the earlieft Accounts of fuch Tranfactions are never entirely reliable, as we witnefs every Day in the Progrefs againft the prefent Rebellion, with all our modern Means of acquiring and conveying Information.

Thofe acquainted with the Work of Dr. Mather, only by Extracts from it, have probably but a faint Idea of its real Value. I would be underftood by its *Value*, to mean, as compared with what is elsewhere to be found concerning Philip's War, and especially as compared with the Work of Mr. Hubbard. To form a Kind of comparative Estimate of the Importance of the *Brief History* in that Relation it may be observed, that while there never has been an Edition of it since the Year of its first Publication before mentioned, to the present Time; yet the Work of Mr. Hubbard had passed through seven Editions many Years ago. And it should be remembered too, that Mr. Hubbard did not Write under the Advantages possessed by Dr. Mather. The former resided a long Day's Ride from Boston where all the Information, especially official, centered; while the latter resided in Boston, and by his Position had Access to the best Sources of Information. Hence, these Circumstances taken into Account, one might be led to expect a much more full and accurate Work from Dr. Mather than Mr. Hubbard. But the historical Value of the two Works are strongly in the inverse Ratio, as will be inferred from what has just been said. Unfortunately for the Reputation of Mr. Hubbard's Work, none of the Editions of it since the second have been accurately reprinted. The third Edition was printed here (in Boston) in 1775. This was so mutilated by Omissions and

Tranfpofitions, that but for the Author's Name in the Title-page its Paternity would fcarcely be conjectured. Yet this Impofition feems never to have been detected; and the Original had become fo rare, that a Comparifon could not be eafily made. From this mutilated Iffue all the later Impreffions are even *bad Copies!*

It was thought that the Addition of Dr. Cotton Mather's Work on the fame War would be an acceptable Accompaniment to that of his Father, as every thorough Student fhould recur to it, although far inferior in Value to his father's Work. I was induced to add this, as it is nowhere extant except in the *Magnalia*, where it is difficult to be confulted. This was compofed about twenty Years after the *Brief Hiftory*, a Time when a good Hiftory of the War was practicable; yet it contains no Marks of Care and Pains-taking. Much of what is delivered in it is drawn from Mr. Hubbard's Work without fo much as a Word in acknowledgment. Nor does the Author appear to have profited to any confiderable Extent from other Sources, notwithftanding he muft have daily come in Contact with the very Men who had ferved through the War in various Capacities.

Prefatory by the Editor.

Having printed the Account from the *Magnalia* in a different Type from that of the *Brief History* it may be read continuously without Regard to the other. I have made the *Magnalia* Account of each Transaction follow the Account of the same Affair in the *Brief History;* it thus serves as a sort of running Commentary throughout. Nor is any Part of either Work omitted. The Reader will therefore be in Possession of both Accounts, which he can read and consult together or separately, as his Convenience may require.

Some of the Notes to the Work were made many Years ago. Those required some Modification, and I have rewritten many of them to adapt them to the present State of the Light which has been shed on the History of this Period for the last five and twenty Years.

Saml. G. Drake.

Boston, 17 June, 1862.

EXPLANATION.

A PASSAGE in the Title Page of the Edition of 1676 requires Explanation. The *Serious Exhortation* therein mentioned was never added to the London Edition of the Work. It was a Sermon, and accompanied the firſt, or Boſton Edition. As it had nothing to do with the Hiſtory of the War, it was omitted by the Author or Publiſher, who heedleſſly retained the Reference to it. The Author refers to it in his Preface, and in one other Place in the Hiſtory.

I have preſerved the Paging of the Originals in Brackets.

References to *The Book of the Indians* are to the eleventh Edition. In References to other Works, the Edition is always deſignated when eſſential.

INTRODUCTORY.

A RETROSPECTIVE Glance, at the prefent Time, may not be thought out of Place. So let us caft our eyes back about two Centuries, and look upon the Country which is now the United States. There were no States at that Time. A few Europeans had exiled themfelves in what was then, and a long Time after, called the American Wildernefs, and could hardly afpire to the Name of Colonies. Thefe Europeans were thinly fcattered along the Coaft, from Cafco Bay to the Waters of the Chefapeake, but at great Diftances one from the other. The Wilds of New England were here and there dotted with a fmall Number of Settlements called Towns. Thefe were furrounded by Indians. Over thefe the Settlers exercifed a fort of Jurifdiction. Hence, when thofe Indians commenced War upon their white Neighbors, the Latter not very inappropriately termed the War a *Rebellion*. The War now upon us is alfo called a Rebellion, but with much less Propriety than the other. In the Case of the Indians there was some Excuse for their opposing the Progress of those whom they believed were Intruders upon their Country; while it is in no Wise a Parallel to the War of Treason now raging. There is, indeed, this in Common between the Indian Rebellion of 1675 and this War—as both may truly be said to be waged in the Cause of Barbarism.

The Peril in which New England was placed by the War with King Philip, was far greater than that in which the Union is placed by this War of Conspirators; notwithstanding New England had then what is denied the Union now, the Sympathy of Old England. Now, no Army of the Conspirators has dared to pass beyond their own desecrated Soil, while the Indians, at the Period under Consideration, made Inroads everywhere, even to within but a few Miles of the largest Town in the Land.

A Comparison between the rebel Indians and the southern Conspirators would result infinitely to the Advantage of the Former. They never understood the Nature of the Government of their English Neighbors; while the Conspirators can have no such Plea. They fully understand our Government, have been made a great People by it, and have over and

Introductory.

over sworn to maintain it, and then with Force and Arms swear to destroy it. Many of the poor rebel Indians were put to death as Traitors, and many more were sold into Slavery. What will be done with the southern Traitors, deserving a thousand times greater Punishment than the Indians, remains to be seen.

The Period between the Close of Philip's War and the American Revolution may not inappropriately be termed the *Middle Ages* of our historical Literature. Historical Students were few, and consequently there were few Persons engaged in collecting Materials for a History of the Past of New England. But there were a few splendid Exceptions, the most prominent (because best known) was the Collection of the Rev. Thomas Prince. That of the Mathers, though not less important, is less known. Of this we will say more presently.

That there were not many historical Students during the Middle Ages of New-England, is easily accounted for. The first and second Generations of the original Founders of New-England, had, in most Instances, few or no Advantages to obtain an Education; owing to the wild and uncultivated State of the Country, and the Necessity of those early Descendants of the first Settlers to devote all their Energies to gain a Livelihood.

Judge Samuel Sewall was Cotemporary with Mr. Prince and several of the Mathers. He made a most valuable Collection of Manuscripts, Tracts, and Newspapers. Mr. Hubbard, the excellent Historian of New-England, had doubtless a valuable Collection, but what became of it is not known to me. Judge Sewall's was scattered all the Way along through a Period of about a hundred Years, so that its utter Dispersion is now believed to be complete. And there are probably few Collectors of curious and ancient New-England Works, who cannot produce some of its Ruins when they wish to tantalize a less fortunate brother Collector.

But the Collection of the Mathers must have been superiour to all others in New-England. It was accumulated during four Generations. It was commenced by Richard Mather of Dorchester, from whom it passed to his Son, Dr. Increase Mather, and from him to his Son, Cotton Mather, from whom it passed with all its augmentations to Dr. Samuel Mather. A valuable part of it was given, as I was informed by a Daughter of the last named Dr. Mather, to the American Antiquarian Society. There is also in Possession of the same

Introductory. xvii

Society a Portrait of the Rev. Richard Mather, the emigrant Anceſtor, the faithful Miniſter of Dorcheſter. And it is ſomewhat remarkable that the People of the Town of Dorcheſter have not held the Memory of that Patriarch in Reſpect enough, to cauſe even a Copy of his Portrait to be placed in any of its Edifices! This may be no Reproach to the Inhabitants of that Town; if it be not, they will pardon this Alluſion to the Subject. Dorcheſter has its Hiſtory in a handſome Octavo, but, the Portrait of Richard Mather is not there! Portraits of the Founders of New England are by no means plenty. A mere Accident or ſlight Caſualty might reduce the Number. On another publick Occaſion I have endeavoured to influence an Action in this Matter; but have thus far failed. I may ſucceed no better now.

Some Letters written by Samuel Mather, D. D., to his Son, Samuel Mather, Eſq., not long before the Deceaſe of the Former, enable us to judge more correctly of the Value of the Mather Collection than we were hitherto able to do. In the firſt Place it will be pertinent to ſtate, that Samuel Mather, D. D., the Writer of the Letters, has been unpardonably neglected by Biographers. The Reaſon of this Neglect is well underſtood by those who take the Pains to inquire into it. No Man in New England was probably as learned as he, and his Learning was of the exactest Kind. He was independent in Matters of Theology as he was in Estate. When the American Revolution began he took a decided Stand on the Side of his Country; and although opposed to the Course of his Brother-in-law, Governor Hutchinson, yet when an infuriated Mob tore the Governor's House to pieces, the Governor fled for Protection to that of Mr. Mather, and was there safe from personal Violence.

Mr. Mather's only surviving Son, Samuel, joined the Army against Canada in 1758, as Deputy Commissary. In that Capacity, and in that of Commissary he served until the final Subjection of Canada in 1763. He remained in that Country several Years after this, and was a prominent Magistrate. In the mean Time he was often urged by his Father to return and reside in Boston, or somewhere near him. He at length wrote his Father that if he could obtain a Place in the Customhouse he would return. With such a Situation the Father was not very well pleased. He viewed the Customhouse Officers as Instruments of kingly Oppression, and signified the same to his Son. However, through the Influence of Gov. Hutchinson, young Mather obtained the Office he desired. Upon this he entered in 1771. He continued in that Office until Washington drove the British out of Boston in 1776. He now became a Wanderer in Europe, suffering many Privations, where he continued until some Time after the Peace of 1783.

Few Letters passed between the Father and Son after this. The Tone of those of the Former are very different from those written before the Latter deserted his Country; which Desertion was the Occasion of Disinheritance. Their political Relationship will be well understood by a few Extracts from their original Letters now before me. Late in the Year 1783 (Nov. 14th), Dr. Mather wrote: "I have little more to write than one of Tully's curt Epistles, 'We are well; if you are well, it is well: Fare you well." He however continues: "Last Monday I finished my 77th Year, and although I find myself not quite so strong as I used to be, I am generally free from Aches and Pains, and can still read the smallest Print or Writing by Candle-light without Spectacles: And my Hearing is exquisite: So that I see no Cause to complain of old Age: But have rather Cause to own with Gratitude, as the learned Drusius said of himself: 'Melior est mihi senectus quam juventus.'"

In another Letter of the next Year the Doctor thus refers to his Son's Conduct in efpoufing the Caufe of the Enemy of his Country: "You cannot but remember, that I was not approving of your Choice to go into the Service in which you engaged: But you chofe to follow the Counfel of your mifguided and avaricious Uncle; whofe Name is generally hated throughout thefe States, and is doomed to perpetual Infamy."

In the fame Letter he faid to his Son: "You mention Numbers of our Name in England. In Connecticut, as appears by a Lift given me by Dr. Mather of Lyme about fifteen Years ago, or more, there were above feventy Relations there; and no doubt there is now a great Addition to them: and yet I cannot learn that one of them has taken the Side of wicked and miferable Brittain."

We can better appreciate thefe fharp and cutting Rebukes now than we could five or more Years ago; when our long Years of Profperity had foftened the Defcendants of the Men of thofe Days towards the Oppreffors of our Fathers. For now (in 1862), if there are any in the United States who can hold milder Language towards thofe who would deftroy us as a Nation, I am ready to confefs that I am not of the Number.

Introductory. xxi

Dr. Mather had published a political Pamphlet, entitled a *Legacy*, in which he did not spare the Tories and Traitors to their Country. In a Letter which the Son wrote to him he refers to the *Legacy*, complaining of its Severity. To which the Doctor replied: " You seem to dislike one Passage in my Legacy; wherein it is proposed and counselled, that the Deserters of the American Cause returning here, should never be employed in any Place of Consequence. I wrote this in the Sincerity of my Heart: And really think, that they, who discovered themselves inimical to the American Cause, and they also who deserted it from Cowardice or Fear, are not fit to be entrusted with public Offices. For, it is to be feared, that they would not be faithful in them; and if new Difficulties and new Hazards should present, it is likely that they would behave, as indeed they have always done: so that no Dependance is to be placed on them.

" As for the Body of the Tories and Refugees, I look on them in the same Light as your new Mr. Pitt does, who calls them *the most infamous Scoundrels on the Face of the Earth*. And as to those who left us and went over to the Enemies, they were guilty of a criminal Desertion of our Cause: and I pity them for the Effects of their unpitiable

Conduct. Nor have they Reason to blame any but themselves for them."

It is apprehended that the Reader will not require an Apology for this seeming Digression, as it to some Extent illustrates the Spirit of Times which have much in common with our own, as well as what is to follow. The Tory Son, it appears, during his Exile had been led to reflect upon Matters connected with his Ancestors, and wrote to his Father making some Inquiries, the Nature of which will be sufficiently explained in a Reply, dated June 9th, 1784. After informing him (the Son) that "the Sermon preached on the Death of his Grandfather [the Author of the *Brief History*] was by Dr. Colman," he says: "That Paper which you mentioned, I have no more. There were several Letters I had, original Letters, written by the renowned Oliver Cromwell, to my Great-grandfather, Mr. John Cotton, which I lent to your careless Uncle, Mr. Hutchinson, and, as I suppose, they are irrecoverably lost and gone: I furnished him, as I suppose you know, with most of the Materials, of which his History was composed: And I am sorry that he made no better Use of them: For he has misrepresented and misapplied several Things, of which I had given him better Information."

These Facts have never before been given to the World. They show that we are indebted in no small Degree, if not entirely, to the Collections of the Mather Family for Hutchinson's History, and the valuable Volume of *Original Papers* bearing his Name.

To form a better Appreciation of the Mather Collection, I give an Estimate of its Value by the Tory Son: "My Father's Library was by far the most valuable Part of the family Property. It consisted of 7000 or 8000 Volumes of the most curious and chosen Authors, and a prodigious Number of valuable Manuscripts, which had been collected by my Ancestors for five Generations." These he considered worth at least *eight thousand pounds sterling*.

Thus we are enabled to judge of the Mather Collections from a nearer View, probably, than any others, since the Time of Governor Hutchinson.

The meagre Notices we have had of Dr. Samuel Mather, at a Time when full Information was attainable, is doubtless owing to sectarian Intolerance and Jealousy. He may have been bigoted—that is an Attribute of Sectaries. He could never countenance Innovations in Religion, or what he considered such. Hence Mr. Whitefield and his

Followers found no Admirer in Mr. Mather or his Followers. This Stand against "Disorganizers of regular Worship" became unpopular among a Majority of the People in Boston, and consequently Mr. Mather found himself in a somewhat overshadowed Minority; and thus remained for the Remainder of his Life.

Thus has been given a Sort of mirror View of him whom some have been pleased to denominate "the last of the Mathers." He was, it is true, the last hereabouts of the illustrious Mathers. But his Works will ever keep his Memory fresh as long as New England has a Literature. Had he written nothing but his *America Known to the Ancients*, that would have been sufficient to perpetuate his Name in the Annals of his Country. His *Apology for the New England Churches*, published in 1738, when he was thirty-two Years of Age, is a very able Work, and several others might be mentioned; all showing him to have possessed an enlightened Mind and extensive and profound Erudition.

So much has been written about the two celebrated Authors of the ensuing History of the Great Indian War of 1675 and 6, that even a Sketch of their Lives would be unnecessary here. The tabular Pedigree annexed hereto shows, in the most

Introductory.

compact Form, all that will be required to illustrate this Introduction.

In the Time of the Mathers there were few Authors in New England, not Ministers; hence the Works of that Day all partake of their peculiar religious Sentiments. These they constantly brought into their Subject, whatever that Subject might be. They could see the Hand of Providence as well in a Defeat as in a Victory. Thus we are told in the *Brief History*, that God would not suffer the Heathen to destroy Meetinghouses. It was not long however before they did destroy them, and then the Author says, "now he begins with the Sanctuary." The first burnt was at Springfield in October, 1675. And, when, soon after, another was burned, the Fact was passed over with the Remark, that, "another Candlestick had been removed." It does not seem to have occurred to the Writer, that the Reason that the Churches were not sooner destroyed, was, simply, because they yielded no Plunder.

It may be questioned if there were in the Country any Men equally learned with the two Mathers, Dr. Increase and Dr. Cotton. They were not only learned in some particular Studies, but they were learned in all Branches of Knowledge of their Time.

The Father was not endowed with so much Genius as the Son, and yet he was a Scholar of the first Order.

The Mathers were firm Believers in the Doctrines they taught, and were not very charitable towards those who held to different Doctrines. They have been charged with Bigotry in Religion. This Charge may be allowed, and yet not to their exclusive Disadvantage; for it must be remembered that their immediate Ancestors had come out from a Bigotry far greater than that now visible. A Bigotry and Superstition which had enchained the human Mind through previous Ages. Their chief Error was, as regards their Position in religious Belief; that they deemed themselves removed beyond the Confines of that Bigotry and Superstition, which their new Light enabled them to look back upon, and to imagine that they had arrived at that desirable Point safely beyond them. They do not seem to have had any Notion that a similar Error had been the Incubus of religious Progress up to their own Times. Hence naturally grew Uncharitableness and Intolerance. We of this Day should keep this Subject in View, and inquire of ourselves whether we are entirely safe beyond the Bounds of Bigotry and its kindred Faces of Deformity; keeping in

Introductory.

View also what John Robinson wrote to the Pilgrims of Plymouth, who, he had some Reason to fear, might consider themselves as having attained Perfection in the Matter of Religion.

This is considered all the Defence necessary to be made for the Authors of the Works now reproduced; and we may here take Occasion to remark, that if many of this Age shall not require as much of a Defence in a future Age, their Representatives or Successors may congratulate them, and cherish their Memory, for having arrived at Perfection so long before them.

Dr. Cotton Mather was not so well calculated for a Historian as his Father was. His active Brain could hardly be confined to the Drudgery necessary for the Collection and nice Arrangement of Facts. Had Novel-writing been in Fashion among our Puritan Fathers, Cotton Mather would, no doubt, have greatly excelled in that Department. Take, for Example, his Account of the Witchcraft Delusion of his Time. Nothing can exceed the Flights of Imagination to be met with in that work, especially in that Part where he describes the Manœuvres of the Devil in his Intrigues among his deluded Followers. It would be impossible to conceive of any almighty Power, superior, or even equal to that attributed to the contemptible Miscreant we are assured that he is.

Notwithstanding the Peculiarities of Cotton Mather's Writings, he has left us much for our Benefit as well as for our Amusement. But for his singular Pen thousands of Facts would never have been preserved. His *Magnalia* is a stupendous Monument of Learning, Piety, Absurdity, and I had almost said, Frivolity. Though he entitles it an Ecclesiastical History of New England, had we met with it without a Title, we might have been exceedingly puzzled to assign one for it. Before it was published the Author had issued many Works: principally Sermons and Tractates. All, or nearly all of these he put into his *Magnalia*; though some of them he very much altered and abridged. Especially did he garble his *Wonders of the Invisible World*; but wherefore is not very apparent. His Section on Philip's War was never issued in a separate Work, but appears to have been composed expressly for the *Magnalia*; because he would bring into his Work the entire History of the *Wars of the Lord*, as he terms the War with the Indians. And as there were extant Histories of Philip's War, both by Mr. Hubbard and his Father, he treats it in a more general Way than he would otherwise have done. Neverthelefs it muft be confulted by the Hiftorian; and it will always be curioufly interefting, from the peculiar Style of the Author. It is rather in the Manner of an Effay upon that War than a Hiftory of it; yet, it gives us fome Facts not elfewhere to be found. His chief Authority was Hubbard's *Narrative;* often copying its very Language; but he never once refers to that Author. On this I have already remarked in the Preface.

A few Words here refpecting the Population of New England, in 1675, may be of Affiftance to the Reader.

The white Population of New England at the Time of Philip's War is not accurately known, nor is that of the Indians; yet we may judge from various Data near enough for hiftorical Ufes. There were probably between 30,000 and 40,000 white Inhabitants in the United Colonies. Of thefe from 6000 to 8000 were able to bear Arms. Of thefe from 600 to 800 were killed by the Enemy. Dr. I. Mather gives the former Number, and the Author of the *Narrative* in the *Chronicle,* p. 101, the latter. Of the Number of the Indians it is not fo eafy to make an Eftimate. Thefe were probably about equal to the Englifh. About fifty Towns were partially or wholly deftroyed. Up to the End of

May, 1676, the Writer of *News from N. England,* says there had been 444 of the English killed, and 55 taken captive. Of the Indians 910 are enumerated killed.

Having great Advantages of the English in some respects, it is not strange that they were confident in their Ability to rid the Country of them; but for want of System and a Form of Government among them, they lost in one Day what they gained the preceding Day. They had a Sort of Philosophy, but it was too crude to be of any Service to them when it was most needed. Their Regulations or Laws for conducting an Expedition were all out of Joint if they failed in the first Onset. Subordination with them might well be compared to a " Rope of Sand."

A good while before the War with Philip began, the Indians, having possessed themselves with Firearms, did not hesitate to give out Threats on some Occasions that they were able to drive the English out of the Country, and might do it at some future Day. Governor Bradford tells us that they had " fair Muskets, which they kept neat and brave, all English," too; and that " the English were not furnished so well as they." These Remarks of the good Bradford were made long before Philip's War.

He refers to the Charge against the Dutch and French, of supplying the Indians with Arms; to which he replies, "it is English Guns we see in their Hands; for the French and Dutch Guns are more slight, and are such, that these Indians are now grown so knowing as to despise."

When Mrs. Rowlandson was a Captive among them, they told her they would knock all the English on the Head, drive them into the Sea, or make them fly the Country. This was when it was full *Sea* with their Affairs, and their Hands were made strong with the English Implements of Destruction.

One of the greatest and most regretted Defects in our early Histories is the almost entire Absence of personal History. Prominent Persons receive sufficient Laudation and Notice of what they do, but seldom have we any Account of them saving in the immediate Action for which they were noticed. It does not seem ever to have occurred to the old Writers that the Posterity of those Men might desire to know something of their Ancestors, beyond that some One of them led a Company against the Enemy, and that Others were killed by them. Seldom indeed was Pains taken even to give the Names of those who fell. And even Captains and other Officers of Companies are known only by their paternal or family Name, as Capt. Wadsworth, Capt. Beers, Capt. Turner, &c., &c. If we would know *what* Capt. Wadsworth, &c., we must look elsewhere than in the Histories before us.

Though the Officers are only alluded to here, it is not much less important that we have Lists of the Rank and File, and the poor Pioneers, who from limited Means had been compelled to take up their Abodes on the Borders or Frontiers of Settlements; and thus exposing themselves to the Tomahawk and scalping Knife, and standing as a Barrier between a merciless Enemy and their more opulent Countrymen. The Names of all such should be sought out and placed upon the Pages of the History of their Times. In this Service the Writer of this Introduction has devoted much Time for many Years, and although he has done much, much remains to be done. Until these Labors are fully accomplished our Materials are defective for a general History of New England, and consequently that History cannot be satisfactorily written, either to the intelligent Reader or to the Author. Such a History may be compared to a House built on an insufficient Foundation, and although often rebuilt, is still without the necessary Substructure.

A BRIEF HISTORY OF THE WAR WITH THE INDIANS IN NEW-ENGLAND.

From *June* 24. 1675. (when the firſt *Engliſhman* was Murdered by the *Indians*) to *Auguſt* 12. 1676. when *Philip*, alias *Metacomet*, the principal Author and Beginner of the War was ſlain.

Wherein the Grounds, Beginning, and Progreſs of the War, is ſummarily expreſſed. Together with a ſerious EXHORTATION to the Inhabitants of that Land.

By *INCREASE MATHER*, Teacher of a Church of Chriſt in *Boſton* in *New-England*.

Lev. 26. 25. *I will bring a Sword upon you, that ſhall avenge the quarrel of the Covenant.*
Pſal. 107. 43. *Whoſo is wiſe and will obſerve theſe things, even they ſhall underſtand the loving Kindneſs of the Lord.*
Jer. 22. 15. *Did not thy Father do Judgment and Juſtice, and it was well with him?*

Segnius irritant animos demiſſa per aures,
Quam quæ ſunt occulis commiſſa fidelibus.   *Horat.*
Lege Hiſtoriam ne fias Hiſtoria.   *Cic.*

London, Printed for *Richard Chiſwell*, at the Roſe and Crown in St. *Pauls* Church-Yard, according to the Original Copy Printed in New-England. 1676.

Licensed, *Decemb.* 2. 1676.
Roger L'Estrange.

To the Reader.

ALTHOUGH I was not altogether negligent in Noting down such Occurrences, respecting the present *War* with the Heathen in *New-England*, as came to my knowledge, in the time of them; yet what I did that way, was meerly for my own private use; nor had I the least thought of publishing any of my *Observations*, until such time as I read a *Narrative* of this *War*, said to be Written by a Merchant in *Boston*, which it seems met with an *Imprimatur* at *London*, in *December* last.[1] The abounding Mistakes therein, caused me to think it necessary, that a true *History* of this Affair should be published. Wherefore I resolved (σὺν Θεῶ) to *Methodize* such scattered *Observations* as I had by me, so were the *Horæ subsecivæ* of a few days improved. Whilst I was doing this, there came to my hands another *Narrative*[2] of this War, written by a *Quaker* in *Road-Island*, who pretends to know the Truth of things; but that

---

[1] The *Narrative* referred to is the first of the *Tracts* on Philip's War contained in the *Old Indian Chronicle*. The "mistakes" complained of are neither numerous nor extraordinary, taking the circumstances into account under which the Author of that Narrative must have written.

[2] The Author has reference, no doubt, to JOHN EASTON, whose *Narrative* seems to have lain in MS. until 1858, in which year Mr. MUNSELL of Albany printed it in a sumptuous manner, elaborately edited by Dr. HOUGH. It is difficult to understand wherefore our Author accuses Easton of making false state-

Narrative being fraught with worfe things than *meer miftakes*, I was thereby quickened to expedite what I had in hand. I moved that fome other might have done it, but none prefenting, I thought of [t]his faying, *Ab alio quovis hoc fieri mallem quàm à me, fed à me tamen potius quàm à nemine.* And I hope that in one thing (though it may be in little elfe) I have performed the part of an *Hiftorian*, viz. In endeavouring to relate things truly and impartially, and doing the beft I could that I might not lead the *Reader* into a Miftake. *Hiftory* is indeed in itfelf a profitable ftudy. Learned men know that *Polybius*, and the great Philofopher call it, Αληθινωτάτην παιδεῖαν καὶ χρησιμην γυμνασιαν. And there is holy Scripture to encourage a work of this nature; For what was the *Book of the Wars of the Lord?* Num. 21. 14. And that Book of *Jafher*, which we read of in *Jofhua* and in *Samuel?* Yea, and the Book of the *Chronicles*, mentioned in the Book of *Kings* (for we find not fome of thofe things referred unto in the *Canonical* Book of *Chronicles*). What were thefe Books but the faithful *Records* of the Providential Difpenfations of God in the Days of old? Yea, and it is proper for the Minifters of

---

ments, as that narrator fcarcely goes beyond what paffed under his own obfervation; and although he appears before us under all the difadvantages of a want of education, yet his Narrative was well intended, and is as free from errors doubtlefs as any work of the kind. As to the work as a literary performance it is perfectly monftrous. Its Author probably never intended it for publication, although from the mention of it by our Author, he might be fuppofed to have reference to a printed work. Eafton was a man of good ftanding, and was Governor of the Colony in 1690.

God, to engage themselves in services of this nature; Witness the *History* or *Commentary* מדרש *of the Prophet Iddo*, 2 Chro. 13. 22. Whether my defective manner of management in this History renders it unprofitable, I know not. Considering the other employments that are always upon me, together [iv] with my personal inabilities, I have cause to suspect it may be so in a great measure. If any one shall hereby be incited to do better, I hope I shall rather thank than envy him, πλεόνων ἔργον ἄμεινον. And I earnestly wish that some effectual Course may be taken (before it be too late) that a just *History of New England*, be written and published to the World. That is a thing that hath been often spoken of, but was never done to this day, and yet the longer it is deferred, the more difficulty will there be in effecting of it.[1]

Moreover the thing which I mainly designed, was the subsequent *Exhortation*, which is annexed herewith, wherein I have desired to approve myself as in the sight of God, speaking what I believe God would have me to speak, without respect to any person in this world. And there is one thing insisted on therein, concerning which I could wish that I had said more, I mean that which doth respect endeavours for the *Conversion* of the *Heathen* unto Christ. There are some that make a wrong use of a notion of Mr. *Cottons* touching this matter,

---

[1] The Author ignores entirely Capt. JOHNSON's History, published in 1654. It is more generally known as *Wonder Working Providence of Sion's Savior in New England.*

alledging that he taught that a general *Conversion* of *Indians* is not to be expected before the seven Vials[1] are poured forth upon the Antichristian State, nor before the conversion of the *Jewish* Nation. It is far from my purpose to contradict that *Great Author*, unto whose dust (in respect of near Affinity[2] as well as on the account of his Eminency in Grace and spiritual Gifts) I owe a sacred Reverence, and it is known that I have my self asserted the same notions both in Sermons, and in a printed *Discourse concerning the Salvation of the Tribes of Israel*. But it was never intended that that Assertion should be improved so as to discourage from the prosecution of that which was the professed, pious, and a main design of the *Fathers* of this *Colony;* viz.

---

[1] This now curious Book is of great rarity. It was written in New England, and published in London, in 4to, 1642. A part of its title is *The Powring out of the Seven Vials; or an Exposition of the* 16. *Chapter of the Revelation, with an Application of it to our times. Wherein is revealed Gods powring out the full Vials of his fierce Wrath,* &c., &c.

This work, we are told, was preached in several Sermons to his "owne priuate auditorie and was not intended, when first deliuered, for any more publike use." It was probably well adapted to the state of opinions and the times in which it was produced, but in these days, and perhaps in all future time, it will be looked upon as very curious among the curiosities of ancient Theology. Of God's seven "full vials of fierce wrath," he "powrs" out four of them "upon the lowest and basest sort of Catholicks, their worship, Priests, and the Popes Supremacy."

The people to whom Mr. COTTON preached were just from Old England, and he assures them, that, as they came here to enjoy "purity of ordinances," it would be matter of great reproach if they were not true to their professions; "all England (he says) will judge your reformation but a delusion, and you cannot poure forth a viall of more wrath on religion."—*Seven Vials*, p. 23.

[2] The Author married the daughter of Mr. Cotton, as will be seen by the pedigree annexed.

To propagate the Gospel and Kingdom of Christ among these Indians, *who in former Ages had not heard of his fame and Glory.* It is indeed true, that although a *Fulness of the Gentiles* in respect of *Apostasy*, shall be accomplished (so must they *fulfill their Times*) before the calling of the *Jews*, yet the fulness of the *Gentiles* in respect of *Conversion*, will not come in before that. Nevertheless a glorious Sprinkling, and great success of the Gospel may be in particular places at present, even amongst Heathen. And the Salvation of a few immortal Souls is worth the labour of many all their lives. And happy experience hath confirmed this; for here in *New-England*, six Churches have been constituted amongst the *Indians*.[1] And the labours of *Robert Junius* forty years since amongst the *East Indians* in Formosa, were wonderfully successful; for (as *Caspar Sibellius*, Pastor of the Church in *Daventry* in *Holland*, writing the History of that affair doth relate) there were no less than five thousand and nine hundred *Indians* that became professedly subject to the Gospel, and [v] were all, together with their children, baptized into the Name of *Jesus Christ*. *Junius* having learned the *Indian* Language, and being a Man of exemplary Piety in his conversa-

[1] Those who would learn the condition of the converted Indians of this period will find much satisfaction by consulting the two works of the worthy General GOOKIN. These works are printed, one in the first volume of the Collections of the Massachusetts Hist. Society, and the other in the second volume of the American Antiquarian Society's publication. An edition of them, in a handsome volume, would be a valuable addition to our libraries. Their editorship would afford a delightful employment to one qualified for the undertaking.

tion, and one also that excelled in wisdom and spiritual Abilities, God was with him and made him an happy Instrument of winning Souls. He translated some part of the Scripture, and wrote Catechisms, and other profitable Books in their Language. He caused Schools to be erected among those blind *Barbarians*, so as that *six hundred* of them were able to read and write, and about *fifty* who excelled in knowledge, and were of approved godliness, became *Instructors* of others in the Principles of the true Christian Religion: Yea, in *three and twenty Towns*, there were *Indian* Christian *Churches Planted*. And learned men were sent out of Holland, in order to a further propagation of the interest of the Gospel in those remote parts of the World. Also *Justus Heurnius*, who was at first a *Physitian*, being inflamed with a singular zeal after God's Glory, and the Salvation of Souls of Men, left his practicing in *Medicinal Cures*, and betook himself wholly to the study of *Divinity*; after which he engaged in a Voyage towards the *East-Indians*, designing their *Conversion*, and having learned their *Language*, spent fourteen Years amongst them: and as the great *Voetius* (in his Disputation, *De Vocatione Gentium*) testifieth, was instrumental to the *Conversion* of many of those *Indians*, so as to erect Churches of them in divers places, yea, and took care for the *learned Education* of divers Youngmen, even amongst the *Indians* themselves, so as that they were able to instruct the several Churches, which by the blessing of God upon his Labours had been lately formed. It is great pity then, that we in *New-England,* who do not come behind others in Profeſſion, and Pretences to Religion, ſhould fall ſhort in real endeavours, for the promotion and propagation of Religion, and Chriſtianity amongſt thoſe that have been for ages that are paſt, *without God and without Chriſt, and Strangers to the Common-wealth of Iſrael.* It troubleth me, when I read how the *Papiſts* glory in that they have converted ſo many of the *Eaſt* and *Weſt-Indians* to the Chriſtian Faith, and reproach *Proteſtants,* becauſe they have been no more induſtrious in a work of that nature. Though I know they have little cauſe to Glory, if the whole truth were known. For as for many of their *Converts,* inaſmuch as they are become *Vaſſals* not only to the Hereſies, but to the Perſons of thoſe who have Proſelyted them, they are as Chriſt ſaid concerning the Proſelytes of the Scribes and Phariſees, *twofold more the children of Hell,* than they were before; and many of them know little of *Chriſtianity* beſides the *Name.* Witneſs the celebrated Story of that *Franciſcan,* who wrote a Letter to a Friend of his in *Europe,* wherein he glorieth that having lived ſix and twenty years amongſt the Indians, he had converted many thouſands of them to the [vi] Faith, and he deſired his Friend to ſend him a Book called the *Bible,* for he heard there was ſuch a Book in *Europe;* which might be of ſome uſe to him. Surely, *Francis* himſelf did not excel this *Franciſcan,* in profound ignorance. It is alſo true, that the *Hollanders* have formerly (as was in part intimated but now) done something towards the *Conversion* of those *Indians* where they have Plantations settled. For they have caused some part of the Scripture to be Translated into the *Indian* Language, and have out of their Publick Treasuries maintained some learned and meet Persons, on purpose, that they might become *Preachers to the Indians*: Nevertheless, *Voetius* in his dissertation *de plantatoribus Ecclesiarum*, greatly bewaileth it, that no more care hath been taken about that concern of the Gospel and Kingdom of Christ; and declareth what were the unhappy obstructions, hindring the *Belgick* Churches from attaining a further progress in a work so desirable; but (as he there speaketh) *Infanda illa nihil attinet hic referre*. And I know not, but that the Lords holy Design in the *War* which he hath brought upon us, may (in part) be to punish us for our too great neglect in this matter. I would not detract from what hath been done that way, but rather with my Soul bless God for it. It is well known, that sundry of the Lords Servants in this Land, have laboured in that work: Especially Reverend Mr. *Eliot* hath taken most indefatigable pains, having Translated the whole Bible into the *Indian Language*, in which respect *New England* (let Christ alone have the praise of it) hath out-done all other places, so far as I have heard or read. But it cannot be long, before that faithful, and now aged servant of the Lord rest from his Labours: Sad will it be for the succeeding Generation, if they shall suffer the Work of Christ amongst the *Indians*, to die with him who began it.¹ *Sed meliora speramus.*

I shall add no more, but leave the success of this undertaking to him, who alone can give it. And I earnestly desire the Prayers of every Godly Reader.

Increase Mather.

---

¹ The Rev. John Eliot, since known as "The Apostle to the Indians," or "The Indian Apostle," died in Roxbury 20 May, 1690, aged 86. Hence he lived 14 years after this work was published. A pedigree of his family has been published.

Twenty-five years after this war, our author published a little work which he entitled *Ichabod, &c.* For some now amusing reflections on the State of New-England and the Indians, the reader is referred to that work, commencing at p. 66.

A BRIEF HISTORY OF THE WAR WITH THE INDIANS IN NEW-ENGLAND.

[The following is the title which Dr. COTTON MATHER gives to that part of the Seventh Book of his *Magnalia*, &c., containing the hiſtory of King Philip's War.]

Arma Viroſq; Cano: Or, The Troubles which the Churches of New-England have undergone in the Wars, which the People of that Country[1] have had with the Indian Salvages.

[Under this title he narrates the events of the Pequot War, and ſlightly touches upon a few other events concerning the Narraganſets and other Indians.

---

1 The *Magnalia* being publiſhed in London, the author ſeems to have intended to give the impreſſion that he wrote it there.

This part of his history does not belong to our present work, but may be used with his father's history upon the Pequot war; which I propose hereafter to republish, uniform with this.]

THAT the Heathen People amongst whom we live, and whose Land the Lord God of our Fathers hath given to us for a rightful Possession, have at sundry times been Plotting mischievous Devices against that part of the *English Israel*, which is seated in these goings down of the Sun,[1] no man that is an Inhabitant of any considerable standing, can be ignorant. Especially that there have been (*Nec Injuria*) Jealousies concerning the *Narragansets* and *Wompanoags*, is notoriously known to all men. And whereas they have been quiet until the last Year, that must be ascribed to the wonderful Providence of God, who did (as with *Jacob* of old, and after that with the Children of *Israel*) lay the fear of the English, and

[1] Not only our Fathers who came first to New-England used to speak of the Country as the "End of the Earth," but their children considered it as such, as numerous instances might be cited to show. And whatever the hopes of the first settlers might have been of its importance in a Christian point of view, it is pretty evident that they had no expectations of any great National importance, to be attained in after time. Our Author says in his Election Sermon of 1677, "Our Fathers did not in their coming hither propound any great matter to themselves respecting this world," &c. But this was the land they hoped to make so pure and holy, that Christ would take up his abode here on his "second appearing."

In the same Sermon, page 77, our Author says, "it was once Dr. Twiss his opinion, that when New Jerusalem should come down from Heaven, America would be the seat of it." The present learned gentleman of the same name and country is, possibly, of a different way of thinking.

the dread of them upon all the *Indians*. The terror of God was upon them round about. Nor indeed had they such Advantages in former Years as now they have, in respect of Arms and Ammunition; their Bows and Arrows not being comparably such weapons of death and destruction, as our Guns and Swords are, with which [2] they have been unhappily furnished. Nor were our sins ripe for so dreadful a Judgment, until *the Body of the first Generation* was removed, and another Generation risen up which hath not so pursued, as ought to have been, the blessed design of their Fathers, in following the Lord into this Wilderness, whilst it was a land not sown.

As for the Grounds, Justness, and Necessity of the present *War* with these Barbarous Creatures which have set upon us, my design is not to *inlarge* upon that Argument, but to leave that to others whom it mostly concerns, only in brief this. The irruption of this flame at this time was occasioned as followeth.

Read the Postscript at the end of this History.

In the latter end of the Year 1674. An *Indian*, called *John Sausaman*, who had submitted himself unto, and was taken under the protection of the *English*, perceiving that the *profane Indians* were hatching mischief against the *English*, he faithfully acquainted the Governour of *Plymouth*, with what he knew, and also what his fears were, together with the grounds thereof, withal declaring; that he doubted such and such *Indians*, belonging to *Philip* the Sachem of *Pokanoket* or *Mount-hope*, would murder him; which quickly happened accordingly: For soon after this, *John Sausaman* was barbarously murdered by an *Indian*, called *Tobias* (one of *Philip's* chief Captains and Counsellors) and by his son and another *Indian*, who knocked him on the head and then left him on the Ice on a great Pond. Divine Providence, which useth to bring Murder to light, so ordered, as that an *Indian* unseen by those three that killed *Sausaman*, beheld all that they did to him, and spake of it, so as that a *Praying* (and as there is cause to hope) a godly *Indian, William Nahauton* by name, heard of it, and he forthwith revealed what he knew to the *English*. Whereupon the three *Indians* who had committed the murder were apprehended, and the other *Indian* testified to their faces, that he saw them killing *Sausaman*. They had a fair Tryal for their Lives, and that no appearance of wrong might be, *Indians* as well as *English* sate upon the *Jury*, and all agreed to the condemnation of those Murtherers, who were accordingly Executed in the beginning of the 4th Month called *June*, Anno 1675. They stoutly denied the Fact, only at last *Tobias's* son confessed, that his Father and the other *Indian* killed *Sausaman*, but that himself had no hand in it, only stood by and saw them do it.[1]

No doubt but one reason why the *Indians* murdered *John Sausaman*, was out of hatred against him for his Religion, for he was Christianized and

---

[1] The Records of Plymouth throw much new light on the affair of the Murder of Sassamon. They are extracted in the *Book of the Indians*.

baptiz'd, and was a Preacher amongst the *Indians*, being of very excellent parts, he translated some part of the Bible into the *Indian* language, and was wont to curb those *Indians* that knew not God, on the account of their debaucheries; but the main ground why they murthered him seems to be, because he discovered their subtle and malicious designs, which they were [3] complotting against the *English*. *Philip* perceiving that the Court of *Ply-*

In the year 1674, one *John Sausaman*, an Indian, that had been sent forth from the English to preach the Gospel unto his countrymen, addressed the governor of Plymouth with information that *Philip*, with several nations of the Indians besides his own, were plotting the destruction of the English throughout the country. This *John Sausaman* was the son of Christian Indians; but he apostatizing from the profession of Christianity, lived like an heathen in the quality of a secretary to *King Philip*, for he could write, though the King his master could not so much as read. But after this, the grace of our Lord Jesus Christ recovered him from his apostasie, and he gave such notable evidences and expressions of his repentance, that he was not only admitted unto the communion of the Lord's table in one of the Indian churches, but he was also employed every Lord's day as an instructer among them. Nevertheless, because there was but this one testimony of an Indian, and therefore of a suspected original, there was little notice taken of it, until the artificial arguments of some too probable and unhappy circumstances confirmed it. But before the truth of

G

mouth had Condemned and Executed one of his Counſellors, being (as is upon ſtrong grounds ſuppoſed) conſcious of the murder committed upon the matter could be enquired into, poor *John* was barbarouſly murdered by certain Indians, who, that the murder might not be diſcovered, cut an hole through the ice of the pond where they met with him, and put in the dead body, leaving his hat and his gun upon the ice, that ſo others might ſuppoſe him to have there drowned himſelf. It being rumored that *Sauſaman* was miſſing, the neighbors did ſeek, and find, and bury his dead body; but upon the jealouſies on the ſpirits of men, that he might have met with ſome *foul play* for his diſcovering of the Indian plot, a jury was empannelled, unto whom [46] it appeared that his neck was broken, which is one Indian way of murdering, and that his head was extreamly ſwoln, and that he had ſeveral other wounds upon him, and that when he was taken out of the pond, no water iſſued out of him. It was remarkable, that one *Tobias*, a Counſellor of *King Philip's* whom they ſuſpected as the author of this murder, approaching to the dead body, it would ſtill fall *a bleeding afreſh*, as if it had newly been ſlain; yea, that upon a repetition of the experiment it ſtill happened ſo, albeit he had been deceaſed and interred for a conſiderable while before.

Afterwards an Indian called *Patuckſon*, gave in his teſtimony that he ſaw this Tobias, with certain other Indians, killing of *John Sauſaman*; and it was further teſtified that *John Sauſaman*, before he died, had expreſſed his fears that thoſe very Indians would be his death. Hereupon *Tobias*, with two other Indians, being apprehended, they were, after a fair trial for their

John Saufaman, muſt needs think that ere long, they would do to him (who had no leſs deſerved it) as they had done to his Counſellor: Wherefore he,

lives, by a jury confiſting half of Engliſh, and half of Indians, convicted, and ſo condemned; and though they were all ſucceſſively turned off the ladder at the gallows, utterly denying the fact, yet the laſt of them happening to break or ſlip the rope, did, before his going off the ladder again, confes, that the other Indians did really murder *John Saufaman*, and that he was himſelf, though no actor in it, yet a looker on.[1] Things began by this time to have an ominous aſpect. Yea, and now we ſpeak of things ominous, we may add,

---

[1] From ſome unpubliſhed MSS. in my poſſeſſion, it appears that in 1670 *Saſſamon* was one of the counſellors to *Squaumaug*, "Sachem of the Maſſachuſetts." *Squaumaug* was the brother and ſucceſſor of *Joſias Wampatuck*, who (the ſame year, 1670) was killed in an expedition againſt the Mohawks, and grandſon of Chickataubut, Sachem of that tribe, when the Engliſh came. *Squaumaug* had a ſon *Jeremy*. He lived at a place called Mattacheeſeets.

There had been difficulty between *Philip* and *Wampatuck*, about their bounds or the limits of their dominions. When it was known that the latter had been killed, *Squaumaug*, as his ſucceſſor, undertook to have the matter ſettled by treaty; and by the aſſiſtance of the Engliſh the parties were got together on the 12 July, 1670, at the houſe of Capt. *William Hudſon*, at Wading River, and there Articles were ſigned, by which they agreed, that henceforth the line which ſeparated Maſſachuſetts from Plymouth colony, ſhould alſo be the line between them. *Saſſamon* ſigned this treaty as a witneſs. He ſoon after much incurred the diſpleaſure of *King Philip*, by being a tale bearer between his tribe and the Engliſh. In 1671 *Philip* complained that he had reported that he *(Philip)* was entertaining at Mount Hope certain Narraganſet Sachems. The Indian name of Wading River is *Coweſet*. Clarke's *Hiſt. Norton*, 39.

From the ſignature of *Saſſamon* (ſee *Hiſt. and Antiqs. Boſton*, p. 37) it is evident he could write tolerably well. In my former work I have ſhown that his name was originally *Wooſaujaman*, or that it ſo appears in very early papers of his time.

contrary to his Covenant and Faith engaged to *Plymouth* Colony, yea, and contrary to his promise unto some in this Colony (for about five years ago, *Philip* made a disturbance in *Plymouth* Colony, but was quieted by the prudent interposition of some in our Colony, when he engaged, that if at any time hereafter he should think the *English* among whom he lived did him wrong, he would not cause any disquietment before such time as he had acquainted the *English* of *Mattachusets*, but contrary to these solemn engagements he) doth

some time before this, in a clear, still, sunshiny morning, there were divers persons in Maldon who heard in the air, on the south east of them, a great gun go off, and presently thereupon the report of small guns like musket shot, very thick discharging, as if there had been a Battel. This was at a time when there was nothing visibly done in any part of the colony to occasion such noises; but that which most of all astonished them was the flying of bullets, which came singing over their heads, and seemed very near to them, after which the sound of drums passing along westward was very audible, and on the same day, in Plymouth colony, in several places, invisible troops of horses were heard riding to and fro. Now, reader, prepare for the event of these prodigies, but count me not struck with a Livian superstition in reporting prodigies, for which I have such incontestible assurance.

[Much of the above is nearly verbatim with the account contained in our first author's other work on the earlier Indian wars, entitled a *Relation of the Troubles*, &c., before referred to.]

call his Men together and *Arm* them, and refused to come when sent for, by the Authority of *Plymouth*, unto whose Government he had subjected himself.

Philip, conscious of his own guilt, pusht on the execution of his plot as fast as he could; he armed his men, and sent away their women and entertained many strange Indians that flock'd in unto him from several parts of the country, and began to be tumultuous. The English, whose innocency and integrity had made them too secure, neverthelefs, on these alarms made several friendly applications unto Philip, with their advice that he would no more allow of anything that should look like tumult among his people; but they were entertained with a surly, haughty, and provoking insolence.[1]

The Indians proceeded in the month of June unto the riffling of several houses in the plantations near Mount Hope, which was the seat where *Philip* was kennell'd with the rest of these horid salvages; and hereupon the governor of Plymouth sent forth a small army for the defence of the exposed plantations.

[1] Apprehensions were very great among the English, especially among those of Plymouth, in 1671, that the Indians had their destruction in view. It would seem that the author has reference to that period. Gov. *Prince* sent a letter to *Philip*, and the bearer was treated in a manner described above. *Philip* had been holding a dance, and when the latter found him he had just ended his frolic, and is reported to have been somewhat intoxicated, which accounts for his rudeness. Some words passed between the messenger, *James Brown*, and *Philip*, and *Philip* struck off Mr. *Brown's* hat. What the "some words" were it is not stated, but it is probable that *Brown* used insolent language to the chief. "*Philip* exclaimed much against *Sausaman* for reporting that any of the Narragansets were there" (at Mount Hope). See 1 *Cols. Mass. Hist. Soc.*, vi, 197, 198.

Hereupon the *English* in *Plymouth* Jurisdiction, sent a small Army to those Towns next *Mount hope*, in order to reducing *Philip* to his obedience, and for the security of those places which were in great danger, and in no less fear, by reason of the insolency of the Heathen.

June 24. (Midsummer-day) was appointed and attended as a day of solemn Humiliation throughout that Colony, by fasting and praying, to intreat the Lord to give success to the present Expedition respecting the Enemy. At the conclusion of that day of Humiliation, as soon as ever the People in Swanzy were come from the place where they had been praying together, the *Indians* discharged a volley of shot, whereby they killed one man, and wounded others. Two men were sent to call a Surgeon for the relief of the wounded, but the *Indians* killed them by the way: And in another part of the Town six men were killed, so that there were Nine *Englishmen* murthered this day.[1]

On June 24, a day of solemn humiliation was kept through the colony for the success of the expedition; and, reader, behold what a solemn humiliation the displeasure of heaven then dispensed unto them; for at the conclusion of the day, as the inhabitants of Swanzy were coming from their prayers, the lurking Indians discharged a volley of shot upon them, whereby one

---

[1] The account of this first opening of the great Drama of Philip's War is given with much variation, by both early and late writers. We have taken special pains to collect and arrange the facts, and they will be found printed in the *N. E. Hist.-Gen. Reg'r*, xv, p. 156-160. It was intended to extend those Notes into a minute history of the war.

Thus did the *War* begin, this being the first English blood which was spilt by the *Indians* in an Hostile way. The Providence of God is deeply to be observed, that the Sword should be first drawn upon a day of Humiliation, the Lord thereby declaring from Heaven that he expected something else from his People besides Fasting and Prayer.[1]

Plymouth being thus suddenly involved in trouble, send to the other united Colonies for aid, and their desires were with all readiness complied with.

Souldiers marched out of *Boston* towards *Mounthope*, June 26th, and continued marching that man was killed, and another wounded; and the two men that were sent for a chirurgeon to relieve the wounded, were also killed: which slaughter was accompanied with the murder of six men more in another part of the town. So that now the war was begun by a fierce nation of Indians, upon an honest, harmless, Christian generation of English, who might very truly have said unto the aggressors, as it was of old said unto the Ammonites, *I have not sinned against thee, but thou dost me wrong to war against me; the Lord the judge be judge this day between us!*

Plymouth colony being thus involved in a war, immediately sent unto the other United Colonies for their aid, who according to the articles of the Union whereinto they were confederated, immediately approved themselves true to the colony in adversity.

---

[1] It is not improbable that the Author had heard of Cromwell's wife and justly celebrated recommendation to his Soldiers in regard to keeping their powder in good condition. And although Cromwell doubtless believed as much in praying as any man, yet he did not require it at the expense of dry powder.

night, when there hapned a great Eclipfe of the Moon, which was totally darkned above an hour. Only it muft be remem[4]bred, that fome days before any Souldiers went out of *Bofton*, Commiffioners were fent to treat with *Philip*, that fo if poffible, ingaging in a war might be prevented. But when the Commiffioners came near to *Mount-hope*, they found divers *Englifhmen* on the ground, weltering in their own blood, having been newly murdered by the *Indians*, fo that they could not proceed farther. Yea, the *Indians* killed a man[1] of this Colony as he was travelling on the road before fuch time as we took up arms: In which refpect no man can doubt of the *juftnefs* of our Caufe, fince the Enemy did fhed the blood of fome of ours who never did them (our Enemies themfelves being judges) the leaft wrong before we did at all offend them, or attempt any act of hoftility towards them.

June 29th was a day of publick *Humiliation* in this Colony, appointed by the Council in refpect of the war which is now begun.

On June 26, a company of troopers under the command of Capt. *Thomas Prentice*, and footmen under the command of Capt. *Daniel Henchman*, marched out of Bofton towards Mount Hope; and though fome

---

[1] Reference is here made, probably, to the murder of *Zachary Smith*, which was in 1671. The particulars concerning the affair are to be found in the *Book of the Indians*, 263. The murder of *Smith* does not appear to have been in any way countenanced by the Tribe to which the murderers belonged, or by any other Indians, and probably had nothing at all to do with this war.

This morning our Army would have ingaged with the Enemy. The *Indians* shot the Pilot who was directing our Souldiers in their way to *Philips* Country, and wounded several of our Men, and ran into Swamps, rainy weather hindred a further pursuit of the Enemy. An awful Providence hap-

of a melancholy complexion had their dark thoughts, that a total and central eclipse of the moon in Capricorn, which gave them some *dark hours* the first night of their march, might be ominous of ensuing disasters; yet the soldiers were generally of the mind of *Marcus Crassus*, the great Roman general, *That there was more cause to be afraid of Sagittarius than of Capricornus.* A company of brisk volunteers under the command of Capt. *Samuel Moseley* quickly overtook them, and so joined with the Plymouth forces under the command of Capt. *Cudworth* at Swansey, June 28. Twelve of our men, unwilling to lose a minute of time, went that very evening to discover the enemy, who from the bushes fired upon them, killed one and wounded another, but were soon by our handful of men, put unto a *shameful flight.*

Our army the next morning [June 29,] made a resolute charge upon the enemy, who presently fled from their quarters, and left their whole territory open to us; entering whereof we found the mangled bodies of some of our countrymen, whose heads they had also stuck upon poles; and we found Bibles torn to pieces in defiance of our holy religion; but we found in the wigwams of the enemy all the marks of an [47] hasty departure; nor was Philip any more seen in his country, till he returned thither the next year to receive the recompence of his perfidy.

H

pened at this time: For a Souldier (a stout man) who was sent from *Water-town*, seeing the *English Guide* slain,[1] and hearing many profane oaths among some of our Souldiers (namely those Privateers, who were also Volunteers) and considering the unseasonableness of the weather was such, as that nothing could be done against the Enemy; this man was possessed with a strong conceit, that God was against the *English*; whereupon he immediately ran distracted, and so was returned home a lamentable Spectacle.[2]

In the beginning of *July*, there was another Skirmish with the Enemy, wherein several of the *Indians* were killed, amongst whom were *Philips* chief Captain, and one of his Counsellors.[3]

Now it appears that *Squaw-Sachem* of *Pocasset*,

[1] "The forces arriving there, some little time before night, twelve of the troop, unwilling to loose time, passed over the bridge for discovery into the enemies territories, where they found the rude welcome of eight or ten Indians firing upon them out of the bushes, killing one William Hammond, wounding Corporal Belcher" &c.—Hubbard, *Ind. Wars*, 18. "When the English drew off, the pilot [Hammond] was mortally wounded, Mr. Belcher received a shot in his knee, and his horse was killed under him. Mr. Gill was struck with a musket ball on the side of his body; but being clad with a buff coat and some thickness of paper under it, it never broke his skin."—Church's *Entertaining Hist.*, 33.

[2] Among the files in our Commonwealth Archives I find a paper shedding some light on this passage. It is an order of Court in these words:

"Oct. 1675. The Court order that Desire Sherman, whose husband, William Sherman Junr, whose sell destracted in the service of the country, be allowed £20. towards the reliefe of them and their family."

There were several families of the name of Sherman belonging to Watertown between 1635 and 1685, but I have learned nothing of this particular family, beyond this.

[3] This event was on July 1, and the party of English who performed the exploit was under Lieut. Oakes.

her men were conjoyned with the *Womponoags* (that is *Philips* men) in this Rebellion.[1]

[No notice being taken by our author of the events of the early part of July, the *Magnalia* supplies some of them as follows:]

The English little army scoured the woods, and with some loss to ourselves, we now and then had opportunity to inflict a greater loss upon the enemy. But we took this opportunity to march over into the Narraganset country, that with a sword in our hands we might renew and confirm our peace with a most considerable nation of Indians there, of whose conjunction with Philip and his Wompanoags (for so were *Phillip's* nation called) we had more than ordinary cause to be afraid. The effect of which was, that the sachems of the Narragansets, did, on July 15, sign and seal articles of peace with us, wherein they engaged that they would not only forbear all acts of hostility against the English, but also use their utmost ability, by all acts of hostility to destroy *Philip* and his adherants, calling the God of Heaven to witness for the true performance of these articles.

In the mean time Capt. *Cudworth*, with his Plymouth forces, went upon the like account unto another small nation of the Indians, at a place called Pocasset, with a design to hasten further a field for the help of the two little villages of Middlebury and Dartmouth, now suffering under the depredations of a sculking ad-

The number of Indians killed was three. They were scalped and their Scalps sent to Boston as Trophies! One of the Indians killed gave cause for exultation. His name was *Thebe*, and of considerable note.

[1] Her name was *Weetamoo*. Her defection is fully explained in Easton's *Narrative*, though the learned Editor mistakes another for her. Some early writers call her name *Weetamore*.

About this time they killed several *English* at *Taunton*, and Burnt divers Houses there.¹ Also at versary. Capt. [*Matthew*] *Fuller* and Capt. *Church*, with two small detachments, had spent some time in the woods of Pocasset, befor a great company of Indians compelled Capt. *Fuller* with his men to seek some shelter from a shower of bullets in an house near the water side, where they defended themselves, till a sloop from Rhode Island fetch'd them off; but Capt. *Church* was got into a Peas-field, where he with his 15 men, found himself suddenly surrounded with an hundred and almost five times *fifteen* terrible Indians: Nevertheless, this gentleman, like another *Shamgar*, had courage enough in himself alone to have saved an army; he assured his men with a strange confidence, that not a bullet should hurt them; which one, that was more faint-hearted than the rest, not believing, his valiant commander set him to gather a few rocks together for a little barricado to them; in the doing whereof, as he was carrying a stone in his arms to a bank intended, a bullet, which else would have killed him, struck upon that very stone, and missed him, which experiment presently restored *manhood* unto him: So they fought it out bravely that whole afternoon, without the least *hurt* unto any *one* of their number, but with death given to as many as *their number* of their enemies. And at last, when their guns by often firing were become unserviceable, a sloop of Rhode Island fetched them off also. This action was but a whet unto the

---

¹ They burnt the houses of *John Tisdell* and *James Walker*. Tisdell was killed; also *John Knolles* and *Samuel Atkins*, Soldiers, of Eastham. Baylies' *Mem. Plym. Col.*, iii, 54.

There are no Histories of the Towns mentioned in this paragraph, to which we might turn for the names and circumstances of the persons slain.

Swanzy, they caused about half the Town to be consumed with merciless Flames. Likewise *Middlebury* and *Dartmouth*, in *Plimouth* Colony, did they burn with Fire, and barbarously murdered both men and women in those places, stripping the slain, whether Men or Women, and leaving them in the open Field, as naked as in the day wherein they were born.[1] Such also is their Inhumanity, as that they flay off the skin from their Faces and Heads of those they get into their hands, and go away with the hairy Scalps of their Enemies.

July 19. Our Army pursued *Philip*, who fled unto a dismal Swamp for refuge:[2] The *English* courage of Capt. *Church*, who hastening over to the main, borrowed three files of men from the Massachuset forces, and returned unto Pocasset, where he had another skirmish, in which he slew 14 or 15 of the enemies, and struck such a terror into the rest, that if they could have got away, those Quarterers would for a while have heard no more of them.

[The above is from *Hubbard*, as will be seen on a reference to his history. *Hubbard* very probably had it from *Church* himself, as it agrees substantially with *Church's* own account, which was not published when Dr. C. Mather wrote.]

[1] There is much confusion and uncertainty about what was really done by KING PHILIP and his warriors, to which allusion is made in very vague terms, as well by other authors as ours. *Hubbard* has some facts, and others since his time elucidate him but poorly. The reader will find all that is known at present in Mitchell's *Bridgwater*, Baylies' *Plymouth*, and *Cols. M. H. Soc.*

[2] It was 18 miles from Taunton, and seven miles in length. Baylies' *Mem. Plym. Col.*, iii, 52. Its exact locality is not pointed out.

Souldiers followed him, and killed many of his men, alfo about fifteen of the *Englifh* were then flain. The Swamp was fo Boggy, [5] and thick of Bufhes, as that it was judged to proceed further therein would be but to throw away Mens lives. It could not there be defcerned who were *Englifh*, and who the *Indians*. Our Men when in that hideous place if they did but fee a Bufh ftir would fire prefantly, whereby 'tis verily feared they did fometimes unhappily fhoot *Englifh Men* inftead of *Indians*.[1] Wherefore a Retreat was founded, and night coming on, the Army withdrew from that place. This was becaufe the defperate Diftrefs which the Enemy was in was unknown to us, for the *Indians* have fince faid, that if the *Englifh* had continued at the Swamp all night, nay, if they had but followed them but one half hour longer, *Philip* had come and yielded up himfelf. But God faw we were not yet fit for Deliverance, nor could Health be reftored unto us except a great deal more Blood be firft taken from us: and other places as well as *Plimouth* ftood in need of fuch a Courfe to be taken with them. It might rationally be conjectured, that the unfuccefsfulnefs of this Expedition againft *Philip* would embolden the *Heathen* in other parts to do as he had done, and fo it came to pafs. For *July* 14, the *Nipnep* (or *Nipmuck*) *Indians* began

---

[1] That fome melancholy accidents occurred of the kind mentioned in the text, at this time, there is great probability. Capt. Church mentions one to which he was a witnefs. See *Hift. King Philip's War*, p. 34.

their mifchief at a Town called *Mendam*[1] (had we mended our ways as we fhould have done, this Mifery might have been prevented) where they committed *Barbarous Murders*. This day deferves

The little forces of the two colonies coming together again after the treaty of Narraganfet, they marched from Taunton, July 18, eighteen miles to a mighty fwamp where the Indians were lodged; and the Indians covering themfelves with green boughs, a fubtilty of the fame *nature*, though not of the fame *colour*, that they affirm to be ufed by the *cuttle-fifh*, took the advantage from the thick under-woods to kill feveral of the Englifh. But the Englifh purfuing of them, they prefently deferted an hundred of their wigwams which they had there erected, and retired further into the prodigious thicket, where we prefumed that we had 'em in a pound; and fo, fcarce 200 men being left there to keep an eye upon them, the reft (except fuch as returned unto Bofton) were difpatched unto the relief of Mendham [Mendon] where, about July 14, the Nipmuck Indians, another nation of them that were well willers to *Philip's* defign, began to *philippize* in barbarous murders. Our forces kept a ftrict eye upon the motions of the enfwamped enemy; but finding if once we fqueezed ourfelves into thofe inacceffible woods, we meerly facrificed one another to our own miftakes, by firing into every bufh that we faw to ftir, as expecting *a thief in every bufh*; we were willing rather to *ftarve* the beaft in his den, than go in to fight him

---

[1] Now Mendon. We have not been able to recover the name of but one perfon killed at this time at Mendon. There were two, as appears by the Old *Indian Chronicle*, 138. The name of one of the flain was Richard Poft I am happy to learn that the Hon. J. G. Metcalf is engaged on a Hiftory of the ancient and important town of Mendon.

to have a *Remark* set upon it, considering that Blood was never shed in *Massachusetts Colony* in a way of Hostility before this day.[1] Moreover the Providence of God herein is the more awful and tremendous, in that this very day the Church in *Dorchester* was before the Lord, humbling themselves by Fasting and Prayer, on account of *the day of trouble* now begun amongst us.

The news of this Blood-shed came to us at *Boston* the next day in Lecture time, in the midst of the Sermon, the Scripture then improved being that *Isai.* 42, 24. *Who gave Jacob to the spoil and Israel to the robbers? did not the Lord, he against whom ye have sinned?*

As yet *Philip* kept in the Swamp at *Pocasset,* but there. Heaven saw more blood must be drawn from the colonies, before health could be restored to them. *Philip* would have surrendered himself, if we had gone in to take him ; whereas now becoming desperate, he with his best fighting men taking the advantage of a *low tide*, in the middle of the night, wafted themselves over on small rafts of timber, into the woods that led into the Nipamuck country, while our forces that lay encamped on the other side perceived it not. An hundred of the miserable salvages that were left behind, made a surrender of themselves to our mercy ; but *Philip's* escape now soon after day-light being discovered, the English, assisted with a party of Monhegin Indians, pursued them as fast as they could, and in the pursuit slew about 30 of them e'er the night obliged 'em to give over.

---

[1] I suppose the author intended to be understood that this was the first blood shed in *regular* warfare.

August 1. (being the Lords day) he fled. The *Englifh* hearing that *Philip* was upon flight purfued him with a party of *Monhegins*, i. e. *Vnkas* (who approved himfelf faithful to the *Englifh* almoft forty years ago in the time of the *Pequod* Wars, and now alfo in this prefent War) his *Indians*, they overtook *Philips* Party and killed about thirty of his men, none of ours being at that time cut off.¹ Had the *Englifh* purfued the Enemy they might eafily have overtaken the Women and Children that were with *Philip*, yea and himfelf alfo, and fo have put an end to thefe tumults: but though Deliverance was according to all Humane probability near, God faw it not good for us as yet. Wherefore *Philip* efcaped and went to the *Nipmuck Indians*, who had newly (as hath been intimated) done Acts of Hoftility againft the *Englifh*. In the mean while endeavours were ufed to keep thofe *Indians* from engaging in this war, and that thofe perfons who had committed the Murder at *Mendam* might be delivered up to juftice. Captain *Hutchinfon* with a fmall party was fent to *Quabaog*, where there was a great Rendezvouze of *Nipnet Indians*. They appointed time and place of Treaty to be attended, *Auguft* 2. Accordingly Captain *Hutchin-*

---

1 This memorable retreat of Philip, and the attack on his rear, are pretty minutely recorded in the *Book of the Indians*. The enemy were attacked as they efcaped over Rehoboth Plain. Philip having brought his beft warriors to the rear, feveral of his chief Captains were flain. Among them was Woonafhum, called by the Englifh Nimrod, who had, as one of Philip's chief counfellors, figned the Treaty of Taunton four years before. See APPENDIX A.

ſon rode to the place fixed on to Treat in. But the *Indians* came not thither according to their Agreement, whereupon Captain *Hutchinſon* reſolved to go further to ſeek after them elſewhere, and as he was riding along, the Perfidious *Indians* lying in Ambuſcado in a ſwamp, ſhot at him and wounded him, of which wounds he after dyed, and eight men that were with him were ſtruck down dead upon the place.[1] Captain *Wheeler* who was in that Company was ſhot through the Arm, his dutiful Son alighting to relieve his Father, was himſelf

---

[1] He died at Marlborough, and was the firſt there buried in the old burying-ground, where his aſhes ſtill remain, and over them was placed the following inſcription:

"CAPT. EDWARD HUTCHINSON, Æ. 67 YEARS WAS MORTALLY WOUNDED BY THE INDIANS, AUGUST 2D. 1675; DIED AUGUST 19TH, 1675." *Allen's Hiſt. Northboro.*

There is quite a diſcrepancy between this inſcription and the above for which it is difficult to account:

Captain Edward Hutchinſon
aged 62 years,
was ſhot by
Treacherovs Indians
Avgvſt 2. 1675.
Dyed 12 Avgvſt,
1675.

See *Hiſt. and Antiquities of Boſton*, 406.

He was the ſon of William and Ann (da. of Edward Marbury, min. of London) Hutchinſon, and had been in New England ſince 1634. He was the great grand-father of the afterward celebrated governor Thomas Hutchinſon. Though he left a large family of children, Eliſha was the only ſon living at this time old enough to take charge of his affairs, and he was in his 34th year. This ſon was his executor, and the following account againſt the colony for the ſervices of his father in the war in which he loſt his life, is given as a curious illuſtration of the value of ſervices in thoſe times.

```
Account.                          £  s  d
1675 June. To a Jorney To
   Naraganſet one weeke        2:00:00
   Expences for himſelf & a man 1:10:00
July. To a Jorney to Naraganſet
   2 weekes                    4:00:00
   To Expences for himſelfe & man 2:10:00
Auguſt. To a Jorney to Quabauge
   wher he Recd his death's
   wound, being 3 weeks be-
   fore he dyed                6:00:00
To his Expences & Charges
   ther & at Marlborow         4:10:00
                              ———————
                              £20:10:00
```
ELISHA HUTCHINSON, Execut'r.
Boſton July 29, 1678.

shot and sorely wounded, willingly hazarding his own life to save the life of his Father. The *English* were not in a capacity to look after their dead, but those dead bodies were left as meat for the Fowls of Heaven, and their Flesh unto the Beasts of the Earth, and there was none to bury them.[1]

Captain *Hutchinson* and the rest that escaped with their lives, hastened to *Quabaog*, and the Indians speedily followed, violently set upon the Town, killed divers, burning all the Houses therein down to the ground, except only one unto which the Inhabitants fled for succor, and now also (as since we have understood) did *Phillip* with his broken Party come to *Quabaog*. Hundreds of *Indians* beset the House, and took possession of a Barn belonging thereunto, from whence they often shot into the House, and also attempted to set fire to it six times, but could not prevail, at last they took a Cart full of Flax and other combustible matter, and brought it near the House, intending to set it on fire; and then there was no appearing possibility, but all the *English* there, Men and Women, and Children must have perished, either by unmerciful flames, or more unmerciful hands of wicked Men,

---

[1] Capt. Thomas Wheeler, one of the principal men in the affair at Wackabaog Pond, Brookfield, wrote and published the same year (1675) a faithful and simple account of it, in a small quarto pamphlet of some 20 pages. It is of extreme rarity, and not above two or three copies are known to exist. It was first republished with valuable notes in the *Cols of the N. H. Hist. Soc.*, vol. II, in 1827. It has been reprinted (from this edition) in an edition of the Rev. Mr. Foot's *Historical Discourse on the History of Brookfield*. It is exceedingly valuable, containing the names of the slain, and other particulars.

whose tender Mercies are cruelties, so that all hope that they should be saved was then taken away, but behold in this Mount of Difficulty and Extremity (יהוה יראה) *the Lord is seen*.[1]

For in the very nick of opportunity God sent that worthy Major *Willard*, who with forty and eight men set upon the *Indians* and caused them to turn their backs, so that poor People who were given up for dead, had their lives given them for a prey. Surely this was a token for good, that however we may be diminished and brought low through Oppression, Affliction, and Sorrow, yet our God will have compassion on us, and this his People shall not utterly perish. And this Salvation is the more remarkable, for that albeit the *Indians* had ordered Scouts to ly in the way, and to give notice by [7] firing three Guns, if any English came to to the relief of the distressed; yet although the Scouts fired when Major *Willard* and his Souldiers were past them, the *Indians* were so busie and made such a noise about the House that they heard not the report of those Guns; which if they had heard, in all probability not only the People then living at *Quabaog*, but those also that came to succor them had been cut off.

However, *Philip* now escaping [from Pocasset] to the westward, he enflamed the several nations of the Indians in the west wherever he came, to take part

---

[1] By the kindness of J. CARSON BREVOORT, Esq., of Brooklyn, N. Y., I have been put in possession of copies of two original letters of Maj. John Pynchon, written, as will be seen, immediately after the flight of

Things being brought to this ſtate, the Tumult of thoſe that are riſen up increaſeth continually: with him, until the flame of war was raging all over the whole Maſſachuſetts colony. The firſt ſcene of the bloody tragedy was in the Nipmuck country, whither Capt. *Hutchinſon*, accompanied with Capt. *Wheeler*, went Aug. 2, upon a treaty of peace with the Indians there, who had agreed with him a place of meeting for the conſummation of the treaty, and the renovation of the covenant, wherein they had [48] the month before promiſed under their hands that they would not aſſiſt *Philip* in his hoſtilities. The Indians not coming to the place aſſigned, Capt. *Hutchinſon* rode a little farther, and ſo *far* that the perfidious villains, from an ambuſcado, mortally wounded him, and ſhot eight more dead upon the ſpot; but the reſt fled back by a by path to Quaboag, a ſmall village, where all the inhabitants were juſt got into one houſe, reſolving there to live and die together. The Indians, with *Philip's* army newly arrived unto them, ruſhed in like a ſtorm of lightning upon this diſtreſſed village: and having burnt all the reſt, they furiouſly beſet that one houſe, where a little handful of men bravely defended the little cottage, which was all their caſtle againſt an huge army of cruel tawnies, who kept perpetually pouring in their ſhot upon them for two days together, and thruſting poles with brands and rags dipped in burning brimſtone, and many other tricks, to ſet their cottage on fire. At laſt, after ſix ineffectual attempts to burn this poor hovel, (ſo in *ſix troubles they were delivered*, yea, in

Philip and his men into the country of the Nipmuks. Theſe letters contain an excellent picture of Spring- field at that time, and ſome new items giving them much intereſt. They will be found in APPENDIX B.

For *August* 22. being the Lords Day, the *Indians* about *Lancaster* killed a Man and his Wife and two *seven* the *evil touch'd* 'em not!) they filled a cart with flax, hemp, and other combuſtible matter, and kindling of it, they puſhed it on with very long poles, that were ſpliced one unto another; by which means this *petite flock* muſt have unavoidably become a prey to theſe horid *wolves*, if a mighty ſtorm of rain had not ſuddenly extinguiſhed it. But *bleſſed be the Lord*, (might the ſeventy men, women and children in that houſe anon ſing!) *who hath not giuen us a prey to their teeth; our ſoul is eſcaped as a bird out of the ſnare of the fowlers!*

Our memorable Major *Willard*, on Aug. 4, in the morning, ſetting forth with a party of men to viſit and ſecure a nation of ſuſpected Indians in the neighborhood, received by ſtrange accident ſeaſonable advice of the doleful condition wherein our brethren at Quaboag, 39 miles diſtant from him, were enſnared, and thereupon turning his courſe thither, it came to paſs, that although the Indians had placed ſufficient ambuſhments to cut off any ſuccors that ſhould come that way, yet there was an *unaccountable beſotment* ſo fallen upon them, that this valiant commander with 48 men arrived at night unto the help of theſe beſieged people, and bravely raiſed the ſiege, by driving the beaſts of prey back to their dens after he had firſt ſacrificed many ſcores of them unto the divine vengeance. Thus remarkable was this poor people delivered; but the enemy ſteering further weſtward, Capt. *Lothrop*, Capt. *Beers*, and others, were ſent with more forces to track 'em; and if it were poſſible, to prevent their poiſoning and ſeducing of the Indians upon Connecticut river, whoſe fidelity was now extremely doubted of.

Children in the afternoon Exercise.¹ And we hear that *Philip* and the *Quabaog Indians* are gone more Weftward, not far from *North-hampton, Hadly, Deerfield,* &c. Whereupon Forces are fent from hence under the command of Captain *Lothrop,* Captain *Beers,* and after that Captain *Mofely,* to relieve thofe diftreffed Towns, and purfue the Enemy.² Alfo our Brethren at *Connecticut* afforded their Affiftance, Major *Treat* being fent to *Hadly* with a party of *Englifh,* and fome of *Vnkas* his men. The *Indians* inhabiting about *Connecticut River* pretended great fidelity to the *Englifh,* and that they would fight againft *Philip,* who it feems had been tampering with them in the Spring before the War broke out, endeavouring by money (*i. e. Wampampeag* which is the *Indians* money) to engage them in this bloody defign againft the *Englifh.*

At firft they were fo far credited as to be Armed by the *Englifh,* hoping they might do good fervice as the *Monhegins* and *Natick Indians* had done. But within a while their Treachery was juftly fufpected. Whereupon Souldiers were fent (on or about *Auguft* 25.) to demand their Arms. They were then gone out of their Forts, our Men fearching after them, they fuddenly fhot out of a Swamp, and after that an hot difpute continued for fome

---

1 Mordecai McLeod was the name of the man. Befides him and his wife and two children, at the fame time, or on the fame day, in different parts of the town, were killed, George Bennet, William Fagg, Jacob Farrar, and Jofeph Wheeler. See Whitney's *Hift. Worcefter County,* 37.

2 See APPENDIX C.

hours. How many *Indians* were slain we know not, but nine *English* fell that day: wherein this Providence is observable, that the *nine men* which were killed at that time belonged to *nine several Towns;* as if the Lord should say, that he hath a controversie with every Plantation, and therefore all had need to repent and reform their way.[1]

Now the *English* have a multitude of open enemies more than when this trouble began, so that greater desolations are now expected.

Wherefore *September* 1. the *Indians* set upon *Deerfield* (alias *Pacomtuck*) and killed one man,[2] and laid most of the Houses in that new hopeful Plantation in ruinous heaps. That which added solemnity and awfulness to that desolation is, that it happened on the very day when one of the Churches in *Boston* were seeking the face of God by Fasting and Prayer before him. Also that very day the Church in *Hadly* was before the Lord in the same way, but were driven from the Holy Service they were attending [8] by a most sudden and violent *Alarm*, which routed them the whole day after. So that we may humbly complain, as some-

---

[1] That these nine men belonged to nine different towns, is stated by the author on the authority of the Rev. John Russell, the minister of Hadley, as will be seen a few pages forward. Their names were Azariah Dickinson, James Lewis, Samuel Mason, Richard Fellows, John Plummer, Mark Pitman, Joseph Pearson [Parsons], Mathew Scales, and William Cluffe. Russell's *Account* in Coffin's *Hist. Newbury*, 389.

[2] James Eggleston by name. Prince's *Appendix* to Williams' *Redeemed Captive* (Rev. John Taylor's edition) p. 109. In Mr. Russell's account it appears there were two men killed at this time—"James Eaglestone and Nathaniel Cranberry." Coffin, p. 390.

times the Church did, *How long haſt thou ſmoaked away againſt the Prayers of thy People?* Not long after this Captain *Beers* with a conſiderable part of his men fell before the Enemy. Concerning the ſtate of thoſe parts at this time until *September* 15. I received information from a good hand,[1] whilſt things were freſh in memory, which I ſhall here inſert, as containing a brief *Hiſtory* of the Tranſactions which happened within the time mentioned; thoſe parts being then the Seat of the War: the Letter which I intend is that which followeth.

Reverend and dear Brother

" I received yours, wherin among other things
" you deſire an account of the paſſages of our War
" with the *Indians :* I ſhall in anſwer to your de-
" ſire relate the moſt remarkable paſſages: The
" people here having many cauſes of jealouſie, of
" the unfaithfulneſs of our *Indians* preſented the
" ſame before the Committees of the Militia,
" whereupon it was thought meet to deſire of
" them the ſurendry of their Arms, and by per-
" ſwaſion obtained about nine and twenty: But
" about three days after they being deſirous to go
" forth with ſome Forces from *Hartford*, both *In-*
" *dians* and *Engliſh*, and ſome from the *Bay*[2] in

---

[1] The Rev. John Ruſſell, no doubt, miniſter of Hadley, mentioned in a previous note. He was ordained there in 1659, and is celebrated in Stiles's *Hiſt. of the Judges*, for his ſervices in concealing the two Regicide Judges of Charles I. He died in Hadley in 1692. The communication in the text was written Sept. 15th, probably, by what immediately follows.

[2] The country about Boſton; or that part of Maſſachuſetts bordering on the bay of the ſame name, was uſually then ſo denominated.

"pursuit of *Philip*, their Arms were delivered to
them again; but a while after their return,
jealousies still increasing, there was a general desire
in the People of these three Towns, that they
should be again disarmed, and such things as these
were presented to the Council here, as inducing
thereto: 1. That when they heard of the Massacre
at *Quabaog*, they made in the Fort eleven Accla-
mations of joy, according to the number of our men
that were slain. 2. A *Frenchman* that was going
to *Boston* gave Testimony that he met three *Indians* that told him they were coming to perswade *North Hampton Indians* to fight with
Philip, and that at his return he askt our *Indians*
whether they would fight, they said they could
not tell. 3. One of their *Sachims* owned that
there were several among them false to the
English, but would not tell who they were. 4.
A woman of ours was warned by a *Squaw* to
remove with her Children into the middle of the
Town: told her withal, she durst not tell News,
for if she did the *Indians* would cut off her head.
5. Some of theirs gave out very suspicious Expressions; one upbraided the *English*, that *Coy*
was dead already, and *Eyer* and *Pritchet* were
dead already;[1] said further that the *Indians* went

---

[1] The affair here vaguely referred to was on August 2d, at Wickabaug pond, in the westerly part of
Brookfield. See Wheeler's *Narrative*, p. 9, in *Colls. N. H. Hist. Soc.*
Vol. II. "There were then slain,
to our great grief," says Capt.
Wheeler, "eight men, viz., Zechariah Philips of Boston, Timothy
Farlow [Farley] of Billericay, Edward Coleborn of Chelmsford, Samuel Smedley of Concord, Sydrach

" out to find *Philip* with the *English,* that when
" *Philip* was fighting with them in the front, they
" might fall on them in the rear: another said the
" reason why he went not out with the Army was
" that he might help to destroy the *English* at
" home: another threatened [9] a Maid of our
" Town to knock her on the head. 6. When
" they were out with our Army, they shewed
" much unwillingness to fight, alledging they must
" not fight against their Mothers and Brothers and
" Cousins (for *Quabaog Indians* are related unto
" them.) 7. *Vnkas* his son, who went out the
" same time, complained that our *Indians* had al-
" most spoiled his, and that the *English* were blind
" and could not see the falsehood of these *Indians.*
" 8. They shot bullets five several times at our
" men in divers places. Other things too many
" to numerate were presented, and the Council
" saw cause to demand their Arms, *Aug.* 24. They
" made some Objections, but were fully answered:
" The Sachem left the Council to try whether he
" could perswade the *Indians,* promising however
" to bring in his own. In the afternoon the
" Council sent to the Fort for their answer: they
" told the Messenger that some *Indians* were

Hopgood of Sudbury, Serjeant [John] Eyres, Serjeant [Joseph] Pritchard, and Corporal [John] Coy, the inhabitants of Brookfield. There were also then five persons wounded, viz., Capt. Hutchinson, my self, and my son Thomas, Corporal [John] French of Billericay, who having killed an Indian, was (as he was taking up his gun) shot, and part of one of his thumbs taken off, and also dangerously wounded through the body near the shoulder; the fifth was John Woldoe of Chelmsford, who was not so dangerously wounded as the rest."

" abroad in the Meadows, and they were not will-
" ing to deliver up their Arms without their con-
" fent: but in the morning they fhould have their
" anfwer. The Meffenger was defired to go again
" to them in the evening, to confer with them, to
" try whether he could perfwade them, and coming
" to the other fide of the River, wifht fome of them
" to come over: they bid him come over to them,
" and bid him kifs ——— whereupon Captain
" *Lothrop* and *Beers*, with whom the thing was
" left, intended to take their Arms by force, and
" at midnight fent over to our officers, to draw as
" nigh the Fort as they could without being per-
" ceived, and they would do the like on *Hatfield*
" fide, and fo at break of day come upon them:
" but before they came the *Indians* were fled, hav-
" ing killed an old *Sachem* that was not willing to
" go with them. The Captains refolved to follow
" them, and purfued a great pace after them, with
" about an hundred men, having fent back a part
" of ours for a Guard of the Town. A little be-
" fore they overtook the *Indians*, they heard two
" ftrange claps of Thunder, like two volleys of
" fhot; a length they faw a fingle *Indian*, but fhot
" not at him, though they might have killed him,
" becaufe they intended to parley with them: but on
" a fudden the *Indians* let fly about forty Guns at
" them, and was foon anfwered by a volley from
" our men; about forty ran down into the Swamp
" after them, poured in fhot upon them, made
" them throw down much of their luggage, and

"after a while our Men after the *Indian* manner
"got behind trees, and watcht their opportunities
"to make ſhots at them; the fight continued about
"three hours, we loſt ſix men upon the ground,
"though one was ſhot in the back by our own
"men, a ſeventh died of his wound coming home,
"and two died the next night, nine in all, of nine
"ſeveral Towns, every one of theſe Towns loſt a
"man: Of the *Indians* as we hear ſince by a
"*Squaw* that was taken, and by three Children
"that came to our Town from them the day after,
"there were ſlain [10] twenty ſix: the ſame day
"there was an *Indian* that lodged in our Town
"the night before, taken by our men, and a *Squaw*
"that belonged to our Fort that was coming from
"*Springfield;* they both own that our *Indians*
"received *Wompam* from *Philip* in the Spring, to
"ingage them in the War. The fellow alſo owns
"that there were ſeven of our *Indians* that went to
"*Quababaog,* where they heard that they intended
"to fight. After this fight we heard no more of

The towns belonging unto Maſſachuſetts colony upon Conecticut river, aſſiſted now by forces alſo from Connecticut, under the command of Maj. *Robt. Treat,* ſent ſoldiers on Aug. 25, to demand from their Indians a proof of that faithfulneſs, which they had hitherto profeſſed, but *Philip* had bewitched them; they were fled from their forts, having firſt killed an old ſachem of their own that was not willing to go with them; they fired upon our men from a ſwamp when we were looking after them; and a diſpute continued for ſome hours, wherein we loſt *nine men,* belonging to *nine towns.*

"them till the first of *September*, when they shot
"down a Garrison Souldier of *Pacomptuck* that was
"looking for his horse, ran violently up into the
"Town, many people having scarcely time enough
"to get into the Garrisons. That day they burnt
"most of their houses and barns, the Garrison not
"being strong enough to sally out upon them,
"but killed two of their men from the Forts.
"The next day they set upon several men that
"were gone out of the Fort at *Squakheag*, they
"slew eight of our men,[1] not above one of them
"being slain that we know of, but made no attempt
"upon the Fort. The next day (this Onset being
"unknown) Capt. *Beers*
"set forth with about
"thirty six men and some
"Carts to fitch off the
"Garrison at *Squakheag*,

It seems Capt. Beers and those 36 men that were with him, fought couragiously till their powder and shot was spent, then the Indians prevailed over them so as to kill above 20 of them, only 13 escaped with their lives, at which time a Cart with some Ammunition fell into the hands of the enemy.[2]

Thus the desolations of war were carried into these parts of the country, while small crews of salvages here and there, in other parts of the country, were distressing people wonderfully.

[1] This was Sept. 2d, as mentioned in the text, at a place called Sugar-loaf hill, opposite Sunderland. The persons slain were Serj. Samuel Wright, Ebenezer Jeans, Jonathan Jeans, Ebenezer Parsons, Nathaniel Curtis, Thomas Scott, and John Peck. *Russell's Account*, before cited. *Squakheag* is in what is since Northfield. *Pacomptuck* was a part of Deerfield.

[2] Richard Beers came over in 1630, and settled in Watertown, where he had granted him a lot of an acre and a half of land. He became freeman in 1637, and went against the Pequots, as he himself says, "in two several designes when the Lord delivred them into our hands." Soon after, or, as he says, "vppon his return, such a weaknes fell vppon his boddy that for 8 years space he

the Indians in New-England. 79

" and coming within three miles of the Place, the
" next morning were set upon by a great number
" of *Indians* from the side of a Swamp, where was
" an hot Dispute for some time: They having
" lost their *Captain* and some others, resolved at
" last to fly, and going to take horse lost several
" more, I think above twelve: the most that es-
" caped got to *Hadly* that evening:[1] next morning
" another came in, and at night another that had
" been taken by the *Indians*, and loosed from his

was much disinabled to labor for his famyly; spending a great part of that little hee had upon phesitions." In 1664 he petitioned for a grant of land from the colony, "where he can find it in this wilderness, seeing he hath many children to share in the same." And " hath bin an inhabitant in this jurisdiction ever since the first begining thereof, and according to his weake abilities served the same; not only in times of peace," &c. The government granted him 300 acres. He was a respected citizen, and was a representative from 1663 till the year in which he was killed. His name is written *Beere*, *Beeres*, and *Beers*.

Sixty years after the fight in which Capt. Turner was killed, a list of the descendants of those who fought with him was made out by order of the General Court, and these descendants were rewarded by a grant of a township of land, which was named Fall Town, now Bernardston. In the list we find the name of Richard Beers; doubtless a descendant of the Captain.

[1] This disastrous battle was fought on the 3d of September, " very near the town" of Squakheag. Hubbard, 37. Gen. Hoyt, who knew the ground, says the place where the attack was made, "is to this day called *Beers' Plain*, and the hill where the Captain fell, *Beers' Mountain*. Until lately the mail route from Montague to Northfield, passed over the ground. It now runs a little to the west of it." *Antiquarian Researches*, 104.

Russell says the number slain with Capt. Beers was sixteen; viz., Capt. Richard Beers, John Chenary, Ephraim Child, Benj. Crackbone, Robert Pepper, Joseph Dickinson, William Markham, George Lyrass, John Gatchell, James Miller, John Wilson. Pepper was not killed, as at first supposed, but was wounded in the leg and taken prisoner, and remained some time with the Indians. See *Indian Captivities*, 25-6.

"bonds by a *Natick Indian*, he tells the *Indians*
"were all drunk that night, that they mourned
"much for the loss of a great Captain, that the
"English had killed twenty five of their men. Six
"days after another Souldier came in, who had been
"lost ever since the fight, and was almost famish-
"ed, and so lost his understanding that he knew
"not what day the fight was on.

"On the 5th of *September* Major *Treat* set forth
"for *Squakheag* with above an hundred men, next
"day coming nigh *Squakheag*, his men were much
"daunted to see the heads of Captain *Beers's* Soul-
"diers upon Poles by the way side; but after they
"were come to *Squakheag*, some partyes of them
"went into the Meadow, but hearing some Guns
"about the Fort, they ran up to see what the
"matter was, but by the way were fired upon by

On Sept. 1, the Indians laid most of the houses belonging to the hopeful plantation of Deerfield in ashes, while the garrison was not strong enough to sally forth upon 'em; and on the day following they slew eight men abroad in the woods at Squakhegg, without making any attempts upon the garrison. Capt. Beers, with about 36 men, were sent up to fetch off the people in these little garrisons, but they found *a serpent by the way, and an adder in the path:* hundreds of Indians from a thick swamp fired upon them, whereupon followed a desperate fight, wherein the captain and a score of his men sold their lives at as good a price as they could, but the rest fled into Hadley, leaving Maj. *Treat* a few days after to finish what they had undertaken.

"about fourteen *Indians* as they judge out of the
"Bushes: one or two *Indians* were slain, Major
"*Treat* was struck upon the thigh, the bullet
"pierced his [11] cloaths, but had lost its force,
"and did him no harm: coming to the Fort he
"called his Councill together, and concluded
"forthwith to bring off the garison: so they came
"away the same night, leaving the Cattel there,
"and the dead bodies unburied: since which
"seventeen of their Cattel came a great part of the
"way themselves, and have since been fetcht into
"*Hadly*.[1]

[It was necessary to transpose a paragraph from the Magnalia, owing to the above letter.]

The Inhabitants of Springfield, notwithstanding the firmest assurances which the nations of Indians near to them had given them of their friendship and faithfulness, were awakened by these things to enquire how far they might rest assured thereof [49] when all o'th' sudden the hostages which these Indians had given were fled; and some English going to visit them at their fort, were treacherously saluted with a volley of shot, which miserably wounded them; whereupon the town was, in all the ungarrisoned parts of it, fired by these perfideous catifs. Thirty-two houses, and amongst the rest, the minister's, with his well furnished library, were consumed before the arrival of Maj. *Treat*, Maj. *Pinchon*, and Capt. *Appleton*, put a stop to the fury and progress of an insulting enemy: Nor had the inhabitants themselves escaped a massacre, if an Indian, privy to the plot, had not, just in the *nick of time* discovered it unto them.

[1] For the state of Springfield at this time, see APPENDIX.

"Upon the 12*th:* of this month the Indians made an assault upon twenty two men of *Po-comptuck*, that were going from one garison to the other to *Meeting* in the afternoon: made a great volley of shot at them, but killed not one man, they escaped to the Garison whither they were going, only one man running to the other garison was taken alive: The *Indians* took up their rendezvouze on an hill in the meadow, burnt two more house kiled many horses, carryed away horse-loads of beef and pork to the hill: they sent the same night for more aid, but partly through the strictness of the Commission of our Garison souldiers, or at least their interpretation of it, and partly through the wetness of the weather, there was nothing done that night: the next day we perswaded some of our inhabitants to go Volunteers, and sent to *Hadly* to doe the like, who going up with some of Captain *Louthrops* souldiers, joyned themselves to the garison at *Pocomptuck*, and on Tuesday very early went out to assault the *Indians*, but they were all fled. Last night[1] Captain *Mosely* with his men came into *Hadly*, and this night we expect more Forces from *Hartford*.

"If the Lord give not some sudden Check to these Indians, it is to be feared that most of the *Indians* in the Countrey will rise.

"I desire you would speak to the *Governour*, that there may be some thorough care for a *Re-*

---

[1] September 14th. Hadley was then the head-quarters of the army.

"*formation*, I am sensible there are many difficulties
"therein: many sins are grown so in fashion, that
"it becomes a question whether they be sins or
"no. I desire you would especially mention, *Op-*
"*pression*, that intollerable *Pride* in cloathes and
"hair: the tolleration of so many *Taverns*, espe-
"cially in *Boston*, and suffering home-dwellers to
"lye tipling in them. Let me hear soon from
"you: the Lord bless you and your Labours;
"forget us not at the throne of Grace: It would
"be a dreadfull Token of the Displeasure of God,
"if these afflictions pass away without much spirit-
"ual advantage: I thought to have written some-
"what more large with respect to *Reformation*, but
"I hope I need not, you will I presume be forward
"of your self therein.

After this, the English forces were ordered, by a merciful providence of Heaven, to rendezvous about Northampton, Hadley, Hatfield, until it might be considered what there was further to be done; and now behold, reader, a comfortable matter, in the midst of so many tragedies. The general court then sitting at Boston appointed a committee, who with the assistance of the ministers in the neighborhood, might suggest what were the *provoking evils* that had thus brought the judgements of God in a bloody *war* upon the land, and what laws might be enacted for the reformation of those *provoking evils!* The return of which committee to the general court was kindly received on Oct. 19th, and care taken further to prosecute the intentions of it.

Now as our Martyrologist, Mr. *Fox*, observes, that at the very day and hour when the Act of Reformation,

[12] Not many dayes after this letter was written, the Englifh received a fadder rebuke of Providence, then any thing that hitherto had been. For *September* 18. Captain *Lothrop* (a godly and couragious Commander) with above feventy men were fent to be as a Guard to fome that were coming from *Deerfield* with Carts loaden with Goods and Provifion, to be removed to *Hadly*, for fecurity: But as they were coming, the *Indians*, whofe cruel Habitations are the dark corners of the Earth, lurked in the Swamps, and multitudes of

in the reign of King *Edward* VI was put in execution at London, God gave the nation a fignal victory at Mufcleborough: Thus it was remarked by fome devout men, that on the very day when the vote was paffed at Bofton for the *reformation* of mifcarriages in the land, our forces had a notable fuccefs an hundred miles off againft the common enemy. Seven or eight hundred Indians broke in upon Hatfield at all quarters, but our forces being beyond their expectation lodged in the neighborhood the Indians were fo terribly defeated, that after the killing of but one Englifhman in the fight, they confeffed the town too hot for them, and fled fo faft, that many of them loft their lives in the river. This refolute repulfe gave fuch a chceck to the enemy, that the weftern plantations for a long while heard little or nothing further from them; fome ftraggling parties, indeed, were here and there mifchievous; but as winter drew on, they generally retired unto the Narraganfet country, where the reader muft now expect a confiderable action.

[For the next paragraph of the *Magnalia*, fee the 1ft note to the Poftfcript.]

them made a sudden and frightful assault. They seized upon the Carts and Goods (many of the Souldiers having been so foolish and secure as to put their Arms in the Carts, and step aside to gather *Grapes*, which proved dear and deadly Grapes to them) killed Captain *Lothrop*, and above threescore of his men,[1] stripped them of their clothes, and so left them to lye weltring in their own Blood. Captain *Mosely* who was gone out to range the Woods, hearing the Guns, hasted to their help, but before he could come, the other Captain, and his men were slain, as hath been expressed Nevertheless he gave the *Indians* Battle: they were in such numbers as that he and his company were in extream danger, the *Indians* endeavouring (according to their mode of fighting) to encompase the English round, and then to press in upon them in great numbers, so to knock them down with their hatchets. In the nick of time Maj. *Treat* with above an hundred men, and three of *Unkas* his *Indians* came in to succour those that were so beset with the Enemy, whereupon the Enemy presently retreated, and night coming on there was no pursuing them in the night but few of Captain *Mosley's* men were slain.[2] How many *Indians* were killed is unknown, it being their

[1] The number of slain was seventy-one. He set out with eighty, according to Mr. Hubbard. Hence nine only escaped. Such a wholesale slaughter has few parallels in history.

[2] Of the "few" that were slain we have the names of John Oates and Peter Barron. For some curious facts from original MS., of Mosley in this action, see *Book of the Indians*, 216.

manner to draw away their dead men as faft as they are killed, if poffibly can do it; yea they will venture their own lives for that end, which they do out of policy, that fo their Enemies may think, that few or none of them are killed, when neverthelefs they have loft many. I am informed that fome of the *Indians* have reported, that they loft ninety fix men that day, and that they had above forty wounded, many of which dyed afterwards. However, this was a black and fatal day, wherein there were eight perfons made Widows, and fix and twenty Children made Fatherlefs, all in one little Plantation, and in one day; and above fixty Perfons buried in one dreadful Grave. And this was the ftate of the *Weftern* parts in refpect of the War with the Heathen.[1]

We muft now take a ftep backwards, and a little

---

[1] The place of this ambufh is well known. A village called Bloody Brook is near it. It is about five miles from the North Village of Deerfield. See Dr. Steven W. Williams's Hift. Rev. John Williams, p. 10. The place was formerly called Muddy Brook, but owing to the fanguinary tragedy of Sunday, April 18th, 1675, the name of the brook and village have been changed to Bloody Brook. In 1835, the Hon. Edward Everett delivered an addrefs there commemorative of the event. He has appended a lift of the flain. In 1838 a neat monument was erected on the fpot with an appropriate infcription; a reprefentation of the monument may be feen in Barber's *Hift. Coll. Mafs.* Capt. Thomas Lothrop was about 65 years of age when he was killed. The precife time of his arrival in New-England has not been afcertained. He fettled in that part of Beverly, called *Bafs-river-fide*, where he had a grant of land in 1636. His wife was Bethiah, dau. of Jofhua Rea, who, after the death of her hufband, married *Jofeph Grafton*. Capt. *Lothrop* left no children. He had a fifter, *Ellen*, who came over with him from England, and inherited his property. She was the fecond wife of the well known fchoolmafter, *Ezekiel Cheever* of Bofton. See Stone's *Hift. Beverly*, and *Genealogical Regifter*, i, 138.

consider the *Eastern Plantations*.[1] For in the Month of *September* did the flame break out there.

The towns thereabout [the Connecticut river] being tolerably garrisoned, Capt. Lothrop, with about 80 men carried carts to fetch off the corn that lay threshed

[1] Our Author is exceeding meagre in what he gives of the war at the eastward. The reader will find a comparatively very full and excellent account in Hubbard. To this, if the investigations of Mr. Willis be added, there will not be much to be gleaned. The following brief letters are copied to show how the people were distressed on the breaking out of the war in that region. They are from the originals in the Author's possession.

Sacoe, 18 Sept. 1675.
Major Waldren
 Sir y^{rs} dated 16 Sept. to Capt. Davis came hither this day. One post you have had from us since ye burning of one house; this afternoone five more are consumed, and wee expect ye losse of all before morning. Every town from us Eastward, viz., Scarbarough, Falmouth, Kenĩbeck, have 100 Indians apeece upon them, and we 100 also. As we wrott before we want amunition and men. Pray post away therefore, y^t if ye Lord please, life may be preserved, although wee are like to have many beggers.

 No more but rest yours and ye Countrey's Servent
BRIAN PENDLETON.

 When this letter arrived at Wells on the following night it was opened by Lieut. Littlefield, who endorsed the urgency of Capt. Pendleton, by the following letter on the same small half sheet:

Wells ye 19 Sept. 75, at 9 of the clocke at night.
Major Waldren, Sir
 You will se by ye aboue what a great strat y^a are in at Sacoe, and we look howerly for an assalt here; soe that you can^{n}lt [can not] expect any assistance from us; we being too weak to defend our selues y^{r}fore ye earnest request to you is that you will rase ann army from Pascataqua with all possible speed for the pr'servation of our liues and estats: otherwise we cannott expect in an ordinary way long to hold out. The Lord direct you and us all. We convoid Mr. George Broughton and company safe to the Cape. With outt spedy supply you must expect noe more posts from us. The enimy snapt twice or thrife at this post coming from Saco, butt mist fire, as God would haue it.
 Yours to command
JNO. LITTLEFELD.
To maj^r Waldren in extraordinary post hast.

 Mr. Geo. Broughton mentioned above was at Salmon Falls on the 16th of October when he and Roger Plaisted signed a similar imploring letter to Waldron for help. That letter is printed in Hubbard, Part II, p. 23.

Some who had their hearts exercifed in difcerning things of that nature, were from the beginning of the War, not without fad Apprehenfions concerning the Inhabitants in thofe parts of the Country, in that they were a [13] fcattered people, and fuch in Deerfield; but they fell themfelues into a terrible *tribulation;* for on Sept. 18, a vaft body of 7 or 800 Indians on the road entertained them with an affault, wherein the courageous captain having taken up a wrong notion that the beft courfe was to fight with Indians in their own way, of fkulking behind trees, and thence aiming at fingle perfons, thereby expofed himfelf to ruin. If they had fought more in a body, they might have carried all before them; for it has been obferved, that Indians never durft look Englifhmen in the face; whereas now above three fcore of our men, and moft of them hopeful *young men*, were killed. Captain *Mofely* hearing the reports which the *guns* gave of this battle, came up with an handful of men, tho' too late for the refcue of Capt. *Lothrop;* and feveral times he marched thro' and through that prodigious clan of *Dragons,* and raked them for five or fix hours together, with the lofs of no more than two men of his own; albeit the Indians afterwards confeffed that they loft 96 of themfelves, and had more than 40 wounded. New England had never yet feen fo black a day!¹

---

1 Notwithftanding the author of the *Magnalia* has nearly copied a part of Mr. Hubbard's defcription, yet he falls far fhort of doing juftice to that glowing writer's narrative of the terrible difafter which befel Lothrop and his brave band. The names of thofe who fell are given in Ruffell's account beforementioned, (Coffin's *Newbury,* 390,) which being eafily confulted, are omitted here. The reader fhould alfo confult Gen. Hoyt's work on the Indian wars, where will be found collected fome new facts, and the *Book of the Indians,* 216-17.

the Indians in New-England.

as had many of them Scandalized the Heathen, and lived themfelves too like unto the Heathen, without any *Inftituted Ordinances*, alfo the *Indians* thereabouts were more numerous then in fome other places. They began their Outrages, at the Houfe of one Mr. *Purchafe*,[1] who had been a great Trader with the *Indians*. After that they came to the Houfe of an old Man in *Cafco-bay*, whofe name was *Wakely*. Him with his Wife, Son and Daughter in law (who was great with Childe) and two Grand-Children, they cruelly murdered, and took three Children alive, and led them into Captivity.[2]

This old *Wakely* was efteemed a godly Man. He would fometimes fay with tears, that he believed God was angry with him, becaufe although he came into *New-England* for the Gofpels fake, yet he had left another place in this Country,

---

[1] Thomas Purchafe lived at Pegypfcot, fince Brunfwick. The "outrages" at his houfe were committed "in the beginning of September." Hubbard has told us what the nature of thofe outrages were. *Narrative*, Pt. I, 14-15. He had refided there many years when the war broke out. What time he fettled there does not appear, but it was prior to 1628, as by a certain deed appears, cited by Mr. Willis, *Hift. Portland*, 1, 14. He purchafed his lands of the Indians. He died before 1683. He had children, Thomas, Jane, and Elizabeth.

[2] Thomas Wakely was at Hingham in 1635; freeman in 1636; probably left Hingham about 1647; was at Gloucefter 1661; thence he went to Cafco Bay and fettled at Back Cove. His oldeft fon, John, was killed by the Indians, as was his fon Ifaac; Elizabeth, daughter of John, was carried away captive. But in June of the next year fhe was reftored. She afterwards married Richard Scamman, a Quaker, and was living in 1723, at the age of 59. The deftruction of his family was on September 9th, five days after the hoftile demonftration at Mr. Purchafe's.

where there was a Church of Christ, which he once was in Communion with, and had lived many years in a Plantation where was no *Church nor Instituted Worship*. If a Faithful Minister of Christ happened to Preach in *Casco*, he would with much affection entertain him, saying *Blessed is he that cometh in the name of the Lord*. After this good man was murthered by the *Indians*, they quickly did more mischief: so that in *Falmouth* there were five Houses burnt, four Men, two Women, and two Children killed, and three Children carried away Captive. After this they set upon them where they flew thirteen Men, and at last burnt the town.[1] A principal Actor in the destruction of *Sacoe* was a strange *Enthusiastical Sagamore*, called *Squando*, who some years before pretended that God appeared to him, in the form of a tall Man, in black Cloaths, declaring to him that he was God, and commanded him to leave his Drinking of Strong Liquors, and to pray, and to keep Sabbaths, and go to hear the Word Preached, all which things the *Indian* did for some years, with great seeming Devotion and Conscience observe. But the God which appeared to him, said nothing to him about Jesus Christ;

[1] The enemy next made an attack upon Saco, where they burnt the house of Capt. *Bonython* and the mills of Major *Phillips*, one on the east and the other on the west side of Saco river. The attack on Saco and the noble defence of *Phillips'* garrison, by a handful of men, was one of the most thrilling events of the war—and nowhere is it told so graphically as in *Hubbard's* work, and later writers seem to be unable to add anything worthy of note to the facts given by that author.

and therefore it is not to be marvelled at, that at laſt he diſcovered himſelf to be no otherwiſe then a Childe of him, that was a Murtherer and a Lyar from the beginning. Alſo theſe inraged *Barbarians*, being annimated with their ſucceſs at *Falmouth* and *Sacoe*, they went to *Black-Point*,[1] and there killed ſix Men and a Woman, and burnt two and twenty dwelling Houſes. In the mean time, the *Engliſh* at *Kenebeck* endeavoured that the *Indians* in thoſe parts might be kept from joyning in this *Inſurrection*, whereto they were tempted and ſollicited by their neighbours. The prudent endeavours of the *Engliſh* proved happily ſucceſsful, inſomuch as the *Sachems* there, brought Preſents with great Proteſtations of Amity and Fidelity, and deſired that no more Liquors might be ſold to the *Indians*, profeſſing that that was a principle cauſe of the miſchiefs that had been done, [14] and that they were not able to keep their men in ſubjection, when once they were become mad with drink.

After theſe things, the *Indians* killed two men at *Kittery*, and ſtripped them. Lieutenant *Playſter* [Plaiſted] with twenty two *Engliſh* went out to fetch off the dead bodies, and to bury them; as they were putting one of them into the Cart, ſuddenly a ſmall party of *Indians* ſhot out of a Swamp. And the greateſt part of the *Engliſh* did unworthily forſake their *Leader* in that hazzard, only ſeven remained with him. He thinking his

[1] They went from Saco to Blue Point (Hubbard, Willis), where they killed ſeveral perſons, one of whom was *Robert Nichols*.

men had been near at hand, faced the Enemy, killed and wounded many of them, but the *Indians* perceiving that all but seven of the *English* were fled, took courage and killed Mr. *Plaister* [Plaisted] (who was a good and useful man) and one of his Sons, and another man: the other four seeing that, ran for their lives, and so escaped until they came safe into a *Garrison*, which was not far off.

Behold how great a matter a little fire kindleth. This fire which in *June* was but a little spark, in three months time is become a great flame, that from East to West the whole Country is involved in great trouble; and the Lord himself seemeth to be against us, to cast us off, and to put us to shame, *and goeth not forth with our Armies*. Wherefore the Magistrates of this Jurisdiction, earnestly called upon the Inhabitants thereof, to humble themselves before the Lord, and to confess and turn from transgression. Inasmuch as the expressions contained in that paper, which was at this time published by the Councils order, for a day of publick Humiliation, to be observed through this Jurisdiction, are most serious, and gracious, and greatly expressive of the sinful *Degenerate Estate* of the *present Generation in New-England*, and that Declaration will turn for a Testimony to our faithful Rulers, both now and hereafter; considering also, that it is in but few hands, I shall therefore here insert, and republish it. 'Tis that which followeth.

---

[1] Lieut. Roger Plaisted. The attack in which he was killed was on the 16 of October, and is minutely detailed in Hubbard, Part I, pp. 23 and 24. The killed were Richard Tozer, James Barney & Isaac Bottes.

the Indians *in* New-England. 93

AT A
COUNCIL[1]
Held at *Boston*, Sept. 17. 1675.

IT having pleased the Holy God (all whose works are Truth, and his Wayes Judgement) for our sins whereby he hath been provoked, in special by the undervaluation of our pleasant things; great unthankfullness for, and manifold abuses of our wonderfull peace, and the blessings of it in this good land

---

[1] At the election on the 12th of May, 1675, the following gentlemen were elected:
John Leverett, *Governor*.
Samuel Symonds, *Dep. Gov'r*.
Assistants or Councillors.—Daniel Gooken, Daniel Dennison, Symon Willard, Richard Russell, Thomas Danforth, Wm. Hathorne, John Pynchon, Edward Tyng, Wm Stoughton, Thomas Clark. See *Gen. Court Records*.

which the Lord hath given us; ill entertainment of the Ministry of the precious Gospel of peace: leaving our first love, dealing falsely in the Covenant of the Lord our God: the Apostacy of many from the Truth unto Heresies, and pernicious Errors: great Formality, inordinate Affection, and sinful Conformity to this present evil vain World: and (beside many horrid and scandalous sins breaking forth among us, for which we have cause to be greatly humbled before the Lord) our great unsensibleness of the Displeasure of the Lord, in suffering these abominations to be perpetuated; together with our carnal Security, and unquietness under the judgements of God upon us, our abiding very much unreformed, notwithstanding all Warnings, and Chastisements, whereby the Lord hath been, and is still debating with us, we having greatly incensed him to stir up many Adversaries against us, not only abroad, but also at our own Doors (causing the Heathen in this Wilder\[16\]ness to be as Thorns in our sides, who have formerly been, and might still be a wall unto us therein; and others also to become a Scourge unto us) the Lord himself also more immediately afflicting us by Diseases, whereof so many Children in some of our Towns have died this Summer. His not going forth with our Armies as in former times, but giving up many of our Brethren to the mouth of the devouring Sword, yea, shewing himself angry with the Prayers of his People: threatening us also with scarcity of Provision, and other Calamities, especially if this present War, with the Barbarous Heathen should continue; and that the Lord of Hosts withdraw not the Commission he hath given to the Sword, and other Judgements to prevail against us;

The Governour and Council of this Jurisdiction therefore (being under the sense of these evils; and also of the distressed state of the rest of the Colonies confederate with our selves, and of the Churches of Christ in other parts of the Christian World, in this day of Trouble, Rebukes, and Blasphemy: and fearing the sad issue thereof, unless the Lord help us with our whole heart, and not feignedly, to turn unto himself.) Do Appoint and Order the seventh day of the next Month, to be a Day of publick Humiliation, with Fasting and Prayer, throughout this whole Colony; that we may set our selves sincerely to seek the Lord, rending our hearts, and not our garments before him, and pursue the same with a thorough Reformation of what ever hath been, or is an Image of jealousie before the Lord to offend the eyes of his Glory; if so be, the Lord may turn from his fierce anger, that we perish not: we do therefore require all the Inhabitants of this Jurisdiction to forbear servile labour upon that day, and that they apply themselves respectively to observe the same, as is appointed.

By the Council, *Edward Rawson* Secr't.

Octob. the 7*th.* This day of Humiliation appointed by the Council, was solemnly observed: yet attended with awfull testimonyes of divine displeasure. The very next day after this Fast was agreed upon by those in civill Authority, was that dismal and fatal blow, when Captain *Lothrop* and his company (in all near upon four score souls) were slaughtered, whereby the Heathen were wonderfully animated, some of them triumphing and saying, that so great slaughter was never known: and indeed in their Warrs one with another, the like hath rarely been heard of. And that very day when this Fast was kept, three Persons were killed by the *Indians* near *Dover*, one of them going from the publick Worship. Also that very day at the close of it, the sad tidings of *Springfields* Calamity came to us here in *Boston*. And [17] inasmuch as this news came at the conclusion of a day of Humiliation, surely *the solemn voice of God to New-England* is still as formerly, *Praying without Reforming* will not do. And now is the day come wherein the Lord is fulfilling the word which himself hath spoken, saying, I will send wild Beasts among you, which shall rob you of your Children, and destroy your Cattle, and make you few in number, *and if you will not be reform'd by these things, I will bring your Sactuaryes to Desolation, and I will not smell the sweet Savor of your Odours.* The Providence of God is never to be forgotten, in that *Churches have been signally spared for so long a time.* Although some Plantations wherein Churches have been settled were in most eminent danger, and the Enemy might easily have swallowed them up, yet God so ordered that they received little or no detriment, when other places were laid utterly waſte; the Lord manifeſting how loth he was to diſgrace the Throne of his Glory, but now he begins with the Sanctuary. As for *Springfields* miſery, it thus came to paſs: Whereas there was a body of *Indians* that lived in a *Fort* near to that *Town* of *Springfield*, and profeſſed nothing but Friendſhip towards the *Engliſh;* they treacherouſly brake in upon the Town, when a party of our Souldiers who had been there, were newly gone to *Hadly*. They killed ſeveral, amongſt others their Lieutenant *Cooper* was moſt perfideouſly Murthered by them, without the leaſt occaſion or Provocation given. They burnt down to the ground above thirty dwelling-houſes, and above twenty out-houſes: amongſt others, Mr. *Pelatiah Glover*, Teacher of the Church there, is a great ſufferer, his Houſe, and Goods, and Books, and Writings being all conſumed in one hour. Neverthelefs there was a great mixture of mercy in this dark and diſmal diſpenſation. For God ſo ordered, as that an *Indian* who knew what was deſigned the next day, ran away in the night, and acquainted the *Engliſh* therewith, whence they had time and opportunity to eſcape to an houſe that was Fortified; otherwiſe in probability the Inhabitants had ſurely had their lives as well as their dwelling places cut off.[1]

[1] This overwhelming diſaſter to Springfield was on October 5th. The Indians were at firſt repreſented 500 ſtrong; but as it is almoſt always the caſe, the eſtimate was much too high. The Rev. Mr. Lothrop ſays in his Century Sermon at Weſt Springfield: "The people

October 13. The *General Court* sat in *Boston*, during this Session, a *Committee* was with the concurrance of both Houses appointed in order to a *Reformation* of those Evils which have provoked the Lord to bring the Sword upon us, and to withdraw from our *Armies* from time to time. The Assistance of the *Teaching Elders* in the Churches was desired, as in a case of that nature, it was proper for them to advise and help according to God.

There was a gracious presence of God with them in their consultations, all that were there with one voice agreeing in many particulars, in respect whereof *Reformation* should be, and must be: *e. g.* " That some effectual course should be " taken for the Suppression of those proud Ex- " cesses in Ap[18]parel, hair, &c. which many

of Springfield did not realize their danger, until by a messenger from Windsor they were informed that 300 of Philip's men had joined with the Springfield Indians, and were then in the Indian fort on Long Hill, and that their intention was to destroy the town. This plot was disclosed by one of the Windsor Indians. On this alarming intelligence, the people fled to their fortified houses and thus saved themselves from a general massacre. On this morning two men set out to examine into the grounds of the alarm from Windsor, and in their way towards the Indian fort were fired upon by some in ambush; one is killed, the other mortally wounded."

On the Springfield records I find,

that, besides Lieut. Thomas Cooper named in the text, the deaths of Thomas Miller and Pentecost Matthews are recorded. Serjt. Richard Wait was severely wounded in attempting to recover the body of Lieut. Cooper. *MSS. Petition* of said Wait, 28 Feb. 1680.

In a letter of Col. John Pynchon written at Springfield at the time, he says " about 30 dwelling houses burnt, and 24 or 25 barns, cornmill, sawmill, and other buildings."

In a letter of Mr. John Russell, he thus speaks of Mr. Glover's loss: " Mr. Glover had all his books burnt, not so much as a bible saved; a great loss for he had some choice books and many." And Mr. Hubbard says he had " a brave library."

"(yea and the poorer forte as well as others) are
"shamfully guilty of. That a due teftimony fhould
"be borne againft fuch as are falfe Worfhippers,
"efpecially Idolatrous *Quakers*,[1] who fet up Altars
"againft the Lords Altar, yea who fet up a Chrift
"whom the Scriptures know not. That whereas
"excefs in drinking is become a common Sin,
"meanes fhould be ufed to prevent an unneceffary
"multiplication of Ordinaries, and to keep Town
"dwellers from frequenting Taverns: and that
"whereas Swearing hath been frequently heard,
"they that hear another Swear profanely and do
"not complain of it to Authority, fhall be punifh-
"ed for that concealment. Alfo that fome further
"care fhould be taken, that the fourth and fifth
"Commandments be better obferved than former-
"ly; and that there may be no more fuch Op-
"preffion, either by Merchants or day Labourers
"as heretofore hath been; and that the *Indian*
"Trading-houfes, whereby the Heathen have
"been debauched and fcandalized againft Reli-
"gion, be fuppreffed; and that more care fhould
"be taken refpecting the *Rifing Generation*, then

[1] The Court of Plymouth was rather more fenfibly employed than that of Maffachufetts on this occafion. That Court ordered, "That during the time of public danger, every one that comes to the meeting on the Lord's day, bring his arms with him, and furnifhed with at leaft fix charges of powder and fhot, until further order fhall be given, under the penalty of two fhillings for every fuch defect. Alfo, ordered, that whofoever fhall fhoot off any gun on any neceffary occafion, or at any game whatfoever, except at an Indian or a wolf, fhall forfeit five fhillings for every fuch fhot." Mr. Pulfifer's *Plymouth Colony Records*, v, 176-7. The immenfe importance of ammunition occafioned this law.

"formerly hath been, that they might be brought "under the difcipline of Chrift &c. Thefe things "were unanimoufly confented to.

October 19. The Concluſions of the Committee, refpecting *Reformation* of provoking evils were figned, and delivered in to the General Court, who voted acceptance thereof, and appointed another Committee to draw up Laws in order to the eſtabliſhment of the things agreed on. Now as I remember that famous Martyrologiſt Mr. *Fox*[1] (in *Acts & Monuments,* vol. 2. pag. 669,) obferves, with refpect to the *Reformation* in K. *Edward* the 6*th* his dayes, that that very day and hour when the Act for *Reformation* was put in execution at *London,* God gave the *Engliſh* a fignal victory againſt the *Scots* at *Muſcleborough;* fo it was proportionably with us. For that day when there was a vote paffed for the Suppreffion and Reformation of thofe manifeſt evils, whereby the eyes of Gods Glory are provoked amongſt us, the Lord gave fuccefs to our Forces, who that day encountred with the *Indians* at *Hatfield.*[2] The *Engliſh*

[1] The title of Maſter John Fox's work is briefly this? *Acts and Monuments of Matters moſt ſpeciall and memorable, happening in the Church, with an Univerſal Hiſtory of the ſame....With the bloody times, horrible troubles, and great Perſecutions againſt the true MARTYRS of Chriſt.* Thus runs the title to the edition of 1641.

The *Book of Martyrs* was next to the *Bible* with our Puritan Anceſtors.

[2] At this time Capt. *Moſely* lay at Hatfield with his company, and three days before, he wrote the following letter to the Council of Maſſachuſetts. It appears from an endorfement on ſaid letter, that one of the moſt revolting acts was committed under the countenance of the

loft but one man in the fight[1] (albeit fome that were fent forth as Scouts were killed or Captivated) the Enemy fled before them, and ran into the Englifh, that any people could be guilty of.

"Hatfield, yᵉ 16 Oct. 1675.

"I have fkarce aney ftrang news to acquaint you with all, at this int. Yefterday we thought to go in purfuit of yᵉ enemies at Hadley fide of the river, and as we marched out from Hadley fomething better than a mile, the fkoutes that was fend from this towne did fpeye fome Indians, and therepvon we came this fide of the river, and did march out laft night yᵉ whole body or ftrength of men that we have heare; but att laft we took it to confideration that it was very dangerous to leave the townes imteye without any fouldiers. This day being a very bluftrous and very high winds, I have fent out fome fkoutes, and they difcover fome Indians fome three miles of. And laft night I have fend of my men four to Deerefeeld, and fome two miles from the town wheare there was fome rails, yᵉ enemy have waged them up and made them very faft. I know not whether it be to trepann the fkoutes, or elfe to faight us there if we go in purfueth them; but I intend to bourn all the rails vp, pleafe God to grant me life and health.

"Wee are told by an Indian that was taken att Springfeeld, yᵗ they intended to fet upon thefe three townes in one day. The body of them yᵗ waites this exploite to do, is about 600 Indians, as wee are informed by the afforefaid Indian; and further wee are informed that they are making of a fort fome fixty miles" [off.]

SAMUEL MOSELY.

The captive Indian feems to have been a female, and, from fome caufe now unknown, had incurred the vengeance of the Englifh. Everything regarding the matter, faving the fact of the horrible execution of the prifoner, remains without a fhadow of explanation. There was an *order* given for her execution, but by whom, as we have faid, there is no record. The endorfement on the letter is in thefe words: The captive was "ordered to be torn in pieces by dogs, and fhe was to dealt withal"!

[1] This was on Oct. 19. Our Author is fadly deficient in his details of the affair, while Mr. Hubbard is more fatiffactory. There happened to be then at Hatfield and vicinity a large number of Englifh under Major Samuel Appleton, Maj. Robert Treat, Capt. Jonathan Poole, and Capt. Samuel Mofely. The Indians do not appear to have been aware of the force of the Englifh, and came in great numbers to furprife the town, and were repulfed with confiderable lofs. In their approach, however, they furprifed a fcout of fome ten men, all of whom were killed. Their names are Thomas Mekins, Nathaniel Collins,

River, many of them being seen to fall, but night coming on, it was in vain to follow them further. And after that day, the *Western Plantations* had little or no disturbance by them, but lived in quietness all the Winter. All this notwithstanding, we may say as sometimes the Lords People of old, *the Harvest is past, the Summer is ended, and we are not saved.* The Sword having marched *Eastward, & Westward, and Northward,* now beginneth to face toward the *South* again. The *Narragansets,* who were the greatest body of *Indians* in *New-England;* there being no less then six Sachims amongst them; having not as yet appeared in open [19] Hostility. Nevertheless *Philips* and *Squaw-Sachims* men, when routed by the *English* Forces, were harboured amongst the *Narragansets.* When the Commissioners of the united Colonies sat at *Boston,* in the latter end of *September,* one of the *Narraganset Sachims,* and Messengers from other Sachims there, made their appearance in *Boston;* they pretended nothing but good-will to the *English,* and promised that those Enemies of ours, who had burnt so many houses, and committed so many Murders, and had fled to them for refuge, should be delivered up by the latter end of *October.* But when the time prefixed for the surrendry of the *Wompanoags* and *Squaw-Sachems Indians* was

Richard Stone, Samuel Clarke, John Pocock, Thomas Warner, Abraham Quiddington, William Olverton and John Petts. Serjt. Freegrace Norton was shot down in the town by the side of Maj. Appleton, and a bullet passed through the Major's hair, doing him no other harm.

lapfed, they pretended they could not do as they had ingaged at prefent, but after winter they would do it. In the mean while, when the *Englifh* had any ingagement with the *Indians*, wounded *Indians* came home to the *Narraganfets*, efpecially after the fight at *Hatfield*, *Octob*. 19*th*. about fourty wounded men were feen croffing the woods towards the *Narraganfets:* alfo fome (at leaft two *Indians*) from amongft themfelves, came to the *Englifh*, and told them that the *Narraganfets* were refolved (if they could) to deftroy the *Englifh:* but they were loth to begin to fall upon them before winter, but in the Spring when they fhould have the leaves of trees and *Swamps* to befriend them, they would doe it: wherefore it was judged neceffary to fend out Forces againft them, and preparations were made accordingly.[1]

There was fome agitation amongft thofe whom it did concern, where a perfon fuitable for fo great truft might be found as *General;* and that worthy

The Commiffioners of the United Colonies having manifeft and manifold proofs that the great nation of Narraganfet Indians, with whom the reft were now harbour'd, had not only broken their articles of peace with the Englifh in divers inftances, but were alfo plotting to begin a war againft us in the fpring, when they fhould have the leaves of the trees to befriend them, took up a general refolution in the depth of winter,

[1] From a paper in the *Mafs. Archives*, drawn up as a Petition to the Governor and Council, by the Officers of the Army, and prefented on the 4th of December (1675), we have an idea of the equipments of the men of war of that day. See APPENDIX E.

Gentleman *Josiah Winslow Esq*, who succeeds his Father (of blessed memory) is Governour of *Plimouth*, was pitched upon for this Service.

Under his conduct therefore, an Army consisting of at first a thousand, and at last about fifteen hundred men, were sent forth to execute the vengeance of the Lord upon the perfidious and bloudy Heathen. But before they set out, the Churches were all upon their knees before the Lord, the God of Armyes, entreating his favour and gracious success in that undertaking, wherein the welfare of his people was so greatly concerned. This day of Prayer and Humiliation was observed *Decemb.* 2d. when also something hapned intimating as if the Lord were still angry with our Prayers; for this day all the houses in *Quonsickamuck*[1] were burnt by the *Indians*.

Decemb. 8th. The Army set out from *Boston*. Whilst they were upon this march, an *Indian*

to make a vigorous expedition against them. Accordingly an army of a thousand at first, and afterwards fifteen hundred men, under the conduct of the truly honorable *Josiah Winslow*, Esq., marched into the Narraganset country.

[The paragraph preceding this applying to a passage in the latter part of the work, it will be found there.]

---

[1] In what is since Worcester. Some of the many ways in which this name has been written may be seen in Lincoln's *Hist. Worcester*, p 2. The name is now usually spelled Quonsigamond. The number of houses burned was six or seven. Hubbard.

whose name was *Peter*[1] having received some disgust among his Countrymen, came to the *English*, and discovered the plots of the *Indians*, told where they were, and promised to conduct the Army to them. They were no sooner arrived in the *Narraganset* Country, but they killed and took captive above fourty *Indians*. Being come to Mr. *Smiths* [20] house, they waited some dayes for *Connecticut* Forces. In the mean while a party of the enemy did treacherously get into the house of *Jerem. Bull* (where was a Garison,) burned the house, and slew about fourteen persons.[2]

---

[1] Notwithstanding the great service this Indian rendered the English, he seems to have been subject to great neglect, annoyances and hardships for a long time after the close of the war, as will be seen from the two papers now printed in the APPENDIX. This is the more worthy of remembrance, because it was then acknowledged by the officers of the expedition, and history has since confirmed their opinion, fully, that had not this Indian conducted and guided the march, the army would have been entirely lost. Thus is shown, that on seemingly insignificant circumstances and individuals, sometimes hangs the fate of nations. What became of poor "Peter Indian," the savior of the Narraganset army, it is needless to inquire; for to such inquiry, echo would be the only respondent. Costly monuments have been erected to the memory of thousands less worthy of remembrance than Peter, while of him no one knows the place of burial. That his daughter should have remained a slave ten years after his signal services is a reproach prominent among the reproaches of that trying day. We do not know even the native name of Peter. Perhaps, at some very distant day, steps may be taken by unborn descendants of the Founders of New England, to erect some humble monument on the line of the march of the army suitably inscribed to his memory. Though Peter could not by his eloquence set forth the folly of rebellion among his countrymen like the Rev. Mr. Brownlow of this day, he may, nevertheless, be as worthy of remembrance. See APPENDIX F.

[2] The Christian name of Mr. Bull was probably the scriptural one *Jeriah*, though Mr. Bartlett finds it written in the Rhode Island *Records Jireh*. In Hubbard's *Narrative* it is *Jerry*. Not many years ago,

Decemb. 18. *Connecticut* Forces being come, a March toward the enemy was resolved upon : *Peter Indian* having informed that the *Body of Indians* (only *Ninnigret* being one of their old crafty *Sachems*, had with some of his men withdrawn himself from the rest, professing that he would not ingage in a *War* with the *English*, therefore did he goe into a place more remote) was in a Fort about eighteen miles distant from the place where our Army now was. The next day, although it were the Sabbath, yet, provisions being almost spent by our Souldiers, waiting so long for *Con-*

On December 12, about 40 Indians fell into their hands; among whom, one was a fellow named *Peter*, who having receiued some disgust from his countrymen, proved so faithful and useful a guide unto our forces, that they afterwards found that they could not well haue lived without him.

perhaps ten, I noticed upon a physician's sign in New York the name of *Jeriah Bull*. As the Christian name is an uncommon one, I presumed at the time, that this person was a descendant of the Narraganset sufferer.

Mr. Hubbard, p. 50, is probably correct in his account of the numbers killed at Bull's Garrison; viz., " ten Englishmen and five women and children, but two escaping in all." Mr. Arnold, *Hist. R. I.*, i, 403, adopts Hubbard's account. I have sought in vain for the names of the slain. A brief pedigree of the family of Bull may be seen in Mr.

Potter's *Hist. Narraganset*, 307. The residence of the family was at Petequamscott, now in South Kingston, R. I. As early as 1669, Jireh Bull was appointed " a Conservator of the Peace at Petaquomscut." See Bartlett's *Records of the Colony of R. I.*, ii, 256. Capt. Wait Winthrop was at Bull's house on the 9th of July, from which he wrote, saying there were then in it " about 16 of the neighbours, being a convenient large stone house, with a good stonewall yeard before it, which is a kind of small fortyfication to it." *Colonial Records of Conn.*, ii, 338, Note by Mr. Trumbull.

necticut Forces, the Councill of War resolved to give Battle to the enemy. The *English* Souldiers played the men wonderfully; the *Indians* also fought stoutly, but were at last beat out of their Fort, which was taken by the *English*. There were hundreds of *Wigwams* (or *Indian* houses) within the Fort, which our Souldiers set on fire, in the which men, women and Children (no man knoweth how many hundreds of them) were burnt to death. Night coming on, a Retreat was sounded.

Several mischiefs were done by the Indians whilst our army were here waiting for their brethren from Connecticut, especially their surprisal of a remote garrison belonging to one [*Jireh*] *Bull*, where about fourteen persons were *baited to death* by the terrible *dogs*, [the Indians.]

The Connecticut forces being also arrived on Dec. 18, they presently marched away by break of day, the next morning, through cold and snow, and very amazing difficulties, enough to have *damned* any ordinary fortitude, for eighteen miles together. The Indians had a fort raised upon an island of about five or six acres in the midst of an horid swamp, which fort, besides its palisadoes, had a kind of wall or hedge about a rod thick encompassing of it. The entrance of this fort was upon a long tree over the water, where but one man could pass at a time, that if our men had attempted that passage, they must have perished.

Only by the help of *Peter* they discovered a *vulnerable heel*, as I may call it, yet left in the fort at one corner, where there was a gap supplied only with long

Concerning the number of *Indians* slain in this Battle, we are uncertain, only some *Indians*, which afterwards were taken prisoners (as also a wretched *English* man¹ that apostatized to the Heathen, and fought with them against his own Country-men, but was at last taken and executed) confessed that the next day they found three hundred of their fighting men dead in their Fort, and that many men, women and children were burned in their *Wigwams*, but they neither knew, nor could they conjecture how many: it is supposed that not less then a thousand *Indian* Souls perished at that time. *Ninnigret* whose men buried the slain, affirmeth

trees about four or five foot from the ground, over which men might force their way; though against this they had built a block-house, from whence a bloody storm of bullets (and enough to make every man like the poor man in the twelve signs of the [50] Almanack) was to be expected by them that should make their approaches there.

1 From Hubbard we learn that the name of this "wretched Englishman" was Joshua Tift, or Tiffe. I have given some account of him in the *Book of the Indians*. A writer in the *Old Indian Chronicle*, p. 58, in a letter dated at Boston, on the 8th of February, 1676, says, "our scouts brought in prisoner one Tift, a renegadoe Englishman, who having received a deserved punishment from our General, deserted our army, and fled to the enemy, where he had good entertainment, and was again sent out by them with some of their forces. He was shot in the knee by some of our scouts, and then taken before he could discharge his musket, which was taken from him and found deep charged and laden with slugs. He was brought to our army, and tried by a counsel of war, where he pretended that he was taken prisoner by the Indians, and by them compelled to bear arms in their service; but this being proved to be false, he was condemned to be hanged and quartered, which was accordingly done." *William* and *John* Tift were among the early settlers of Mass.

that they found twenty & two *Indian* captains among the dead bodyes. Of the *English* there were killed and wounded about two hundred and thirty, whereof only eighty and five perſons are dead. But there was a ſolemn rebuke of Providence at this time, in that ſix of our Captains were ſlain,[1] viz, Captain *Johnſon* of Roxbury, Captain *Gardner* of Salem, Captain *Davenport* of Boſton (ſon to that Captain *Davenport* who did great Service in the expedition againſt the *Indians* in the *Pequod* war, Anno 1637) Captain *Gallop* of New-London, Captain *Marſhall* of Windſor, Captain *Seily* of Stratford, who dyed of his wounds ſome dayes after the fight was over. The three Captains firſt mentioned, belonged to *Mattachuſets* Colony, the three laſt to *Connecticut*, of *Plimouth* Colony Captain *Bradford*[2] (one of their faithfull Magiſtrates, and ſon of him that was many years Governour there) was ſorely wounded, but God had mercy on him, and on his people in him, ſo as to ſpare his life, and to reſtore him to ſome meaſure of health, albeit

[1] I took ſome pains to recover the Chriſtian names of theſe Captains, and the reader will find them inſerted in the *Hiſtory and Antiquities of Boſton*. I have alſo there inſerted from an original MS. of the time, the names of the ſoldiers ſlain, in this "great conflict of New England," as it is aptly called by Mr. Arnold in his *Hiſt. of R. I.*

[2] In the *Old Indian Chronicle* it is noted that Capt. Bradford was wounded in the eye. He probably received more than one wound; as Judge Sewall ſays, in his *New Heaven upon the New Earth*, p. 64, that the Captain was then (1697) "more than 73 years old, and hath worn a bullet in his fleſh above 20 of them." This undoubtedly refers to his wound received at the Swamp Fight. Had he been wounded only in the eye he would hardly have carried a ball in that locality for 20 years.

the bullet shot into him is still in his body. 'Also Captain *Goram* of *Barnstable* in Plimouth Colony fel sick of a feaver whereof he dyed.

Thus did the Lord take away seven Captains

Our men came up to the swamp about one a clock, and immediately and courageously pressing through the swamp, from whence the Indians begun to fire upon 'em, they advanced unto that part of the fort which was most accessible: Now having of nothing but *Mors certa, aut victoria læta,* in their eye.

Brave Capt. *Mosely* and Capt. *Davenport* led the van; Capt. *Gardner* and Capt. *Johnson* were in the center, Maj. *Appleton* and Capt. *Oliver* brought up the rear of the Massachuset forces: Gen. *Winslow* with Plymouth forces, under Maj. *Bradford* and Capt. *Goram*, marched in the center; and Connecticut forces under Maj. *Treat* and Capt. *Siely*, Capt. *Gallop*, Capt. *Mason*, Capt. *Wats*, and Capt. *Marshal*, made the reer of the whole body.

Nothing in the world could be more magnanimous than the spirit which now carried on both leaders and soldiers in the enterprise now before them: They leaped over the *trees of death*, into the spot of ground where death in all its terrors was to be encountered; the fall of the valiant leaders, no less than six of them, namely, *Davenport, Gardner, Johnson, Gallop, Siely* and *Marshal* (tho' it rendered the place worthy of the name which the Romans put upon the abhorr'd place where their beloved commander *Drusus* died, namely, *Scelerata Castra*) did but add fire to the rage of the soldiers; they beat the enemy from one shelter to another, till they had utterly driven them out of all their sconces; and at last they set fire to the fort, from whence the surviving Indians fled into a vast cedar swamp at some distance off.

out of that Army. Alfo four *Lieutenants* were wounded in that *Fort fight*, fo that although the *English* had the better of it, yet not without folemn and humbling Rebukes of Providence. At night as the army returned to their Quarters, a great Snow fell, alfo a part of the army miffed their way, among whom was the *General* himfelf with his Life-Guard. Had the enemy known their advantage, and purfued our Souldiers (and we have fince heard that fome of the *Indians* did earneftly move that it might be fo, but others of them through the over-ruling hand of Providence would not confent) when upon their retreat, they might have eafily cut off the whole Army: But God would be more gracious to us. Here then was not only a *Victory*, but alfo a fignal *Prefervation*, for which let the Father of mercyes have eternal Glory.

I wifh I could particularly give an *immortal memory* to all the brave men that fignalized themfelves in this action. But among them all, *O quam te memorem*, thou excellent SAMUEL NOWEL, never to be forgotten! This now *revered*, and afterwards *worfhipful* perfon, a chaplain to the army, was author to a good fermon preached unto the Artillery Company of the Maffachufets, which he entituled, *Abraham in Arms;* and at this fight there was no perfon more like a true fon of *Abraham in Arms*, or that with more courage and hazardy fought in the midft of a fhower of bullets from the furrounding falvages. But,

Longa referre mora eft, quæ confilioq; manuq;
Utiliter fecit fpaciofi tempore belli.

After this God seemed to withdraw from the *English*, and take part with the enemy. The next

No less than 700 fighting Indians were destroyed, as it was afterwards confessed, in this desperate action; besides 300 which afterwards died of their wounds, and old men, women and children, *sans* number; but of the English about *eighty-five* were slain, and an *hundred and fifty* wounded. And now, *sic magnis componere parva!* Reader,

>And now their mightiest quell'd, the battel swerv'd
>With many an inrode gor'd; deformed rout
>Enter'd, and foul disorder; all the ground
>With shivered armour strown, and on a heap,
>Salvage and Sagamore lay overturn'd,
>And fiery, foaming blacks; what stood, recoil'd
>Orewearied, and with panick fear surpris'd.

Had the assault been deferred one day longer, there fell such a storm of snow, that for divers weeks it must have been impracticable; and at the end of those weeks there came so violent and unusual a thaw, that by making the way to the fort unpassable, it would have rendered it still more impracticable. *Just now* was the *time* for this work; and the work being so far accomplished, our forces retreating after day-light was almost spent, found it necessary to go back with many *wounded*, and more *weary* men, unto their head-quarters, near eighteen miles off, in a dismal night, through hardships, that an whole age would hardly parallel; which, if the remaining enemies had known, they might easily have cut off all our enfeebled and bewildered army. However, such a blow was now given to the enemy as never could be recovered! And our forces having in some following weeks made now and then some happy *gleanings* of their late victory, until the enemy was gone, they knew not whither, they returned unto their several homes unto the next occasion.

day the *Indians* finding but few *English men* dead in the Fort amongſt their three hundred *Indians* that were ſlain, were much troubled and amazed, ſuppoſing that no more of ours had been killed; this blow did greatly aſtoniſh them, and had the *Engliſh* immediately purſued the Victory begun, in all likelyhood there had been an end of our troubles: but God ſaw that neither yet were we fit for deliverance. Wherefore *Connecticut* Forces withdrew to *Stonington*, and there being ſo many killed and wounded amongſt thoſe that remained in the *Narraganſet* Country, alſo bread for the Souldiers being wanting by reaſon the extremity of the weather was ſuch, as that the Veſſels loaden with proviſion could not reach them, therefore the army lay ſtill ſome weeks[1]

In this interval of time, the town of *Mendam* (which before that had been forſaken of its Inhabitants) was burnt down by the *Indians*.

Now doth the Lord Jeſus begin ſolemnly to

[1] The Author conveys a wrong impreſſion about the *veſſels with proviſions;* for Capt. Church, who was in that expedition, ſays, "it mercifully came to paſs, that Capt. Andrew Belcher arrived at Mr. [Richard] Smith's [in Narraganſet] that very night [after their march from the battle ground] from Boſton, with a veſſel loaden with Proviſions for the Army, who muſt otherwiſe have periſhed for want." *Entertaining Hiſt.* p. 27, 4to edition. Yet this does not agree with Mr. Hubbard's ſtatement, who ſays, "after they were retired to their quarters, but 16 miles from that place [the battle field] there was ſo great want of proviſion, the veſſels being frozen in at the Harbour about Cape Cod, that ſhould have brought them relief, and the froſt and ſnow ſet in ſo violently, that it was not poſſible for them to have made another onſet." This is all he ſays about "proviſion."

fulfill his word, in *removing Candlesticks* out of their places because of *Contentions*, and loss of first Love. Surely when those places are destroyed where Churches have been planted, Candlesticks are removed out of their places. But to proceed, When the Army was just upon Resolve to return home, because provisions were spent, God so ordered, as that a Vessel loaden with Victuals arrived, whereupon it was determined (σόνΘεῶ) to pursue the enemy. Only it was thought necessary to desist from this pursuit until *Connecticut* Forces could return and joyn with ours. In the *interim*, a strange sudden *Thaw* happened in the midst of *January* (when in *New-England* the season is wont to be extream cold) that the snow melted away in a little time; the like weather hath rarely been known in this land at that time of the year, albeit some of the first Planters say it was so above fifty years agoe: However this made [22] wonfully for the *Indians* advantage, for now they fled out of the *Narraganset* Country, and whereas they had been sorely straightned and distressed for victuals, now the snow being wasted, they lived upon Ground-nuts.

In fine, the Army pursued them several dayes, overtook some of them killed and took about seventy persons, were in sight of the main Body of them, and could they have held out to have pursued them but one day longer, probably this unhappy War had then been ended: but the Souldiers were tired with eight dayes March, and (having spent much of their provision whilst waiting for our *Connecticut* Brethren) their bread faild, so as that they were forced to kill horses and feed upon them.¹

¹ This is the expedition, I presume, which Capt. Church distinguishes as the "long march," in which he was engaged after his wounds were healed, which he had received in the Narraganset fight. (See also *Hubbard*, 142.) But, as usual, Church is considerably out in his chronology. None of the cotemporary Chroniclers precisely inform us when this "march" commenced or when it ended. Hubbard says it continued until "all their provisions were spent;" that it extended "60 or 70 miles up through the woods towards Marlborough and Lancaster." He says nothing about seeing the "main body" of the enemy. *Narrative*, 55.

In that rare and loosely written account entitled *News from New England*, 4to, London, 1676, it is stated that "on the 4th of Feb. [1676], the Christians [English] received private intelligence from the Indians who skulked ever since the last battle in certain woods scituate about 30 miles from Malbury [Marlboro] that they were drawn up into a body, and encamped in a well fortified swamp." They were driven out of this with some loss, and the English had four wounded from an attack in their rear. The English found 150 wigwams, in which they encamped for the night. Early the next morning they set fire to them, and pursued on after the Indians. They "killed divers of them, whom age or wounds rendered incapable of keeping up with their companions." *News*, &c. p. 2-3.

The English soon came upon the main body in "another swamp, whose rocky ascent propounded so great a difficulty to attain it, as would have stagared the resolution of any but a resolved mind." The enemy were again routed, however, with the loss "of all they left behind them." This was on the 16th of February, according to the same author.

The English continued the pursuit two days longer, namely till the 18th of February; by which time they had spent their provisions, tired out their horses, and worn down themselves. Therefore in a council of war it was resolved to discontinue the pursuit. The Connecticut men returned home; the Plymouth and Massachusetts men went to Marlboro'. Gen. Winslow returned to Boston with his mounted men, leaving his foot at Marlboro' and Sudbury. These returned on the Monday following, and were allowed to return home also, except Capt. Wadsworth, who, in an excursion from Marlboro', came upon and destroyed "about 70, old men, women and children." *Ibid*, p. 3.

A more full account in some re-

We have often carried it before the Lord as if we would *Reform* our wayes, and yet when it hath come to, we have done nothing : so hath the Lord carried towards us, as if he would deliver us, and yet hath deferred our *Salvation*, as we our selves have delayed *Reformation*.

So then *February* 5. The Army returned to *Boston*, not having obtained the end of their going forth.¹ It was easie to conjeccture that the *Nar*-

spects of this expedition, will be found in the *Old Indian Chronicle*, p. 57-59. From that we learn that the English army consisted of 1600 men. There accompanied it also a band of Indians under Uncas ; that the place where the four English were wounded was at Pumham's town [now in Warwick, R. I.] ; that the Indians had 1800 fighting men ; that in the fight, at Pumhams town, a great Captain named *Quaqualk* was wounded, and five of his men were killed. The four wounded Englishmen were Connecticut soldiers; that the Indians were pursued " almost as far as Quabog " [Brookfield.]

It is quite impossible to make the contemporary accounts agree one with the other, respecting this expedition in pursuit of the enemy ; nor were the writers particular in bestowing credit where it was justly due. It is plain that Dr. Mather avoided giving the "Friend Indians" the credit they deserved. We learn from the *Chronicle*, p. 116, that it was the Mohegans under Uncas who overtook and slew the 70 Indians before mentioned.

¹ It is an easy thing for those who stay at home in their warm habitations to find fault with those who go forth to battle, not with the enemy alone, but with every privation, and the elements in all their extremes. Who has not heard enough petulant impatience in this our present hour of peril ! As though deep rivers could be momentarily crossed, lakes waded and enemies vanquished with as much ease as the subject can be talked about. At the same time that our Author tells us if the enemy had been pursued another day, an end would probably have been put to the war, another Author writing at the same time and place says, that the men sent from Boston to join that expedition, lost in their march " eleven men who were frozen to death,"—so extreme was the frost of that winter ! *Letter to Lond. (Old Ind Chron.)* 57.

Mr. Hubbard refers to this matte. in a manner incompatible with the opinion we have formed of his enlightened mind. He says: "Fresh supplies of soldiers came up from Boston, wading through a sharp storm of snow, that bit some of them

raganset, and *Nipmuck*, and *Quabaog*, and *River Indians*, being all come together, and the *Army* returned, they would speedily fall upon the *Frontier Towns*. And some of the praying *Indians*[1] who had been sent out as Spies, and had been with the *Indians* beyond *Quabaog*, brought intelligence that a *French Man* that came from *Canady* had been amongst them, animating them against the *English*, promising a supply of Ammunition, & that they would come next summer and assist them: also the *Indian* Spies declared, that there was a designe, within such a time to burn *Lancaster*, which a me to pass both as to the time and manner accordingly.

For upon the 10*th* day of *February* some hundreds of the *Indians* fell upon *Lancaster*, burnt many of the Houses, kill'd and took Captive above forty persons. Mr *Rowlandson* (the faithful pastor of the Church there) had his House, Goods, Books, all burned; his Wife, and all his Children led away Captive before the Enemy. Himself (as God would have it) was not at home, whence his own

by the heels with the frost." *Narrative*, 58. This is speaking with too much levity of the poor men who perished to defend the lives and homes of the Author and his kindred. Had the destruction of the enemy been thus spoken of, little would have been thought of it.

[1] The services of the Praying Indians have nowhere been adequately acknowledged in the histories of this war. Gen. Daniel Gookin, their governor or overseer, wrote an account of them, which remained in MS. near 200 years. And though it has been printed, it is *buried* in a volume of the American Antiquarian Society's works. To that the reader is referred. We hope yet to see the works of Gookin brought together and published as they should be in a volume by themselves.

person was delivered, which otherwise (without a Miracle) would have been endangered. Eight men lost their lives, and were stripped naked by the *Indians*, because they ventured their lives to save Mrs. *Rowlandson*.[1]

Deserted Mendon was this winter laid in ashes. And the French from Canada sending recruits unto the Indians for that purpose, the Indians thus recruited, on February 10, fell upon the town of Lancaster, where they burned many houses, murdered and captivated more than forty persons. The worthy minister of the town, Mr. *Rowlandson*, had been at Boston to intercede for some speedy succours; and though by this journey from home he was himself preserved, yet at his return he found his house on fire, his goods and books all burned, and which was worse, his wife, and children, and neighbours in the hands of the worst barbarians in the world. This good man, like *David* at Ziklag, yet *believed*, for the recovery of his relations out of those horrible hands, which about four or five months after was accomplished with wonderful dispensations of Divine Providence, whereof the gentlewoman herself has given us a printed *Narrative*. Capt. *Wadsworth*, with forty resolute men, compelled the Indians to quit the place; but they soon did further mischiefs at Marlborough, Sudbury, Chelmsford.

[1] In the *History of Lancaster*, by Mr. Willard will be found an interesting amount of facts relative to the families which suffered from this attack of the Indians. See also the *Narrative* of Mrs. Rowlandson, with Notes by the same Author. Of the old Accounts Mr. Hubbard's is the best, as usual, yet the writer of *News from New England* seems to have been intimately acquainted with the facts. He says the Indians carried "no less than 55 persons into their merciless captivity; and because the reader shall understand the damnable antipathy they have to religion and piety, I would have him take notice how they endeavour to

As this good Man returned home (having been at *Boston* to intercede with the Council that something might be done for the safety of that place) he saw his *Lancaster* in flames, and his own house burnt down, not having heard of it till his eyes beheld it, and knew not what was become of the Wife of his bosome, and Children of his Bowels. This was a most awful Providence, and hath made me often think on those words, *though Noah, Job and [23] Daniel were in it, they should deliver but their own Souls, they should deliver neither Sons nor Daughters, they only shall be delivered, but the Land shall be desolate.* And this desolation is the more tremendous, in that this very day the Churches *Westward* were humbling themselves before the Lord. Within a few days after this, certain *Indians* did some mischiefs at *Malbery, Sudbery, Chelmsford.*

February 21. The *Indians* assaulted *Medfield*, and although there were two or three hundred Souldiers there, they burnt half the Town, killed several Men, Women and Children, (about eighteen in all) amongst others their Lieutenant *Adams* was slain. And soon after he was killed, his Wife was casually slain by an *English-man*, whose Gun discharged before he was aware, and the bullet

---

signalize their cruelty, and gratify their enraged spleen; for of these 55 captives, the minister of the Town's relations made no less than 19 of them; viz., Mrs. Rowlandson, the Minister's wife, and three of his children, her sister and seven children, and her sister Drew and four children." p. 3. In the *Chronicle*, p. 117, it is said that the number of persons taken was 42, whereof but 12 were men, the rest women and children. Mrs. Rowlandson was daughter of John White of Lancaster.

passed through the Boards overhead, and mortally wounded Lieutenant *Adam's* wife. It is a sign God is angry, when he turns our Weapons against our selves.[1]

And, Feb. 21 [1676], two or three hundred of them came wheeling down to Medfield, where they burnt near half the town, and killed near a score of the inhabitants.

---

[1] The details of the affair at Medfield are too extensive to be brought within the compass of a Note. The fullest account is to be found in Gookin's work on the Praying Indians. Lieut. Henry Adams was son of Henry Adams of Braintree. His wife was Elizabeth Paine. She was killed at the house of Mr. Wilson, the Minister of the town, as she lay upon a bed in the chamber; the ball passing through the chamber floor and bedding. Gen. Gookin calls it "a very strange accident." Capt. John Jacob was the unfortunate cause of the accident; his gun being "half bent," went off as he was about leaving the house to go to his quarters. He belonged to Hingham.

A noted Indian called One-eyed John led the enemy at Medfield. He was Sachem of Musketequid (Concord) or of a clan of Indians in that vicinity, and his native name was Monoco. Philip was also present and mounted on a fine horse. See Sanders's *Century Sermon* at Medfield, 1817. From that work I take the names of the killed and wounded:

Killed.
John Fusell of Medfield.
John Bowers,   "
John Bowers, Jr.,   "
Thomas Mason,   "
Zechariah Mason,   "
Jonathan Wood,   "
Elizabeth Smith,   "
Henry Adams,   "
Elizabeth Adams,   "
William Williams of Boston.
John Cooper,   "
Edward Jackson, Cambridge.
The three last were soldiers.

Wounded.
Margaret Thurston,
Samuel Thurston,
Daniel Clarke,
Timothy Dwight.
These all belonged to the town, probably.

John Gilbert, Jr., of Boston, "apprentice to Mr. Bozoune Allen, tanner," was so severely wounded that he lost the use of his right arm. *Mass. Archives.*

John Fusell was said to have been 100 years of age. He was burnt in his house. William Williams left a young family, consisting of a wife and four small children, in destitute

the Indians *in* New-England.

February 23. A day of Humiliation was attended in the old Meeting-houſe in *Boſton*, but not without much Diſtraction, becauſe of an Alarm, by reaſon of rumors, as if the *Indians* were doing miſchief within ten miles of *Boſton*.

February 25. This night the *Indians* fired ſeven Houſes and Barns in *Weymouth*.[1]

In the beginning of *March* another ſmall Army was ſent out from *Boſton*, under the conduct of that expert Souldier and Commander Major *Savage*, to ſeek out the Enemy. Connecticut Forces met with ours at *Quobaog*, and they marched together, but not following the direction of the (*Natick*) *Praying Indians*, who were ſent as Pilots, the Army miſſed their way, and was bewildred in the Woods. On a ſudden when they thought on no ſuch thing, a party of *Indians* fired upon them and killed one man, and wounded Mr. *Gerſhom Bulkly*, who is Paſtor of the Church in *Wetherſfield*, where-

---

And Feb. 25 [1676], Weymouth alſo ſuffered from theſe *burners* no little damage.

circumſtances. The firſt houſe attacked was that of Samuel Morſe. Mr. Morſe defended himſelf vigorouſly and beat off the Indians, and then rallied and aſſiſted his neighbors.

In Auguſt, 1676, a committee of the inhabitants of this town, conſiſting of *John Wilſon*, *George Barbour*, *Samuel Bulling* and *John Elice*, petitioned the General Court for a remittance of their rates, in conſideration of their " great loſs by the enemy;" " many of our houſe being burnt, and the proviſions of ſeveral perſons taken away, ſome loſing moſt of their clothes and houſehold goods, as alſo moſt of their cattell, many of which were burnt, others killed or driven away; the amount whereof, vpon a iuſt and due calculation amounts vnto £2145, beſides all other damages ſuſtained." *Original MS. Petition.*

[1] Mr. Hubbard (*Narrative*, 66), ſays ſeven or eight houſes were sburned.

upon thofe *Indians* were immediately purfued, who haftened towards *North Hampton*. The Army following them thither, miffed of the main Body of *Indians*. Neverthelefs, there was a fingular providence of God ordering this matter for the relief of thofe *Weſtern Plantations*, which otherwife, in probability had been cut off.

For upon the fourteenth of *March* a multitude of Indians fell upon *North Hampton*, broke through their fortifications in three places, burned five houfes and five barns; and killed four Men, and one Woman: but the town being full of Souldiers, the Enemy was quickly repulfed, with the lofs of many of their lives.[1]

An army under the command of that [51] expert leader, Major *Thomas Savage* about this time did make after the Indians as far as Northampton; and there was again a fingular Providence of God in ordering this matter: For had it not been for thefe recruits, thofe weftern plantations had probably been cut off by a vaft body of Indians, which on March 14, in three places broke in upon the palifadoes, wherewith Northampton was fortified, and killed five perfons, and burned five houfes, but met with a brave repulfe."

---

[1] "In this attack they killed Robert Bartlett, and Thomas Holton, and two other men and two women, and fet fire to four or five dwelling houfes, and as many barns." Williams's *Hiſt. Northampton*, p 12. Hubbard, 77.

Northampton had fuffered before this by the Indians. On the 20th of Auguſt, 1675, they killed Samuel Mafon; and on the 28th of September following they killed Praifever Turner, Uzacaby Shackfpeer and one other perfon. *Ibid*, and Ruffell's *Letter*, in Coffin, 390. Hubbard, p. 44, mentions the lofs of three perfons, but not their names. On the 29th Oct., Jofeph Baker, Jofeph Ba-

the Indians in New-England. 123

March the 10*th*. Mischief was done, and several lives cut off by the *Indians* this day, at *Groton* and at *Sudbury*. An humbling Providence, inasmuch as many Churches were this day Fasting and Praying,[1]

[24] March 12. This Sabbath eleven *Indians* assaulted Mr. *William Clarks* House in *Plimouth*, killed his Wife, who was the Daughter of a godly Father and Mother that came to *New England* on the account of Religion, (See *July* 6.) and she her self also a pious and prudent Woman; they also killed her sucking Childe, and knocked another Childe (who was about eight years old) in the head, supposing they had killed him, but afterwards he came to himself again. And whereas there was another Family besides his own, entertained in Mr. *Clarks* house, the *Indians* destroyed them all, root and branch, the Father, and Mother, and all the Children. So that eleven persons were

On March 10 [1676], they did mischievous things at Groton and Sudbury. And on March 13, they burnt almost all Groton to the Ground; and then called unto the English in the garrison, *what will you do for a house to pray in, now we have burnt your meeting-house!*

ker, Jr., Thomas Salmon and John Roberts were killed. Two days before, John and William Brooks, and John Dumbleton were killed at Westfield. *Ibid.*

[1] Particulars much more at length may be seen in Hubbard's *Narrative*, p. 73. Mr. Butler was unable to find the names of those who were killed in the several attacks upon the town of Groton. In his History of that Town he tells us that no records were kept from the 10th of December, 1675, for two years. The inhabitants fled to Concord, where they remained till after the war.

murdered that day, under one roof, after which they set the house on fire. The Leader of these *Indians* was one *Totoson*,¹ a fellow who was well acquainted with that house, and had received many kindnesses there, it being the manner of those brutish men, who are only skilful to destroy,

---

1 All that a good deal of patient research could recover respecting the destruction of Mr. Clark's family, will be found in *The Book of the Indians*, 245-6, 11th edition. Totoson was a son of a noted Indian, known now only by the English name, *Sam Barrow*. His residence was at Agawam, in what is now Rochester. I visited the spot on the 12th of Sept. 1825. It is on a piece of upland in a large swamp, well known among the inhabitants in that region. It is near the road as you pass from Rochester village to Mattapoiset. The upland, or island lies on the east side of the road, and is connected with the main land by a kind of neck. Over this neck all must pass to the camp of the Chief. The road now crosses this neck, nearly at right angles. Capt. Church had a most desperate encounter with Totoson, in one of his expeditions; the account of which may be read in his *Narrative*, p. 41. Further notice will be found respecting the party who murdered Mr. Clark's family, as we proceed. Their house was a garrison, and stood about two miles southeasterly from the village of Plymouth. It was considered a strong and safe place, and Capt. Church was urged to leave his family there as the most secure place, while he went to Rhode Island in the service of the country. "But," says he, "let me not forget this remarkable providence, namely, that within twenty-four hours, or thereabouts, after my arrival at Rhode Island, Mr. Clark's garrison, in which I was so much importuned to leave my wife and children, was destroyed by the enemy." When he was afterwards commissioned to pursue and destroy the Indians, he was instructed to give quarter to such as he judged proper, except Philip and all those who had been concerned in the murders at Eel River.

There is some uncertainty hanging over the fate of Totoson, as Mr. Hubbard, when he wrote his *Narrative*, said "he was still out in rebellion." At the time Church took his father (the noted Sam Barrow), he barely escaped, and as Church was preparing to entrap him, an old squaw came into Sandwich and reported his death; saying she had covered his body with leaves, and promised to point out the place; "but never had the opportunity, for she immediately fell sick and died also." Church's *History*, 42.

to deal worst with those who have done most for them.¹

March 13. The *Indians* assaulted *Groton*, and left but few houses standing. So that this day also another Candlestick was removed out of its place. One of the first houses that the Enemy destroyed in this place, was the *House of God, h. e.* which was built, and set apart for the celebration of the public Worship of God.²

When they had done that, they scoffed and blasphemed, and came to Mr. *Willard* (the worthy pastor of the Church there) his house (which being Fortified, they attempted not to destroy it) and tauntingly, said, *What will you do for a house to pray in now we have burnt your Meeting-house?* Thus has the Enemy done wickedly in the Sanctuary, they have burnt up the Synagogues of God in the Land; they have cast fire into the Sanctuary; they have cast down the dwelling place of

But the enemy finding these parts of the country, [about Northampton] too many for them, they again translated the scene of their *tragedies* into Plymouth colony, where, after they had, on March 12, barbarously cut off two families under one roof in Plymouth, and on March 17, laid all Warwick, but one house in ashes, Capt. Pierce, [&c.]

---

[1] The proceedings of the Court of Plymouth against the destroyers of Clark's garrison, being of special interest, are placed in the APPENDIX. See APPENDIX F.

[2] This Mr. Hubbard calls the "removal of the Candlestick, after it had been there seated above twelve years. Hence it was built 1664. The same author has left us the most thrilling as well as the most circumstantial account of the destruction of Groton anywhere to be found.

his name to the Ground. *O God how long shall the Adversary reproach? shall the Enemy Blaspheme thy Name for ever? why withdrawest thou thine hand, even thy right hand: pluck it out of thy bosome.*

March 17. This day the *Indians* fell upon *Warwick*, and burnt it down to the ground, all but one house.[1]

March 20. Some of them returned into the *Narraganset* Country, and burnt down the remaining *English* houses there.

We are now come to the conclusion of the year 1675,[2] which hath been the most troublesome year that ever poor *New-England* saw. What ending the present year shall have, is with God, but it hath a most dolefull beginning.

For *March* 26, 1670, being the *Sabbath-day*, the *Indians* assaulted *Malbery* and consumed a great part of the town: after which the Inhabitants apprehended themselves under a necessity of deserting that place which was [25] done accordingly;

[1] Mr. Hubbard places the burning of Warwick on March 16th, which date Mr. Arnold adopts. *Hist. R. Island*, I, 408. The Indians spared "one house" for the very good reason that it was built of stone. *Ibid.* Warwick stands on a neck of land called by the Indians *Potowmut*, or *Pootowoomet*. See Dr. Parsons' valuable tract on *Indian Names* in R. Island, p. 21. Mr. Hubbard describes Warwick as "near Providence seated upon a Neck of land environed by the sea. It was all burned by the enemy at several times, yet but one man killed." *Narrative*.

[2] The 24th of March was the last day of the year in those times. Soon after Philip's War people began to write what is called a double date. Thus between January 1st and March 25th they wrote 1675-6, 1676-7, &c., which signified the real date. When this was not observed writers often made mistakes of a whole year.

so that here is another Candlestick removed out of his place.¹ This day also, Captain *Pierce* of *Scituate* with a party of about fifty *English*, and twenty *Indians*, who were Friends to the *English*, pursued a small number of the Enemy, who in desperate subtility ran away from them, and they went limping to make the *English* believe they were lame, till they had led them into a snare: for suddenly a vast body of *Indians* did encompass them round; so that Captain *Pierce* was slain, and forty and nine *English* with him, and eight (or more) *Indians* who did assist the *English*, and fought bravely in that engagement.

How many of the Enemy fell we know not certainly, only we hear that some *Indians*, which have since been taken by the *English*, confess that Captain *Pierce*, and those with him killed an hundred and forty of them before they lost their own lives.²

Capt. *Pierce* being fitted with 50 Englishmen, and with 20 Christian Indians, did courageously pursue them. This meritorious captain was unhappily tre-

---

¹ When the Indians came upon Marlborough the people were assembled in their Meetinghouse. The Minister, Dr. Brinsmade (or Brinsmead) was commencing his sermon, when the appalling cry was uttered—"The Indians are upon us." Notwithstanding the terror and confusion which ensued, the inhabitants escaped into a garrison, and none were killed. Outside of that every thing was destroyed. The Minister's house was near the Meeting house. That was first set on fire; the flames from which soon extended to the other, and thus both were consumed. Hudson's *Hist. Marlborough*, 73 Quite a different account of the affair will be found in Hubbard's *Narrative*, 95, where it appears that Mr. [Thomas] Graves was then preacher.

² Here again, for the fullest and best account of the battle at Pawtucket, we must refer the reader to

Upon this Lords-day another sad thing likewise hapned; for near *Springfield*, there were eighteen *English-men* riding to the Town, to attend the solemn Worship of God on his Holy day. And although they were Armed there were seven or eight *Indians,* who lying in Ambuscado, were so bold as to shoot at them. They killed a Man and a Maid that rode behind him, the *English* being surprised with fear, rode away to save their lives; in the mean while the *Indians* seized upon two women and Children, and took them away alive, so that here we have cause to think of Joshuahs words, who said, O Lord What shall I say

panned into an ambushment of the enemy, who, on March 26, 1676, by meer multitude overpowered him; so that, after he had first made a slaughter of an hundred and forty of *them*, he with 49 Englishmen (an *hard battel* truly!) and eight christian Indians, expired on the bed of honor. This was a very disastrous day! For on this day also, the town of Marlborough was all in flames by another assault from this treacherous adversary; and on this day several people at Springfield became a sacrifice unto their fury.

Hubbard. But the *Old Indian Chronicle* should also be consulted. Capt. Pierce, whose Christian name was Michael, was brother of Capt. Pierce of London. *News from New England,* 15. The "Capt. Pierce of London," was perhaps the noted ship-master of previous years who sailed between London and Boston. Capt. Pierce lost 56 men, of whom eight were Indians.

Ibid, p. 16. The accounts all differ as to the number slain. See *O. I. Chron.* p. 83. The next day after the fight, the Rev. Noah Newman of Rehoboth collected the names of the slain of Pierce's men, and transmitted them in a letter to the Rev. John Cotton of Plymouth. The list was printed from the original by Mr. Bliss in his *Hist of Rehoboth,* p. 91-2, which see.

the Indians *in* New-England.

when Ifrael turns their backs before their Enemies? What fhall be faid when eighteen *Englifh-men* well arm'd, fly before feven *Indians?* This feems to argue fomething of a divine forfaking, and difpleafure in heaven againft us.¹ The next day thofe *Indians* were purfued, but when the *Englifh* came in fight thofe barbarous wretches hafted to run away, but before that they knocked the two Children on the head, as they were fucking their Mothers breafts, and then knocked their Mothers on the head: Neverthelefs one of them was alive when the Souldiers came to her, and able to give an account of what the *Indians* had told her. Amongft other particulars, they did affirm to her that there was a Body of about three thoufand *Indians* (no doubt but in that they did hyperbolize) near to *Deerfield,* and that they had newly received a great fupply of powder from the *Dutch* at *Albany*: men that worfhip *Mammon,* notwithftanding all prohibitions to the contrary, will expofe their own and other mens lives unto danger, if they may but gain a little of this worlds good.²

Wherefore methinks, reader, we want fome diverting ftory to entertain us in the midft of fo many horrible

---

¹ There were fix killed near Pecowfick brook in Springfield; three of them as they were paffing from Long Meadow to Springfield town, to meeting. The guard accompanying them are held in remembrance by the following lines, compofed on the occafion:

Seven Indians, and one without a gun,
Caufed Capt. Nixon and forty men to run.

See Sprague's *Hift. Difcourfe*, p. 22.

² Befides the printed accounts of this affair at Springfield, I am able to give quite a near view from an original letter written two days after by Maj. Savage then at Hadley. It being too long for a note, I have placed it in the Appendix. See APPENDIX H.

March 27. Some of the inhabitants of *Sudbury*, being alarumed by what the *Indians* did yesterday to their neighbours in *Malbury*, apprehending they might come upon the enemy unawares, in case they should march after them in the night time,

accidents. I will therefore mention a pleasant stratagem used by one of our christian Indians, in the fight when Capt. *Peirce* lost his life. This Indian, who, I durst say, never had read *Polyenus*, being pursued by an enemy, betook himself unto a great rock, where sheltering himself, he perceived that his enemy lay on the other side ready with his gun to discharge upon him whenever he should stir one step from the place where he stood. He therefore took a stick which he had at hand, and hanging his hat upon it, he gently and slowly lifted it up, until he thought his watchful friend on the other side might be sensible of it: And accordingly the other taking this hat for the head of his adversary, let fly immediately, and shot through the hat; Whereupon he briskly lift up his head, and presently letting fly, not upon the hat, but upon the head of the adversary, laid him dead upon the spot.

In this fight another Indian luckily saved not only himself, but an Englishman too, by pretending to run after the Englishman with his hatchet, as if intending to kill him therewithal. And another Indian as luckily saved himself by besmearing his tawny face with wet gun powder, which made him look so like some of the adverse party, who had blacked their faces, that they distinguished him not.

Many such passages and policies are told of our christian Indians, who in truth showed their christianity by their being wonderfully serviceable unto us in the war which now perplexed us.

they resolved to try what might be done, [26] and that not altogether without succefs. For towards the morning whilft it was yet dark, they difcerned where the *Indians* lay by their Fires. And fuch was their boldnefs, as that about three hundred of them lay all night, within half a mile of one of the garifon houfes in that town where they had done fuch mifchief the day before. Albeit the darknefs was fuch as an *Englifh man* could not be difcerned from an *Indian*, yet ours being forty in number, difcharged feveral times upon the enemy, and (as *Indians* taken fince that time do confefs,) God fo difpofed of the bullets that were fhot at that time, that no lefs than thirty *Indians* were wounded, of whom there were fourteen that dyed, feveral of which had been principal actors in the late bloudy Tragedyes. They fired hard upon the *Englifh*, but neither killed nor wounded fo much as one man in the Skirmifh.[1]

March 28. The *Indians* burnt about thirty Barns, and near upon fourty dwelling Houfes in *Reheboth*, fo that thereby the diffipation and defolation of that Church is greatly threatned.[2]

[1] This affair is told with a little more minutenefs by Mr. Hubbard than by our Author. We learn from him that the Englifh were led by Lieut. [Richard] Jacobs of Marlborough. In other refpects their accounts are fo fimilar that the writers muft have compiled from the fame fource of information. Mr. Hubbard fays "an Indian could not be difcerned from a *better man*."

[2] Some interefting traditions refpecting the burning of Rehoboth will be found in Blifs's Hiftory of that town, 94-5. For his facts he feems to have made ufe of a fpurious edition of Hubbard. I therefore take from the genuine as fol-

The next day they burnt about thirty houses at the town called *Providence*.[1]

In the beginning of *April* they did some mischief at *Chelmsford* and *Andover*, where a small party of them put the town into a great fright, caused the people to fly into Garison-houses, killed one man, and burnt one house.[2] And to shew what barbarous creatures they are, they exercised cruelty toward dumb creatures. They took a Cow, knocked off one of her horns, cut out her tongue, and so left the poor creature in great misery. They put an horse, ox &c. into an hovil, and then set it on fire only to shew how they are delighted in exercising cruelty.

But reader be content that this paragraph relate a few more of the pernicious things done by the barbarians, about this time, in several parts of the country; and for thy comfort we will give in the next a relation of an unexpected *alteration* and *revolution*. Know then, that in March 28 the Indians burnt about 40 houses at Rehoboth, and on March 29, about 30 houses at Providence: For the English retiring into garrisons, could not but leave their houses open to the impressions of the adversary.

In the begining of April they were mischievous at

---

[1] For the best account of this attack on "the town called Providence," see Arnold's *Hist. R. I.*, 1, 409. Some of the worthies of those days could not speak of anything appertaining to Rhode Island without a sneer: "Forty-five dwelling-houses were there burned, whereof thirty-eight were inhabited, and the owners thereby turned out of doors, and left without house or harbour. Besides twenty-one barns, two corn-mills and one saw-mill."

[2] The Author had not been able to get particular information of what

the Indians in New-England.

April 9*th*. This day being the Lords day, there was an alarum at *Charlestown, Cambridge*, and other towns, by reason that sundry of the enemy were seen at *Billerica*, and (it seemeth) had shot a man there.[1] This week we hear from *Connecticut*, that a party of their Souldiers went with many of the *Pequods* and *Monhegins*, and some of *Ninnegrets*

Chelmsford and Andover; and that they might by their cruelty discover whose children they were, they would cut out the tongues of the dumb creatures, leaving them alive in misery; and putting others of those poor creatures alive into hovels, they would set them on fire. And although on March 27, about 40 inhabitants of Sudbury made a salley forth in the night upon a body of 300 Indians, killing 30 of them, without losing one of their own; yet on April 18, the Indians made a fierce affault upon Sudbury, wherein they burnt several houses, and killed a dozen persons that were coming from Concord for the assistance of their neighbors.

had been done in the region towards the Merrimack. "On April 8th, the son of George Abbot was killed, and another son carried away captive, who yet was returned some few months after, almost pined to death with hunger." Hubbard, *Narrative*, 84. The name of the son killed was Joseph; that of the other Timothy. See Abbot's *Hist. Andover*, p. 42, who says the affair was on the 19th of April, but cites no authority. Timothy Abbot was but 14 years old, 11 Sept., 1676, at which time he was a witness against Sam Numphow, or *Nobboth*, as Abbot called him. See *Massachusetts Archives*.

The Indian name of Andover was *Cochichawick*. *Ibid.*

[1] Billerica was the Indian *Shawshin*. On March 10th, two houses were burned there. Hubbard, 84. "On the 9th of April the Indians beset Bilerica round about, the inhabitants being at Meeting." *Letter of John Cotton of Plymouth*, dated 17 April. John Farmer published a *History of Billerica*, but he does not seem to have found anything about this affair.

Indians, to seek after the enemy, and they killed and took captive forty and four *Indians* without the loss of any of ours: amongst whom were several of their *Chief Captains* and their great Sachem called *Quanonchet*, who was a principal ring leader in the *Narraganset* War, and had as great an interest and influence as can be said of any among the *Indians*. This great Sachem was pursued into a River by one of *Ninnegret* his men, and there taken. Being apprehended he was carried away to *Stonington*, where the *English* caused the *Pequods* and *Monhegins*, and *Ninnegrets Indians* to joyn together in shooting *Quanonchet*, and cutting off his head, which was sent to *Hartford*. And herein the *English* dealt wisely, for by this meanes, those three *Indian* Nations are [27] become abominable to the other *Indians*, and it is now their interest to be faithfull to the *English*, since their own Countrymen will never forgive them, on account of their taking and killing the Sachem mentioned: So that there was a gracious smile of providence in this thing, yet not without matter of humbling to us, in that the Sachem was apprehended not by *English* but by *Indian* hands.[1]

But a Polybius will tell me, *non decet Historiæ Scriptorem, duntaxat Res Crudules Legentibus Exponere.*: And, I promised my reader *a turn of our affairs*. The prayers

---

[1] Mr. Hubbard employs several of his quarto pages in this account summed up by our Author in a few lines. It is one of his most happy efforts, and I venture the opinion that there are few passages in history, ancient or modern, equal to that of Mr. Hubbard upon the capture and fate of Nanuntenoo. See also, *A New and Further Narrative*, in

April. 19. The *Indians* killed a man at *Weymouth*, and another at *Hingham.* And they burnt down the remaining deserted houses at *Malbery.*[1]

of many thousands of pious people, poured out with the greatest solemnity, did all this while [52] *Cœlum Tundere,* and now they must, *Misericordiam Extorquere.* The maxim uttered by the renowned King of Sweden, *The greater the army of prayers is, the more certain and glorious will be the victory!* must now be fulfilled; and the supplications for our distressed case, made by not only the churches of New England, which were in the distress, but also by the churches of London, of Suffolk, of Dorset, of Devon, of Somerset, of Lancashire, of Dublin, (for which we now publickly return our thanks) must now be answered.

The time limited by heaven for the success of the Indian treacheries was now almost expired: The blasphemy and insolence, and prodigious barbarity of the salvages, was come to a sufficient heighth, for the Lord God of Zabaoth to interpose his own *revenges;* and the impossibility which there appeared for our people to attend their husbandry in the fields, or to find out their enemy in the woods, did, as the spring advanced, throw

---

the *Old Indian Chronicle,* p. 90-92; or, *The Book of the Indians,* where all the accounts are embodied. The expedition employed about fourteen days. It commenced Mar. 27, and ended April 10. Hubbard, *Narrative,* 140.

[1] From the *Weymouth Records* is obtained the name of the man killed there, "Sergeant Pratt." At Hingham, "John Jacob was slain by the Indians near his father's house; and the next day Joseph Joanes's, Anthony Sprague's, Israel Hobart's, Nathaniel Chubbuck's, and James Whiton's houses were burnt down." Lincoln's *Hist. Hingham,* p. 83-4, from *Hobart's Diary.* The houses at Marlborough were burnt April 17th, but the number destroyed does not appear. See Hubbard, 79. In the *O. Ind. Chron.*, p. 92, are other interesting particulars. The people of Wrentham abandoned the town and thus escaped. *Bean's Cent. Ser.*

April 20*th.* A day of Humiliation was obferved in *Bofton.* The next day fad tidings came to us. For the enemy fet upon *Sudbury,* and burnt a great part of the town. And whereas Capt. *Wadfworth* (a prudent & faithfull man) was fent out for their relief, with about feventy armed men, a great body of *Indians* furrounded them, fo as that above fifty of ours were flain that day, amongft whom was Capt. *Wadfworth* and his Lieutenant *Sharp.* Alfo Captain *Brattlebanck* (a godly and choife fpirited man) was killed at the fame time. Alfo they took five or fix of the *Englifh* and carried them away alive, but that night killed them in fuch a manner

us into an extremity of defpair, to wade through another fummer like the laft.

But Now was the time for deliverance! There was an evil fpirit of diffention ftrangely fent among the Indians, which difpofed them to feparate from one another. The *demons* who vifibly exhibited themfelves among them at their powowing, or conjuring, fignified ftill unto them, that they could now *do no more for them;* the Maquas, a powerful nation in the weft, made a defcent upon them, ranging and raging through the defert with irrefiftable fury; fevers and fluxes became epidemical among them; and their being driven from their planting and fifhing places, drove them into fo much of a famine as brought *mortal ficknefs* upon them. Finally, a *vifible fmile of Heaven* was upon almoft all the enterprifes of the Englifh againft them. And an unaccountable terror at the fame time fo difpirited them, that they were like men under a *fafcination.* It was the promife of God unto his antient people, " The

as none but *Salvages* would have done. For they ftripped them naked, and caufed them to run the Gauntlet, whipping them after a cruel and bloudy manner, and then threw hot afhes upon them, cut

Lord thy God will fend the hornet among thine enemies, until they that are left, and hide themfelves from thee be deftroyed: And I never faw a more fenfible confirmation of that promife, or explication of that *hornet*, than in what now befel the enemies of New England. They were juft like *beafts* that are ftung with a *garabee* or *hornet*; they ran they knew not *whither* they knew not *wherefore;* they were under fuch a confternation, that the Englifh did even what they would upon them.

I fhall never forget the expreffions which a defperate fighting fort of fellow, one of their generals, ufed unto the Englifh after they had captivated him; *You could never have fubdued us, but* (faid he, ftriking on his breaft,) *the Englifhman's God makes us afraid here!* Firft, from Connecticut colony, which the kind Providence of our Lord Jefus Chrift kept almoft untouched in this bloody war, there went forth in the month of April, under the command of *Capt. Denifon*, 66 volunteers, with above 100 friend Indians, who took & flew 76 of the enemy, among whom were fome of their chiefeft princes and made great havock on their ftores, without lofing any of their own:

And a little before this, a party of Connecticut Soldiers, with the like Indian affiftance, took and flew 44 of the enemy, without any lofs on our fide, but among the prifoners was *Quanonchet*, the mighty fachem of Narraganfet, whom the Englifh wifely delivered unto their tawny auxiliaries, for them to cut off his head; that fo the alienation between them and the wretches in hoftility againft us might become incurable.

out the flesh of their legs, and put fire into their wounds, delighting to see the miserable torments of wretched creatures. Thus are they the perfect children of the Devill. What numbers the Indians lost in this fight, we know not, onely a Captive since escaped out of their hands, affirms that the Indians said one to another, that they had an hundred and twenty fighting men kill'd this day.[1]

The same day (as is judged fifty) *Indians* burnt nineteen houses and barns at *Scituate* in *Plimouth* Colony, but were notably encountred and repelled

But the worst part of the story is, that *Capt.* Wadsworth, one worthy to live in our history, under the name of a good man, coming up after a long, hard, unwearied march, with 70 men unto the relief of distressed Sudbury, found himself in the woods on the sudden surrounded with about 500 of the enemy; whereupon our men fought like *men*, and *more* than so; but were so overwhelmed, that he, with another *good man*, one *Capt.* Brattlebank, [*Capt.* Samuel Brocklebank of Rowley] and more than 50 more, sold their *lives* for the *deaths* of about an hundred and twenty Indians. The Indians took five or six of the English prisoners; and that the reader may understand, *crimine ab uno*, what it is to be taken by such *devils incarnate*, I shall here inform him. They stripped these unhappy prisoners, and caused them to run the *gauntlet*, and whip-

---

[1] The 21st of April, 1676, is one of the very memorable days of Philip's War, and memorable as the last great success which the Indians had. Historians are full upon it. See Hubbard, 80-2, Also *A True Account*, &c., *Indian Chronicle* 118-120. A question has been raised respecting the date of this battle. Suffice it to be said it is a very idle question, or rather, there is *no question* about it. In Gage's *Hist. Rowley* are the names of many of the men under Wadsworth.

from doing further mischief by the valor of a few of the inhabitants.¹

Apr. 24*th*, Skulking *Indians* did some mischief in *Braintree*, but the inhabitants received not any considerable damage by them.²

April 27. A small number of them near *Woodcocks* who keeps the *Ordinary* in the roade to *Rehoboth*, watched their opportunity and killed his son, and another man, and greatly wounded another of his sons, and shot himself through the arm, and then burnt his sons house.³

At *Boston* there is a Press in order to sending forth another Army to pursue the enemy, for we

ped them after a cruel and bloody manner; they then threw hot ashes upon them, and cutting off callop's of their flesh, they put fire into their wounds, and so with exquisite, leisurely, horrible torments, *roasted* them out of the world.

[To follow the order of the Magnalia the above note comes before the next preceding. It is necessary occasionally to transpose a paragraph to make the narrative correspond with that of the text.]

---

1 Deane, in his *History of Scituate*, 125, &c., has detailed the burning of that town with much minuteness, to which the reader is referred. He will there also find the names of the owners of the houses.

2 I do not find any further account of the "damage" done in Braintree, although we have *Century Sermons*, and a *History of Quincy*, then included in Braintree. The "damage" was probably committed beyond the limits of modern Braintree.

3 In Mr. Daggett's *Hist. of Attleboro*, p. 47, will be found all the facts known with regard to the attack on Woodcock's family See also Bliss's *Rehoboth*, 77, 102, and the *Old Indian Chronicle*, p. 96. The date of the attack, according to this last author, was April 26.

hear there is a great body of them near *Malbury,* (as is apprehended) of many hundreds.

About this time, in *Connecticut Colony,* Capt. *Dennifon* with fixty fix Volunteers, & an hundred and twelve *Pequod-Indians,* purfuing the common enemy, took and flew feventy and fix Indians. Amongft the flain was the [28] Sachem *Pomham* his Grand-child, who was alfo a Sachem, and another called *Chickon,* and one great Counfellour. They took and fpoiled an hundred and fixty bufhels of the *Indians* corn. None of ours either *Englifh* or *Indians* that did ingage with and for the *Englifh,* were loft when this exploit was done.[1]

In the moneth of *April,* many of the Eaftern *Indians* having been forely diftreffed, and fain to wander up and down for meat, fo as that they lived for fome time upon no other food then the fkins of wild creatures, which they foaked in water till they became foft and eatable ; notwithftanding the outrages and murthers (for they have fhed the blood of about forty feven perfons) by them committed, they did in confidence of favour from the *Englifh* come and fubmit themfelves, alleadging that the

---

[1] The only other writer on this war who mentions this expedition is Hubbard. No date is affigned to it by him, who fays it was "not long after" the capture of Canonchet. *Narrative,* 68. Hence it was doubtlefs about the middle of April. Dr. Trumbull fays, that before the end of April, the Connecticut men had killed and taken about 120 in one month ; which number includes the 44 taken with Canonchet. "They made, in the Spring, Summer and Fall, ten or twelve expeditions, in which they killed and captivated 230 of the enemy, took 50 mufkets, and brought in 160 bufhels of their corn. They drove all the Narragansets out of their country, except thofe under Ninigred, at what is fince Wefterly." *Hift. Connecticut,* I, 345.

the Indians in New-England.   141

injuryes done by them were grounded upon a mistake. For when a party of *English* came in a Warlike posture upon some of their *Webbs* (as they call them) *i. e. Women* as they were gathering corn, an *Indian* seing it, ran to the other *Indians* and told them that the *English* had (though it were not at all so) killed all those *Indian* women, and therefore they took up arms to revenge the supposed injury. Also they plead for themselves, that a Fisher-man told one of them, that the *English* would destroy all the *Indians*, and when inquiry was made of another *English man* (thought to be more discreet then the former) he confirmed what the other had said, and that some rude *English* did purposely overset a *Canoo* wherein was an *Indian* Lad; and that although a *Squaw* dived to the bottom of the River and fetched him up alive, yet that the Lad never came to himself again. It is greatly to be lamented that the heathen should have any ground for such allegations, or that they should be scandalized by men that call themselves Christians.[1]

May 3*d.* Was the day of *Election* for Governour and Magistrates in the *Mattachusets Colony*.[2] This

---

[1] The troubles with the Eastern Indians are well detailed in Hubbard's *Narrative*, to which inquirers are referred. To which much elucidation will be derived from the *Hist. of Portland*, and other works of the Hon. Wm. Willis.

[2] Gov. Leverett was rechosen; Mr. Samuel Symonds, Deputy Governor; Symon Bradstreet, Daniel Denison, Richard Russell, Thomas Danforth, Wm. Hathorne, John Pynchon, Edward Tyng, William Stoughton, Thomas Clark, and Joseph Dudley, Assistants.

At the May election in Connecticut Wm. Leet was chosen Governor, Robert Treat, Deputy Governor, and Capt. John Mason, famous in the Pequot War, was chosen a Magistrate.

day the Lord by a wonderfull hand of providence, wrought Salvation for *Mrs. Rowlandſon* & returned her to *Boſton*, after ſhe had been eleven weeks in Captivity amongſt the heathen. This is a Token for good, being a great anſwer of Prayer. For by reaſon of her near relation to a *Man of God*, much prayer had been particularly made before the Lord on her behalf. Nevertheleſs did the Lord manifeſt his holy diſpleaſure, inaſmuch as at *Haveril* and *Bradford*, a ſmall company of *Indians* killed two men and carryed away a man and a woman, & five Children alive.[1]

May 6th. Our Forces which are abroad met with a party of *Indians*, and killed about thirteen of them, and had probably deſtroyed many more of them, had not an *Engliſh-man* unhappily ſounded

---

[1] Ephraim Kingſbury is killed at Haverhill, the firſt perſon killed there by the Indians. Myrick's *Hiſt. Haverhill*, 53. The next day (May 3d), a party led by a noted Indian rogue, named *Simon*, came ſtealthily upon the family of Thomas Kimball at Bradford, killed him, and took his wife and five children and carried them into captivity. At the ſame time they carried off Philip Eaſtman from Haverhill. All theſe, however, were, through the kind offices of Wonaſancet, chief of the Pennicooks, ſet at liberty and returned home, after a ſhort captivity; or, as Eaſtman himſelf ſays, they were detained "ſome conſiderable time." He petitioned the General Court, Sept. 6th, 1676, to have his "rates" abated, for " by his captivity he was not able to plant his land, and now a want of ſtrength and bodily ability rendered him unable to labor." The Court remitted his tax. *Original Petition.*

Mrs. Kimball alſo preferred a ſimilar petition. October 16th, 1676, who had been rated "upwards of £4, the which mony I am not able in nowe wais to pay, I am ſo impoveriſhed throw the loſs of my huſband, and our eſtate, being carried away and with my children, wher by wee have bene holy proſtrated of produſeing any thing from oure land." &c. Upon which petition being preſented, ſhe was alſo excuſed from payment of the ſaid rate. *Original Petition in poſſeſſion of the Editor.*

a trumpet, whereby the enemy had notice to efcape. The *Praying Indians* did good Service at that time, infomuch as many who had hard thoughts of them all, begin to blame [29] themfelves, and to have a good opinion of thofe *Praying Indians* who have been fo univerfally decryed.

May 8. About feventeen Houfes and Barns did the *Indians* fire and deftroy at *Bridgwater*.[1] But the Lord in the nick of time, fent thunder and Rain, which caufed the Enemy to turn back.

There were ftill here and there little mifchiefs done by the enemy; Plymouth, Taunton, Chelmsford, Concord, Haverhill, Bradford, Woburn, and other places, did fuftain fundry damages: But the main character of the occurrents not happening on our part, was *victory over them*. Remarkable was the fate of Bridgewater, a moft praying and moft pious town, feated in the very midft of the dangers of the war; that although they were often affaulted by formidable numbers of the enemies, yet, in all their fharp affaults, they *never loft one* of their inhabitants, young or old. They were folicited ftrongly to defert their dwellings, but they refolved that they would keep their ftations.

And now on May 8, the Indians began to fire the town, but the inhabitants with notable courage iffued forth from their garrifons to fight the enemy, and God from Heaven at the fame time fought for them, with

---

[1] All the particulars which could be recovered of the burning of Bridgewater, will be found in the Hiftory of that town by Hon. Judge Mitchell, 39 and 398. "It is very remarkable," fays Hubbard, *Narrative*, 68, "that the inhabitants of Bridgwater, never yet loft one perfon by the fword of the enemy, yet have they helped to deftroy many of the enemy." The fame will be found ftated by our author.

About this time they killed four men at *Taunton*, as they were at work in the field, by whose death about thirty Children were made fatherless.¹

May 9. A day of Humiliation by Fasting and Prayer, was attended in the Town-house at *Boston*, by the Magistrates, and Deputies of the General Court, with Assistance of so many Teaching Elders as could be obtained. Although many such solemn occasions have at times been attended in former

a storm of lightning, thunder and rain, whereby a considerable part of their houses were preserved. Thou, Church of Bridgwater,

O minium Dilecta Deo, cui militat Æther,
Et conjurati veniunt ad Classica Venti.

One that was no Christian so sang the favors of Heaven to the emperor *Theodosius*, and so might the Pagan foe now sing of thy salvations.

On May 6, our forces, assisted with some Christian Indians, did good execution upon the enemy near Medfield, and on May 11, did the like at Plymouth.

---

¹ There is, or was, a letter among the Hinckley MSS. in the library of the Mass. H. Soc., written by Gov. Bradford, in which this mention is made of the sufferings of Taunton: "The enemy have killed four stout men at Taunton, and carried away two lusty youths; Mr. Henry Andrews, James Bell, Sergt. Phillips, and the two youths, all at one time, being securely planting two or three miles from the town. The other one, Leonard Babit, killed at another place. The four men leaving thirty two fatherless children." The place where the four men were killed is since Raynham, called by the Indians *Nesquabinausit*, and after by the English *Squawbety*. The graves of the slain were to be seen when the Rev. Mr. Forbes wrote his account of Raynham. They were upon the bank of Tehticut, or Taunton River. He also tells us that the Christian name of Sergt. Phillips was Henry. He says another was Henry *Andross*, but Baylie's *Memoir Plym. Colony*, III, 122, adopts the name Henry *Andrews*, which agrees with Bradford's letter.

years, yet it hath been obferved by fome, that God did always fignally own his Servants, upon their being before him in fuch a way and manner: And fo it was now, for the very next day after this, a Letter came from *Connecticut* to *Bofton*, informing, that God had let loofe the *Mohawks* upon our Enemies, and that they were fick of Fluxes, and Fevers, which proved mortal to multitudes of them. And whereas a fpecial requeft left before the Lord this day, was that he would (as a token for good) caufe our poor Captives to be returned to us again, and efpecially thofe that were taken from *Haveril* the laft week, God gave a gracious and fpeedy Anfwer, bringing home thofe very Captives in particular, and many other, yea at leaft fixteen of our poor fighing Prifoners, who were appointed to death, did the Lord loofe and return unto us, within eight weeks after this day, and divers of them within three dayes after this folemn day of Prayer.[1] There are who have dated the turn of Providence towards us in this Colony, and againft the Enemy in a wonderful manner, from this day forward: yet fome leffer and more inconfiderable devaftations happened foon after in *Plimouth* Colony. For,

May 11. A company of *Indians* affaulted the Town of *Plimouth*, burnt eleven Houfes and five

---

[1] The Author makes quite a revelation about the return of captives, but leaves us entirely in the dark as to what captives were returned. Doubtlefs the family of Thomas Kimball were among them, and probably among thofe who came eight weeks after the Faft. The facts, as far as known, refpecting thefe captives are ftated elfewhere.

Barns therein :[1] ten *English-men* were going to seek after the Enemy, and having an *Indian* with them, who was true to the *English*, he spied a party of *Indians* lying in .Ambush, who in probability had otherwise cut off many of them, but the *English* having the opportunity of the first shot, struck down several *Indians*, one of which had on a great Peag Belt. But he and the other that fell were dragged away, and the *Indians* fled, when they saw themselves pursued, though but by a few.[2] Nevertheless two days after this, they burnt seven Houses and two Barns more in *Plimouth*, and the remaining Houses in *Namasket*.

May 18. This day that happened which is worthy to be remembred. For at *North-hampton*, *Hadly*, and the Towns thereabouts, two *English* Captives[3] escaping from the Enemy, informed that a considerable body of *Indians* had [30] seated themselves not far from *Pacomtuck*, and that they were very secure : so that should Forces be sent forth against them, many of the Enemy would (in

---

[1] It should be borne in mind that Plymouth then comprised a large territory ; including that now contained in Plimpton, Carver, Kingston, part of Halifax and Wareham. Those burnt were scattered over the town, and had probably all been deserted. The notorious Tispaquin, or Watuspaquin, who lived near Assawomset Pond, was the leader in this devastation. See Hubbard, 106.

[2] Hubbard adds very little and Baylies nothing to this. No names of those engaged in the affair appear to have been preserved.

[3] English lads, says Hubbard, *Narrative*, 87. Their names were Edward Stebbins and John Gilbert. When the Rev. Mr. Breck of Springfield, preached his Century Sermon there in 1775, he mentions grandchildren of Edward Stebbins then present. *Cent. Serm.*, p. 22.

probability) be cut off, without any difficulty. Hereupon the Spirits of Men in thofe Towns were raifed with an earneft defire to fee and try what might be done. They fent to their neighbours in *Connecticut* for a fupply of Men, but none coming, they raifed about an hundred and four fcore out of their own Towns, who arrived at the *Indian Wigwams* betimes in the morning, finding them fecure indeed, yea all afleep without having any Scouts abroad, fo that our Souldiers came and put their Guns into their Wigwams, before the *Indians* were aware of them, and made a great and notable flaughter amongft them. Some of the Souldiers affirm, that they numbred above one hundred that lay dead upon the ground, and befides thofe, others told about an hundred and thirty, who were driven into the River, and there perifhed, being carried down the Falls, *The River Kifhon fwept them away, that ancient River, the river Kifhon, O my foul thou haft troden down ftrength.* And all this while but one *Englifh-man* killed, and two wounded. But God faw that if things had ended thus, another and not Chrift would have had the Glory of this Victory, and therefore in his wife providence, he fo difpofed, as that there was at laft fomewhat a tragical iffue of this Expedition. For an *Englifh* Captive Lad, [1] who was found in the Wigwams, fpake as if *Philip* were coming with a thoufand *Indians:* which falfe report being famed (*Famâ bella ftant*) among the

---

[1] Perhaps John Gilbert, the lad of whom Mrs. Rowlandfon gives fo pitiful a picture in the *Narrative of her Captivity*, p. 42, edition of 1811; or Willard's edition, p. 52. Gilbert belonged to Springfield.

Souldiers, a pannick terror fell upon many of them, and they hafted homewards in a confused rout: Πολλὰ νενὰ τȣ̃ πολέμȣ. In the mean while a party of Indians from an Ifland (whofe coming on fhore might eafily have been prevented, and the Souldiers before they fet out from *Hadly* were earneftly admonifhed to take care about that matter) affaulted our men; yea, to the great difhonour of the *Englifh*, a few *Indians* purfued our Souldiers four or five miles, who were in number near twice as many as the Enemy. In this *Diforder*, he that was at this time the chief Captain, whofe name was *Turner*, loft his life, he was purfued through a River, received his fatal ftroke as he paffed through that which is called the *Green River*, & as he came out of the *Water* he fell into the hands of the *Uncircumcifed*, who ftripped him (as fome who fay they faw it affirm) and rode away upon his horfe; and between thirty and forty more were loft in this Retreat.¹

Within a few days after this, Capt. *Turners* dead Corps was found a fmall diftance from the River; it appeared he had been fhot through his thigh and back, of which its judged he dyed fpeedily without

---

¹ The brave Capt. Wm. Turner was of Bofton. The details of the farfamed Fall Fight are fo full in the publifhed accounts, that little can be added at this day from other fources. In the *Hiftory and Antiquities of Bofton*, p. 418, will be found a lift of the names of Capt. Turner's men, not elfewhere publifhed. Befides the contemporary printed Hiftories, Gen. Hoyt's work, entitled *Antiquarian Refearches*, fhould be read. It is remarkable that Mr. Mather fhould omit all mention of Capt. Samuel Holioke of Springfield, who acted a confpicuous part in the Fall Fight, though fecond in command. For fome interefting perfonal narratives, See APPENDIX I.

any great torture from the enemy. However it were, it is evident that the *English* obtained a victory at this time, yet if it be as some *Indians* have since related, the [31] Victory was not so great as was at first apprehended: For sundry of them who were at several times taken after this slaughter, affirm that many of the *Indians* that were driven down the Falls,[1] got safe on shore again, and that they lost not more than threescore men in the fight: also that they killed thirty and eight *English men*, which indeed is just the number missing. There is not much heed to be given to *Indian* Testimony, yet when circumstances and Artificial arguments confirm what they say, it becometh an impartial *Historian* to take notice thereof; nor is it to be doubted but the loss of the enemy was greater then those Captives taken by our Forces abroad did acknowledge. Some other *Indians* said that they lost several hundreds at this time, amongst whom there was one Sachem. I am informed that diverse *Indians* who were in that battell, but since come in to the *English* at *Norwich*, say that there were three hundred killed at that time, which is also confirmed by an *Indian* called *Pomham*, who saith that of that three hundred there were an hundred

---

[1] These Falls we once suggested should have been named *Massacre Falls:* but in all recent geographies and histories they are known as *Turner's Falls,* and we heartily acquiesce in thus designating them, as it commemorates a brave and excellent man. I do not remember to have met with an Indian name for these Falls. In early accounts they are called simply *The Falls,* the *Falls in the Connecticut,* &c. They were by some called *Miller's Falls,* as they were not far from Miller's river; they have also been called *Deerfield Falls.*

and seventy fighting men. Whatever the victory or success of that ingagement might be, it was the Lords doing, and let him alone have all the Glory.

May 23. Some of our Troopers fell upon a party of *Indians* (about fifty in number) not far from *Rehoboth*, and slew ten or twelve of them, with the loss of onely one *English-man*. The Indians betook themselves to a River, and had not some Foot-Souldiers on the other side of the River, too suddenly discovered themselves, probably there had been a greater slaughter of the enemy, who hasted out of the river again, and fled into a Swamp where there was no pursuing of them.[1]

On May 18, two captive lads escaping from the hands of the enemy, informed the towns about Northampton, that a considerable body of the Indians were securely clanning together a few miles further up the river; whereupon about an hundred and four score active men went out immediately, and so surprized them, that they killed, as was judged, about an hundred on the spot, and they drove as many more into that *ancient river*, that swept them away. But the English in the retreat were unhappily circumvented by a parcell of the enemy, who slew *Capt Turner*, and upwards of thirty more, although not without the loss of three hundred of their own, as was afterwards by some of themselves acknowledged.

On May 30, the enemy lost five and twenty in one onset which they made upon Hatfield, five being slain

---

[1] Hubbard is quite as brief on this Affair as our Author, but he informs us that Capt. Brattle led the English. From the account in the *O. Ind. Chronicle*, p. 122, it seems that Brattle's men were mounted.

May 30*th*. The enemy appeared at *Hatfield*, fired about twelve houses and barns without the Fortification, killed many of their Cattle, drave away almost all their sheep, spread themselves in the meadow between *Hatfield* & *Hadly*. Whereupon twenty five active and resolute men went from *Hadly* to relieve their distressed Brethren. The *Indians* shot at them ere they could get out of the Boat & wounded one of them. Ours nevertheless charged on the enemy, shot down five or six at the first volley near the River. Then they made haste toward the town fighting with a great number of the enemy, many falling before them. And though encompassed with a numerous swarm of Indians, who also lay in Ambush behind almost every Tree, and place of advantage, yet the *English* lost not one man, till within about an hundred Rod of the Town, when five of ours were slain, among whom was a precious young man, whose name was *Smith*, that place having lost many in losing that one man. It speaketh sadly to the rising Generation when on our part in the action; as the week before [53] this twelve of them were slain about Rehoboth, with the loss of but one of ours.

New forces, both in Massachuset Colony and in Connecticut Colony, were now sent forth to distress the enemy in their places of planting and fishing. The Massachuset forces quickly took and kill'd near forty Indians, and the Connecticut forces took and kill'd an hundred, which exploits were performed without losing a man of our own.

such are taken away. After this the enemy fled, having loft five and twenty in this fight.¹

[32] In thefe two laft months of *May & April*, befides the *Sword of War*, in refpect of the Heathen, *the Sword of the Lord* hath been drawn againft this Land, in refpect of Epidemical Difeafes, which fin hath brought upon us; Sore and (doubtlefs) *Malignant Colds* prevailing every where. I cannot hear of one Family in *New-England* that hath wholly efcaped the Diftemper, but there have been many Families wherein every one in the Houfe was fick and ill-difpofed. So as that there have been many fick and weak, and fome are fallen afleep, yea fome eminent and ufeful Inftruments hath the Lord removed, and made breaches thereby upon divers of the Colonies of *New-England*.

Connecticut is deprived of their Worthy and publick-fpirited Governour *Winthrop*.² This Colony of *Mattachufets* hath been bereaved of two

---

¹ This account of the Indian expedition againft Hatfield and the brilliant attack upon them by the Hadley men is here more circumftantial than in any of the other printed works. Yet in all of them there is the fame want of that minutenefs of detail which renders fuch narrations of living intereft. We have not even the name of the leader of the Englifh. Capt. Benj. Newbury, then at Northampton, wrote to the Council of Connecticut, "There is five killed and three wounded; two of our men killed, Jobama Smith and Richard Hall; John Stoe wounded in the foot, and Rodger Alvis is alfo wounded in the foot, John Smith of Hadley kild, and two of the Garrifon Souldiers." *Colonial Records of Connecticut*, II, 450.

² He was fon of the fecond governor of the Maffachufetts Colony; was a man of learning and ability. He died in Bofton, April 5th, 1676, aged 71.

(*viz*, Major *Willard*,[1] and Mr. *Ruffell* [2]), who for many years had approved themselves faithful in the Magistracy. And the death of a few such is as much as if thousands had fallen: yet many other righteous and useful ones are gone, leaving us behind in the storm. And amongst the common people, not a few have been carried to their Graves in these two last months. We have heard of no less then eight in one small Plantation, buried in one week, wherein also twenty persons died this Spring. And in another little Town nineteen persons have died within a few weeks. We in *Boston* have seen (a sad and solemn spectacle) Coffins meeting one another, and three or four put into their Graves in one day. In the month of *May* about fifty persons are deceased in this Town. By which things, God from Heaven speaks to us, and would give us to understand, that if the Sword will not reform us, he hath other judgments in store, whereby he can suddenly and easily bring us down. The Lord help us to apply our hearts unto Wisdome, and make us thankful, in that he hath been entreated graciously and wonderfully to restore Health unto us again.

In the latter end of *May*, and beginning of *June*, the *Indians* have been less active in the pursuit of

---

[1] Major Simon Willard. He distinguished himself in the beginning of this war, in timely raising the siege of Quabaog [Brookfield]. He died at Charlestown, April 24th, 1676.

[2] The Honourable Richard Ruffell. He was of Charlestown, had been in the country since about 1640, died on the 14th of May, 1676.

their mischievous designes against the *English*. One reason whereof hath been in that it was now their Planting and Fishing time: for at this time of the year, they supply themselves with fish out of the Ponds and Rivers. wherewith this good Land doth abound, and dry it against the Sun, so as that they can lay up in store, for to serve them the year about. But it would have been no wisdome for the *English* to suffer them so to do. Wherefore about four or five hundred Souldiers were sent out of this Colony, and as many (*English* and *Indians* together) of *Connecticut*, to seek out and disrest the Enemy.

June 7. Our Forces now abroad came upon a party of *Indians* not far from *Lancaster*, and killed seven of them, and took nine and twenty of them [33] Captive: some of which not long since had *English* Captives under them. Thus did they that had led into Captivity, go into Captivity; and they that killed with the Sword were themselves killed with the Sword.[1]

Also *Connecticut* Forces, whilst upon their march, killed and took above fifty *Indians*, and not long after that, a small party of *Connecticut* Souldiers with the assistance of a few of those *Indians* who

---

[1] Hubbard, though he does not give the date of this exploit, is more particular upon it. The English owed their success to one of the Praying Indians of Natick, named (by the English) Tom Dublet. The Indians were surprised while fishing in "Weshacom Ponds towards Lancaster." *Narrative*, 90. See also Gookin's *Hist. Praying Indians;* Hoyt's *Ant. Researches*, 134; but he was wanting even in printed works, to make his account intelligible.

have been friends to the *English*, flew and took forty and four of the Enemy in the *Narraganset* Country; all these exploits being performed without the loss of any of ours.[1]

June 12. The Enemy assaulted *Hadly*, in the morning, Sun an hour high, three Souldiers going out of the Town without their Arms, were diswaded therefrom by a Serjeant, who stood at the Gate, but they alleadging that they intended not to go far, were suffered to pass, within a while the Serjeant apprehended, that he heard some men running, and looking over the Fortification, he saw *twenty Indians* pursuing those three men, who were so terrified, that they could not cry out; two of them were at last killed, and the other so mortally wounded, as that he lived not above two or three dayes; wherefore the Serjeant gave the *Alarme*. God in great mercy to those *Western Plantations* had so ordered by his providence, as that *Connecticut* Army was come thither before this onset from the enemy. Besides *English*, there were near upon two hundred *Indians* in *Hadley*,[2] who came to fight with and for the *English*, against the common enemy, who was quickly driven off at the *South end* of the Town, whilst our men were pursuing of them there, on a sudden a great Swarm of *Indians* issued out of the bushes, and made their main assault at the *North end* of the Town, they fired a

[1] For the best accounts of the expeditions of the Connecticut men, Mr. Hubbard and Dr. Trumbull must be consulted. Gen. Hoyt has added something.

[2] Hubbard says there were "about 500 in all." *Narrative*, 94.

Barn which was without the Fortifications, and went into an house, where the inhabitants discharged a great Gun upon them, whereupon about fifty *Indians* were seen running out of the house in great haste, being terribly frighted with the Report and slaughter made amongst them by the great Gun. Ours followed the enemy (whom they judged to be about five hundred, and by *Indian* report since, it seems they were seven hundred) near upon two miles, and would fain have pursued them further, but they had no Order so to do. Some in those parts think, that as great an opportunity and advantage as hath been since the war began, was lost at this time, the Lord having brought the enemy to them, and there being *English* and *Indians* enough to pursue them: But others supposing that then they should impede the design of coming upon them at the *Falls*, nothing was done untill it was too late; only the Towns in those places were eminently saved, and but few of ours that lost their lives in this Skirmish,[1] nor is it as yet known how many the enemy lost in this fight. The *English* could find but three dead *Indians*: yet some of them

---

[1] The following minutes of depositions among the *Mass. Archives* probably relate to this affair at Hadley. The paper is dated July 1st, 1676.

"Depositions, from Hadley against John Belshar of Braintree for not taking Isaack Harrison a wounded soldier on his horse, and who thus lost his life. To this effect from Thomas Irons of Boston, soldier, aged about 30 years; Steven Balden, aged about 17 yrs. William Smith of Bradford, aged about 19; Jonathan Walls of Hadley, aged about 17.; Joseph Warrine of H., age about 31. Martha Harrison, widow of the said Isaac, who was in Capt Turner's company." Not in the *Mass. Archives* as published.

who have been taken Captive, confefs that they had thirty men kill'd this [34] day. And fince we have been informed by *Indians,* of that which is much to be obferved, *viz.* that while the *Indian* men were thus fighting againft *Hadley,* the hand of the Lord fo difpofed, as that the *Mohawks* came upon their Head-Quarters, and fmote their women and Children with a great Slaughter, and then returned with much plunder. If indeed it was fo (and the *Indians* are under no temptation to report a falfehood of this nature) it is a very memorable paffage.[1]

June 15. This day was feen at *Plimouth* the perfect form of an *Indian Bow* appearing in the aire,

On June 12, feven hundred Indians made an affault upon Hadley, but they were driven off with much lofs to them, and very *fmall* to our felves; and at the very time when the Indians were thus diftreffing of Hadley, the Maqua's fell upon their head-quarters, and flaughtered their women and children, and carried away much plunder with them. Thus the conqueft of the Indians went on at fuch a rate, that whereas, June 29, 1675, was the *firft* Faft publickly obferved in this colony, on the occafion of the Indian troubles now, June 29, 1676, was appointed a day of thankfgiving through the colony for the comfortable *fteps* and *hopes* that we faw towards the end of thofe troubles.

[1] Mr. Hubbard mentions the rumor, that the Mohawks had fallen upon Philip, but not with that confidence in its truth expreffed by our Author. There is however nothing improbable in it. None of the early Chroniclers have given fo good an account of the affault on Hadley as he; who probably received his information from the Rev. Mr. Ruffell, minifter of the Town, then in the place.

which the Inhabitants of that place (at least some of them) look upon, as a *Prodigious Apparition*. The like was taken notice of, a little before the Fort Fight in the *Narraganset* Countrey. Who knoweth but that it may be an *Omen* of ruine to the enemy, and that the Lord will break the bow and spear asunder, and make warrs to cease unto the ends of the earth? Nor is this (may I here take occasion a little to *digress*, in order to the inserting of some things, hitherto not so much observed, as it may be they ought to be) for the first *Prodigy* that hath been taken notice of in *New-England*. It is a common observation, verified by the experience of many Ages, that *great and publick Calamityes seldome come upon any place without Prodigious Warnings: to forerun and signify what is to be expected*. I am slow to believe Rumors of this nature, neverthelefs some things I have had certain Information of.[1]

It is certain that before this Warr brake out; viz. on Sept. 10, 1674. In *Hadley*, *Northampton*, and other Towns thereabouts, was heard the report of a great piece of Ordinance, with a shaking of the

---

[1] It is scarcely conceivable in this age, that the world was under such grofs superstition scarcely two hundred years ago. And yet there are absurdities groaned under now, which may be as much a marvel to those who may be in existence two centuries hence, there can scarcely be a doubt. Yet it is too much to expect that the world will ever be all Franklins. There was more superstition in Old than in New England, if possible, during our Author's time; and it would not be a difficult task to refer our readers to works publifhed by learned men, to prove it. See *Notes* onward. Indeed the belief in prodigies seems to have been almost universal, in those days.

earth, and a confiderable Echo, whereas there was no ordinance really difcharged at or near any of thofe Towns at that time. Yea no lefs than feven years before this warr there were plain prodigious *Notices* of it.[1] For

Anno 1667. There were fears on the fpirits of many of the *Englifh*, concerning *Philip* and his *Indians*, and that year, Novemb. 30, about 9, or 10 *ho*. A. M. being a very clear, ftill Sun-fhine morning, there were diverfe Perfons in *Maldon*, who heard in the air on the South-eaft of them, a great Gun go off, and as foon as that was paft, they heard the report of fmall Guns like mufket fhott, difcharging very thick, as if it had been at a general Training; but that which did moft of all amaze them, was the flying of the Bullets which came finging over their heads, and feemed to be very near them, after this they heard drums paffing by them and going Weftward. The fame day, at *Scituate*, (and in other places) in *Plimouth* Colony, they heard as it were the running of troops of horfes.

I would not have mentioned this relation, had I not received it from ferious, faithfull, and Judicious

[1] If one has an inclination to fee how extenfive was the belief in prodigies, apparitions, &c., &c., he may find fatisfaction in the perufal of Holinfhed. At page 1313 he tells us how fhips were feen in the air; at the fame page are the forerunners of earthquakes; what blazing ftars portended may be feen at page 1344: how cannon were heard in the air may be found in Winthrop's *Journal*, II, 307; *England's Warning Pieces* is a remarkable book in the fame line, as is alfo our Author's work entitled *Remarkable Providences*, recently reprinted in England.

hands, even of those who were ear witnesses of these things.

[35] And now that I am upon this *Digression*, let me add, that the monstrous births which have at sundry times hapned, are speaking, solemn providences. Especially that which was at *Woburn*, Febru. 23. 1670. When the wife of *Joseph Wright* was delivered of a Creature, the form whereof was as followeth. "The head, neck and arms in true "Form and shape of a child; but it had no breast "bone nor any back bone; the belly was of an "extraordinary bigness, both the sides and back "being like a belly, the thighs were very small "without any thigh bones; It had no buttocks, "the *Membrum virile* was a meer bone; it had no "passage for nature in any part below; the feet "turned directly outward, the heels turned up, "and like a bone; It being opened, there were "found two great lumps of flesh on the sides of the "seeming belly: the bowels did ly on the upper "part of the breast by the Vitalls.[1] This was testified before the Deputy Gouernour Mr. *Willoughby* [2] on the 2d of March following, by Mrs. *Johnson* Midwife, *Mary Kendal, Ruth Bloghead,*[3] *Lydia Kendall.* Seen also by Capt. *Edward Johnson,* Lient. *John Carter, Henry Brook, James Thomson, Isaac Cole.*

There are judicious persons, who upon the con-

---

[1] If the reader desires anything further upon matters of this sort, and that in the next paragraph, he can refer to Winthrop's *Journal.*

[2] Francis Willoughby, Esq,, of Charlestown.

[3] It appears that *Bloghead* is since *Blodget.*

sideration of some relative circumstances, in that monstrous birth, have concluded that God did thereby bear witness against the *Disorders* of some in that place.¹ As in the dayes of our Fathers, it was apprehended that God did testifie from heaven against the monstrous Familistical Opinions that were then stirring, by that direfull Monster which was brought forth by the wife of *William Dyer*, Octo. 17, 1637, a description whereof may be seen in Mr. *Welds* his History of the Rise and Ruine of Antinomianisme.² p. 43, 44, and in Mr. *Clarks Examples*, vol. 1, p. 249.³

[1] This had reference, as my friend, the Rev. Samuel Sewall of Burlington, informs me, to certain of the inhabitants having joined the Anabaptists, then usually called Antinomians.

[2] Mr. Mather was careless in this reference. We have elsewhere shown that Gov. Winthrop was the principal author of that work. Mr. Thomas Welde, at one time of Roxbury, had something to do in re producing, or republishing the book erroneously ascribed to him. See *Hist. & Ant. of Boston*, chap. xxiv.

[3] From this citation one can have but a faint notion of Clarke's work. Its title runs thus; *A Mirrour or Looking-Glass book for Saints and Sinners, held forth in some Thousands of Examples*, &c., in two volumes in folio. The fourth edition was printed in 1671, and it is to that edition Mr. Mather refers. Clark or Clarke (for his name is printed both ways in his work here used) was a very voluminous writer, "sometime Pastour in Bennet Fink, London," a dissenting minister, son of "Master Hugh Clark," of Burton in Staffordshire, also a dissenter. He died in 1682, aged 83. He was father of the celebrated author of *Annotations on the Bible*, of the same name; a work pronounced by competent judges, "as the best single book upon the Bible in the world." See Granger, *Biog. Hist. England*, v, 73-4. By reference to the *Examples*, as cited in the text, will be found the shocking stories about poor Mrs. Dyer and Mrs. Hutchinson, detailed very nearly as found in Winthrop's *Journal*. In the British State Paper Office I saw an original letter of Winthrop containing a similar relation. It has not been published.

Certainly God would have such providences to be observed and recorded; He doth not send such things for nothing, or that no notice should be taken of them, And therefore was I willing to give a true account thereof, hoping that thereby mistakes and false Reports may he prevented.

To goe on then with our History.

June 16. Our Forces marched towards the Falls, ours on the *East* and *Connecticut* on the *West* side of the river. When they were about three miles out of the Towns a vehement storm of rain, with thunder and lightening overtook them, yet continuing but a while, they passed on, till they came to the *Falls*, but the enemy was then gone. The next day it rained again, and continued a cold *Euroclidon*, or, *North-East* storm all that day and night, so that our Souldiers received much damage in their arms, ammunition and provision, and the next day (being Lords day) returned to the Towns, weary and discouraged, the Lord having seemed to fight against them by the storm mentioned. Thus doth the Lord in Wisdome and Faithfulness mix his [36] Dispensations towards us.[1]

June 19. A party of *Indians* set upon *Swanzy*, and burnt down the remaining houses there, except five houses whereof four were Garisons.[2]

---

[1] This account is amplified a little in Gen. Hoyt's *Antiquarian Researches*, 126-7, but he fixes no date to it. "While our forces lay about Deerfield, some of our soldiers ranging, lighted upon the body of Capt. Turner about Green's River, in passing of which stream he was supposed to have received his mortal wounds." Hubbard, *Narrative*, 90.

[2] Mr. Hubbard says this de-

June 20. *Connecticut* Forces returned home in order to a recruit, intending to meet with ours the next week at *Quabaog*.

June 21. was kept as a day of solemn *Humiliation* in one of the Churches in *Boston*, so was the next day in all the Churches throughout the Colony of *Plimouth*. After which we have not received such sad tidings, as usually such dayes have been attended with, ever since this *Warr* began (as the precedent *History* doth make to appear) but rather such Intelligence from diverse parts of the Countrey as doth administer ground of hope, and of rejoycing, the Lord seeming to return with mercy to his people, and to bring the enemy into greater distresses than formerly.

June 28. About thirty of ours adventured to go up the River towards the Falls at *Deerfield*, to see what *Indians* they could espy thereabouts, but coming they found none. They went to an Island where they found an hundred *Wigwams*, and some *English* plundered Goods, which they took, and burnt the *Wigwams*. Also they marched up to a Fort which the *Indians* had built there, and destroyed it. Digging here and there they found

---

struction was on the 16th of June; and that "*six* houses are yet standing." On the 26th of June he records the murder of "Mr. Hezekiah Willet, in Swanzy, an hopeful young gentleman as any in those parts." He also gives the circumstances of "the horid and barbarous murder." *Narrative*, 92, 132. Mr. Willet was the son of Capt. Thomas Willet, and was 25 years of age. His father was the first English Mayor of New York, and great grand-father of Col. Marinus Willet, distinguished in the war of the Revolution, and also as Mayor of New York. See *N. Eng. Hist. and Gen. Reg.*, II, 376.

several *Indian* Barns, where was an abundance of Fish, which they took and spoiled, as also thirty of their *Canoos*; so that it appears that the Heathen are distressed and scattered, being no more able to continue together in such great Bodyes as formerly.

June 29. Was observed as a day of publick *Thanksgiving* to celebrate the praises of that God, who hath began to answer Prayer. And although there is cause for Humiliation before the Lord, inasmuch as the Sword is still drawn against us, nevertheless we are under deep engagement to make his praise glorious; considering how wonderfully he hath restrained and checked the insolency of the Heathen. That Victory which God gave to our Army, *December* 19, and again *May* 18,[1] is never to be forgotten: also in that divers *Indian Sachims* (especially their great Sachim *Quanonchet*) having fallen before the Lord, and before his Servants. And in that things have been no worse with us, since the year of trouble hath been upon us, that no more *Indians* have been let loose upon us, but many of them have been our friends; that no more *Plantations* have been made *desolate*, which nothing but the restraining gracious providence of God hath prevented, for the Enemy might easily have destroyed ten times as many Towns as they have done, had not he that sets bounds to the raging of the Sea, restrained them; yea, *one whole Colony* hath been in a manner untouched, saving that one small deserted

---

[1] Capt. Turner's surprise of the enemy at the Falls.

plantation therein was burnt by the *Indians*,[1] also sundry Towns [37] that have been fiercely assaulted by the Enemy, having obtained help from God, do continue to this day, as brands plucked out of the fire, and as monuments of the sparing mercy of God, although they have been in the fire they are not consumed. And God hath returned many of our *Captives*, having given them to find compassion before them who led them Captive, and caused the Enemy to entreat them well, in the time of affliction, and in the time of evil, and by strange wayes at last delivered them. He hath also sent in a supply of Corn from beyond Sea,[2] this Spring, and before winter, without which we could not easily

---

[1] The Author has reference to Connecticut Colony, and the town of Simsbury, which was burnt on the 26th of March, 1676. See Phelps's *Hist. Simsbury*, 24. Some interesting additions will be found in Barber's *Historical Collections of Connecticut*.

[2] The Colony of Connecticut contributed nobly to supply the wants of the sufferers by the war in Rhode Island, Plymouth and Massachusetts. A letter was written by order of the Council of that Colony, dated at Hartford, June 24, 1676, respecting the donation from the Colony, directed " to the Worshipful Mr. James Richards, the Rev. Mr. Thacher, Mr. [Increase] Mather [our author], and Mr. Thomas Shepherd," which may be seen in the valuable published Records of Connecticut, II, 457; in which the Council say, they " have appointed the Collectors in the several Churches, to transmitt it to yourselves by the first opportunity, in full confidence of your answeringe the end proposed, in sutable distribution of what is collected in this Colony for our distressed brethren."

It was on occasion of this war that Ireland laid New England under great obligations, by contributions for its sufferers. The Author's elder brother, the Rev. Nathaniel Mather, then minister in Dublin, exerted himself with good success among the benevolent of that country, and the contributions arrived in the Spring of 1677. See an Account of the Irish Charity in the *N. Eng. Hist. and Gen. Reg'r*. II, 245.

have sent out such Armies (however small and not worthy the name of *Armies* in other parts of the World, yet with us they are Armies) as have been pursuing the Enemy. Its wonderful to consider, how that the Lord hath visited his people in giving them Bread, when a Famine was expected. And this Summer, God hath caused the showre to come down in its season, there have been showres of Blessing when some beginnings of a Drought were upon the Land. And sore Diseases hath the Lord rebuked; whereas the *small Pox* and other *Malignant* and *Contagious Distempers* have been amongst us since this *War* began, God hath been entreated to have compassion on us, and to restore health unto his people. Moreover, we are still under the enjoyment of our *Liberties*, both Civil and Spiritual: for such causes as these, the day mentioned was observed (by order of the Council) as a day of publick Thanksgiving throughout this Colony: And behold, when we began to sing and to praise the Lord whose mercy endureth for ever, he hath as it were set Ambushments against the Enemy, and they were smitten, yea they have since that been smiting and betraying one another.

There are two things here observable:

1. Whereas this very day of the Month (*viz. June* 29) was kept as a day of publick *Humiliation* the last year, being the first *Fast* that was observed in this Colony on the account of the present *War*, God hath so ordered, as that the same day of the month was in the year after set apart to magnifie

his Name on account of mercies received, being the firſt publick day of Thankſgiving, which hath been attended throughout this Colony ſince the *War* began.

2. The Lord from Heaven ſmiled upon us at this time: for the day before this *Thanks-giving*, as alſo the day after, he gave us to hear of more of our Captives returned: particularly Mr. *Rowlandſons* Children are now brought in as anſwers of Prayer. It is not a ſmall mercy, that the mother and children (only one childe was killed when the other were taken) ſhould all of them be ſaved alive and carried through the Jaws of ſo many deaths, and at laſt brought home in peace,[1] that ſo they and all that ever ſhall hear of [38] it, might ſee and know, that the Lord Jehovah, is a God that heareth prayer. Alſo the night after this *Thanks-giving*, intelligence came to *Boſton*, that a chief *Narraganſet Sachim*, is now ſuing to the *Engliſh* for peace, and that an *Indian* was come in to the *Engliſh* near *Rehoboth*, who informed that *Philip* was not far off, and that he had but thirty men (beſides Women and Children) with him; and promiſed to conduct the *Engliſh* to the place where *Philip* was lurking, and might probably be taken; Moreover

---

[1] On the 11th of May, two of our captives were returned by ranſom from the Indians, who had been taken at the deſtruction of the town of Lancaſter; the one of them the ſiſter of the wife of Mr. Rowlandſon [Mrs. Drew,] and another woman taken out of the ſame houſe," [Mrs. Joſlin?] *Chronicle*, 121-2. The Author probably refers to theſe captives as well as to thoſe particularly named. See Mrs. Rowlandſon's *Narrative*, 24, 29, Mr. Willard's edition.

the *Indian* affirmed, that thofe *Indians* who are known by the name of *Mauquawogs* (or *Mohawks, i. e.* Man eaters) had lately fallen upon *Philip,* and killed fifty of his men. And if the variance between *Philip* & the *Mauquawogs* came to pafs, as is commonly reported & apprehended, there was a marvellous finger of God in it. For we hear that *Philip* being this winter entertained in the *Mohawks* Country, Made it his defign to breed a quarrel between the *Englifh* and them; to effect which divers of our returned Captives do report that he refolved to kill fome fcattering *Mohawks,* & then to fay that the *Englifh* had done it; but one of thofe whom he thought to have killed, was only wounded, and got away to his Country men giving them to underftand that not the *Englifh* but *Philip* had killed the Men that were Murdered, fo that inftead of bringing the *Mohawks* upon the *Englifh,* he brought them upon himfelf.[1] Thus hath he conceived mifchief and brought forth falfehood, he

---

[1] This affair between Philip and the Mohawks is fomewhat different from that in the *Chronicle,* which is as follows: "King Philip and fome of thefe Northern Indians being wandered up towards Albany, the Mohawks marched out very ftrong, in a warlike pofture upon them; putting them to flight, and purfuing them as far as Hofficke river, which is about two days march from the Eaft fide of Hudfon's river to the N. E., killing divers, and bringing away fome prifoners with great pride and triumph, which ill fuccefs on that fide where they did not expect any enemy, having lately endeavored to make up the ancient animofities, did very much daunt and difcourage the faid Northern Indians." p. 99-100. See other particulars further onward in this work. See alfo a Letter of Sir Edmund Androfs, printed by Mr. Trumbull in *Colonial Records of Ct.,* II, 461. Mrs. Rowlandfon's *Narrative* (Willard's edition) p. 52. Alfo Hubbard's *Narrative,* p. 91.

made a pit and digged it, and is fallen into the ditch which he hath made, his mifchief fhall return upon his own head, and his violent dealing fhall come down upon his own pate. The Heathen are funk down into the pit that they made, in the net which they had hid, is their own foot taken; the Lord is known by the Judgment which he executeth, the wicked is fnared in the work of his own hands. *Higgaion*. Selah.

June 30. This day Souldiers marched out of *Bofton*, towards the place where *Philip* was fuppofed to be. But when they came thither, they found that he was newly gone. We hear that he is returned to *Mount-hope*, and that a confiderable body of *Indians* are gathered to that place, where the *War* began, and where (it may be) way muft be

Reader after this day of thankfgiving I fhall have little to report unto thee but what is caufe of thankfulnefs! The Maquas now fall upon *Philip*, and kill him fifty men at a time; upon as odd an occafion too as has been ordinarily heard of. He, as it is affirmed, being entertained among the Maquas the laft winter, ufed many means to feduce 'em, and perfwade 'em unto a war againft the Englifh; and one of thofe means it feems was this: *He* killed fome fcattering Maqua's in the woods, and then told the reft that the Englifh did it; but one of them whom he thought killed, was only wounded, who getting home unto his countrymen, gave 'em to underftand who was the true murderer! And fo the Maqua's, whom he would have brought upon the Englifh, he only brought upon himfelf: *Nec enim lex juftior ulla!*

made towards an end of these troubles. Yet who knoweth how cruelly a *dying Beast* may bite before his expiration? Also *Plimouth* Companies being abroad under the conduct of Major *Bradford*, the Lord went forth with them, this day causing the enemy to fall before them. They were in danger of being cut off by a party of *Indians* who lay in Ambush for that end, but some of the *Cape-Indians*, who have been faithful to the English, discovered the *Stratagems* of the Adversary, whereby their intended mischief was happily prevented.¹ Divers of them were killed and taken, without the loss of so much as one of ours. And whereas, three Messengers from *Squaw-Sachem* of [39] *Sakonet*, were gone to the *Governour* of *Plimouth*, offering to submit themselves, and engaging Fidelity to the *English* for the future, if they might but have a promise of life, and liberty, before the Messengers returned from their treaty, that *Squaw-Sachem*¹ with about

---

¹ The daring and skilfully managed expeditions of Capt. Church, during the month of June (1676), seem not to have been known to the Author; or if known, were not deemed worthy of record. Perhaps the Captain was too much of a Rhode Islander to be favorably considered. For it must be borne in mind that long after this period, there were prominent men in Massachusetts, averring that no good could come from Rhode Island.

In this connection Church's graphic but homely narrative of his operations should be read; commencing on page 20, original edition. Mr. Hubbard, in his *Narrative*, p. 104, *et alibi*, has endeavored to do justice to Capt. Church, and has succeeded very well, considering the disadvantages he labored under for obtaining information.

² This was Awashonks, and the treaty spoken of had been arranged by Capt. Church. See Church, *History*, p. 25-6. Awashonks had been forced into the war, and was glad of the first opportunity to get out of it; and so were the best of her men, the Sogkonates.

ninety persons, hearing that *Plimouth* Forces were approaching to them, came and tendred themselves to Major *Bradford*, wholly submitting to mercy, so that this day were killed, taken, and brought in no less then *an hundred and ten Indians*. And the providence of God herein is the more observable, in that the very day before this, the Lords People in *Plimouth* did unanimously consent to renew their Covenant with God, and one another, and a day of Humiliation was appointed for that end, that so a work so sacred and awful might be attended with the more solemnity; also in the week before these signal smiles from Heaven upon that Colony, most of the Churches there, had *renewed their Covenant*, viz. on the day of *Humiliation* which was last attended throughout that Jurisdiction. God then saith unto us, that if we will indeed hearken unto his voice, the haters of the Lord shall soon submit themselves.

Philip now returns to Mount-Hope, and finds it *Mount Misery, Mount Confusion!* A prince in Germany long since hearing that a neighbor prince intended war upon him, immediately set himself upon the reforming of the people under his government; but his adversary within a while after enquired what preparation his neighbor was making to oppose him? And being informed that his chief *preparation* was *reformation*, he replied, *Nay then, let the Devil fight him for all me; if he be at that, he'll be too hard for me to meddle with him.* The churches of New England, now more than ever, began to be at that; and now see the effects of it.

The churches in Plymouth colony agreed upon a

July 8. Whereas the Council at *Boston* had lately emitted a Declaration, signifying that such *Indians* as did within fourteen dayes come in to the *English*, might hope for mercy, divers of them did this day return from among the *Nipmucks*. Amongst others, *James* an *Indian*, who could not only reade, and write, but had learned the Art of Printing, notwithstanding his Apostasie, did venture himself upon the mercy and truth of the *English* Declaration which he had seen and read, promising for the future to venture his life against the common Enemy.¹ He and the other now come in affirm day solemnly to renew their COVENANT with God, and one another; on the very next day, *Major Bradford*, with his Plymouth forces, was not only by a strange providence delivered from the stratagems of the ambushing adversary, but also took and slew many of them, without the loss of one Englishman: And the *Squaw-Sachem* of [53½] Saconet, with ninety of her subjects, hearing of his approach, submitted themselves to his mercy. *Major Bradford* was the *Oedipus* by whom that *Sphinx* was conquered.

1 This Indian was usually known as *James-the-printer*. His Indian name was *Wowaus*. He learned the business of a printer, and was for a considerable period established in Boston, in the exercise of his calling, and was for a time a partner with Bartholomew Green. A fac-simile of his sign manual may be seen in the *History and Antiquities of Boston*, p. 422, and some particulars respecting his history. Concerning those who came in with *Printer*, the Council ordered Maj. Gookin "to take care for the security of the Squaes and papooses, lately come in with James Printer and Nehemiah, and to improve the said James and Nehemiah to prove their fidelity by bringing some of the enemies heads." *MS. Archives.*

It is believed, that but for this Indian, Eliot would not have been able to produce the Indian Bible.

that very many of the *Indians* are dead fince this *War* began: and that more have dyed by the hand of God, in refpect of Difeafes, Fluxes, and Feavers, which have been amongft them, then have been killed with the Sword.

July 2. This day *Connecticut* Forces being in the *Narraganfet* Country met with a party of *Indians*, purfued them into a Swamp, killed and took *an hundred and fourfcore* of them (amongft whom was the old *Squaw-Sachem* of *Narraganfet*) without the lofs of one *Englifh-man*. Only an *Indian* or two that fought for the *Englifh*, was killed in this engagement. The *Englifh* would gladly have gone further, and have joyned with *Bofton* and *Plimouth* Companies to purfue *Philip* at *Mount-hope*, but the *Connecticut Indians* would by no means be perfwaded thereunto, until fuch time as they had returned home with the booty they had taken. And as they were on their march homeward, they took and flaughtered *threefcore* more *Indians*.[1] In the

---

In writing to the Hon. Robert Boyle, Mr. Eliot faid, "we have but one man, viz. the Indian Printer, that is able to compofe the fheets, and correct the prefs with underftanding." See *Book of the Indians*, 115.

[1] To have a juft idea of the expeditions of the Connecticut forces, the valuable *Records of Connecticut* as edited by Mr. Trumbull muft be confulted; efpecially the fpirited letter of Major John Tallcott, in that work, vol. II, p. 459. The movements of that officer feem to have been conducted with great celerity; by that means the enemy were furprifed, and fell an eafy prey into his hands. On July 1ft, at a place called Nipfachooke, he feized four Indians; on the 2d, "being the Sabbath, in yᵉ morning about fun an hour high," he difcovered the enemy, "who prefently infwamped themfelves in a great fpruce fwamp." This he was able to furround (which he called dreffing it) "and within 3 hours flew and tooke 171," of whom 45 being women and children, "yᵉ Indians faved

mean while the other Colonyes are fending out Souldiers towards *Mount-Hope*, where *Philip* with a multitude of *Indians* lately flocked thither is reported to be: defigning fpeedily to fall upon the neighboring towns.

[40] *July* 6. Five or fix *Indian Sachems* did make peace with the *Englifh* in the Eaftern parts of this Colony.[1] They have brought in with them

On July 2, [1676] our brethren of Connecticut, in the Narraganfet country, took and killed an hundred and four fcore of the Indians, without lofing a man of their own; and in their march home they deftroyed three fcore more. Quickly after this, two hundred Indians in Plymouth colony were compelled by the neceffities upon them to furrender themfelves; and upon advice from *them* of another party abroad, eight Englifhmen, accompanied with fourteen of *them*, feized upon twenty more, without any hurt unto themfelves.

alive and the others flayne." Among the killed were 34 men. They [Tallcott and his Indian allies] took 15 arms; "among which flaughter, that ould piece of venum, Sunck Squaw Magnus was flaine, and our old friend Watawaikefon, Peffecus his agent, who had in his pocket Capt. Allyn's Ticket for his free paffage up to his head quarters. On July 3d, we turned down to Providence, dreft Providence Neck, and Warwick Neck the fame day, took and flew 67, of which 18 were men, and took 11 armes; and of this number is 27 captiues, and the whole number taken and flayne in thefe two engagements is 238." Maj. Tallcott mentions the following officers in his command: Mr. Fitch [Chaplain], Capt. Denifon, Capt. Newbury, Capt. Standley, Capt. Mansfeild, Capt. Selleck, and Mr. Bulkly [Chaplain]. Dr. Ufher Parfons informs us, that *Nippfatchuck* (the fame doubtlefs mentioned by Tallcott, is a hill, two miles N. E. of Greenville, in Smithfield, R. I., now probably Wolf's Hill. *Indian Names*, p. 19. In the Council's letter to Sir E. Andros, 8th July, 1676, it is called *Nipfachoog*. *Colonial Recs. Ct.*, II, 461. For fome account of the old Queen Magnus, fee *Book of the Indians*, 248.

[1] The "peace" referred to was fettled by a Treaty which is printed

three hundred men befides women and Children. One of the *Sachims* did earneftly defire, that the *Englifh* would promife that no more *liquors* fhould be fold or given to the *Indians*, that fo they might not be in a Capacity of making themfelves drunk, having found by wofull experience, that that hath been a ruining evill to many of them. This week alfo about *two hundred Indians* more came & fubmitted themfelves to mercy, in *Plimouth Colony*, being partly neceffitated thereunto by the diftreffes which God in his holy providence hath brought them into, and partly encouraged by a promife from the Government there, that all fuch *Indians*, as would come in, and lay down their armes fhould have life and liberty granted to them, excepting only fuch as had been active in any of the murthers which have been committed. When thefe *Indians* were in the hands of the *Englifh*, a certain *Squaw* amongft them, perceiving that it would be pleafing to the *Englifh*, if the murderers were difcovered, fhe prefently told of one who had a bloudy hand in the murthers which were done in Mr. *Clarks* houfe *March* the twelfth, the *Indian* immediately confeffed the Fact, only faid that there was another who had as great an hand therein as he, which other *Indian* being examined, confeffed the thing alfo, and he revealed a third *Indian* Murderer, who upon Examination owned the thing, whereupon they were all three forthwith executed, thus did

from the original in the *Appendix* to the *Book of the Indians*, p. 699. Maj. Richard Waldron and Wananlanfet were the chief figners to it.

God bring upon them the innocent blood which they had fhed. Alfo the *Indians* who had furrendered themfeves, informed that a bloody *Indian* called *Tuckpoo*[1] (who the laft fummer murdered a Man of *Bofton* at *Namafket*) with about *twenty Indians* more, was at a place within 16 miles of *Plimouth,* and manifefted willingnefs to go and fetch him in, whereupon eight *Englifh* with fourteen *Indians,* marched out in the night, and feized upon them all, none of ours receiving any hurt at this time. Juftice was fpeedily executed upon the *Indian,* who had been a Murderer; the other having their lives granted them.

July 7. A fmall party of our *Indians* having fome *Englifh* with them, took and killed feven of the Enemy in the Woods beyond *Dedham,* whereof one was a petty *Sachem.*[2] The two *Indians* which were then taken Prifoners, fay that many of their men who were fent to *Albany* for a fupply of Powder, were fet upon in the way by the *Mohawks* and killed. It is certain, that about this time, fome of thofe *Indians* who are in *Hoftility* againft the *Englifh* (amongft whom the *Sachim* of *Springfield Indians,* was one) came to *Albany* to buy Powder, and that they might effect their defigne, they lyed and faid, that now they had made peace with the *Englifh,* and defired Powder only to go an hunting in the Woods; we hear that the other *Indians* [41]

---

[1] It will have been feen by an original paper in the Appendix, that *Tuckpoo* was already difpofed of.

[2] Mr. Hubbard fays he was a "Narraganfet Sachim." *Narrative,* 98.

were very defirous to have flain them, but the Governour of *New-York*[1] fecured them, and gave notice to the Council at *Hartford:* fince that we have Intelligence that many of our enemies, yea and fuch as have been notorious Murderers, are fled for refuge to thofe about *Albany.*

July 11. A Party of *Indians* (tis conjectured that there were about two hundred of them) affaulted *Taunton.* And in probability, that Town had at this time been brought under the fame defolation other places have experienced, had not the Lord in his gracious providence fo ordered, that a Captive *Negro,*[2] the week before efcaped from *Philip* and informed of his purpofe fpeedily to deftroy *Taunton,* whereupon Souldiers were forthwith fent thither, fo that the enemy was in a little time repulfed, and fled, after they had fired two Houfes: but not one *Englifh* Life was loft in this Ingagement. What lofs the enemy fuftained is as yet unknown to us. There was a fpecial providence in that *Negroes* efcape, for

---

[1] At this time Sir Edmund Andros was Governor of New York; having been placed there in 1674, by the Duke of York. See Note p. 168, *ante.*

[2] He was, according to Baylies, of the "houfehold of Mr. Willett" of Swanfey. *Memoir of Plymouth,* III, 140. Mr. Hubbard is more particular. About thirty Indians, on the 26th of June, ambufhed the houfe of Mr. Hezekiah Willett, and after killing Mr. Willett, as before noted, took this Negro captive. He was doubtlefs a flave to Capt. Thomas Willett. See Hubbard, *Narrative,* 92, or 88, old Bofton edition. The reader might expect with confidence to find in Mr. Baylies' work, a more particular account of the attack on Taunton, his place of refidence, but he will look only to be difappointed. He fays the Indian who fhot Mr. Willett was named *Croffman.* As he was killed by three fhots at the fame time, it is no doubt true, as Mr. Hubbard ftates, that he was killed by "three of the enemy firing on him at once."

he having lived many years near the *Indians*, understood their Language, and having heard them tell one another what their designs were, he acquainted the *English* therewith, and how *Philip* had ordered his men to lie in *Ambuscadoes* in such and such places, to cut off the *English*, who by means of this intelligence escaped that danger which otherwise had attended them.

About this time we hear that there are three hundred *Mohaugs*, who have armed themselves, as being desirous to be revenged upon those *Indians* who have done so much harm to *New-England* (if they receive no discouragement as to their designed Expedition) And that they purpose to *color* their heads and make them *yellow*, that so they may not upon their approach to any of our Plantations, be mistaken for other *Indians*.

There is another thing which though it doe not concern the Warr, yet hapning this week, it may not be amiss here to take notice of it. At *Saco-*

In the woods near Dedham there was more execution done upon them; and a Negro that had been taken captive by them, informed us, that near two hundred of them had formed a design of an attacque upon Taunton, which information proved the preservation of the town: For auxilliaries being seasonably sent thither, the enemy met with a vigorous repulse, without the loss of one Englishman in the engagement. The Massachuset forces returned unto Boston, July 22, having taken and killed one hundred and fifty Indians, with the loss of but *one* Englishman.

neſſet[1] in *Plymouth* Colony, a female Child was born with two heads, perfectly distinct each from other, so that it had four eyes, and four ears, and two mouths and tongues, &c.

July 22. Some of our Companies returned from *Mount-hope* to *Boſton*, And albeit they have not attained that which was the main end proposed in their going forth, *sc.* the Apprehension of *Philip*, nevertheless God was in a gracious measure present with them: for they killed and took about an hundred and fifty *Indians* in this expedition, with the loss of but one *Engliſh-man*. One night they lodged very near unto *Philip*, but he kept himself private and still in a *Swamp*, ours not imagining that he had been so near, as afterwards (by *Indian* Captives) they perceived he was:[2] after this an *Indian* that was taken prisoner engaged that if they would spare his life, he [42] would forthwith bring Philip all the country over, having tired themselves with many long and tedious marches through the desert woods: before they returned home, some of them were sent toward Mount-hope, yet was their labor well improved, and followed with good success at last: for in ranging those woods in Plimouth Colony, they killed and took, by the help of Capt. Moſley's company, and Capt. Brattle's troop joyning with Major Bradford's company of Plimouth Colony, an hundred and fifty Indians, with the loss of never an Engliſhman." *Narrative*, 99.

---

[1] Wood's Hole, in Falmouth, a small distance to the eastward of Sogkonate Point.

[2] There is an implied censure in Church's account of the proceeding of the "army" at this time. "This with some other good opportunities of doing spoil upon the enemy, being unhappily missed." *Hiſt. King Philip's War*, 28. Under this same date, July 22, Mr. Hubbard gives an additional view of operations. "The companies sent from Concord, May 30, up towards Hadly, having spent much time and pains in pursuit of

them to *Philip*, but our Souldiers were not able to go the nearest way towards him, yet in about two hours space, they came whither the *Indian* conducted them, and found that a great many *Indians* were newly fled, having for haste left their *Kettles* boyling over their fires, and their Belts and Baskets of *Wampampeag*, yea and their dead unburied. At that time did the *English* take and kill about seventy persons: since an *Indian* that came into *Rhode-Island*, informeth, that *Philip* is gone to a Swamp near *Dartmouth*: and that when our Forces were pursuing of him, he with a few hid himself in *Squanakunk*[1] Swamp, till our Souldiers were past, and then with one *Indian* in a *Canoo* crost the river to *Pocasset*. It seems the body of the *Indians* belonging to him, went over on two Rafts, in which passage they lost several Guns, and wet much of their Ammunition. The reason who *Philip fled* to this place, was because if he went *Northward*, the *Mohawks* would be upon him, if *Southward* he was in danger of the *Monhegins*, and he durst not hide himself any longer about *Metapoiset*, because the Woods thereabouts were filled with Souldiers. This

---

[1] A swamp famous throughout the part of the country where it is situated; being in the southeasterly part of Rehoboth. In it is the famous *Annawon's Rock;* and here was the last retreat of Old Captain Annawon, from whom it received its name. Here the old Chief was surprised by Church, August 28th, 1676. The Rock is about 8 miles from Taunton Green, and nearly in a right line between Taunton and Providence. The Swamp contains about 3000 acres. See my Edition Church's *Hist*, 136-7. In 1826 I visited Annawon's Rock and made a sketch of it, from which an engraving was made for the second edition of that work. Its name probably signified, the *Swamp of night*, or *Night-Swamp*. A strikingly appropriate name.

week alſo, Captain *Church* of *Plimouth*, with a ſmall party conſiſting of about eighteen *Engliſh*, and two and twenty *Indians*, had four ſeveral engagements with the Enemy, and killed and took Captive ſeventy nine *Indians* without the loſs of ſo much as one of ours; it having been his manner, when he taketh any *Indians* by a promiſe of favour to them, in caſe they acquit themſelves well, to ſet them an hunting after more of theſe Wolves, whereby the worſt of them, ſometimes do ſingular good ſervice in finding out the reſt of their bloody fellows.[1] In one of theſe ſkirmiſhes, *Tiaſhq Philips* chief Captain ran away leaving his Gun behind him, and his *Squaw*, who was taken.[2] They came within two miles of the place where *Philip* hideth himſelf, and diſcerned at a diſtance about fifty *Indians* with Guns, thought to be *Philips* Hunters for Proviſion, and were deſirous to have engaged with them, but being loaden with Captives and Plunder they could not then attend it. Alſo a *Sachim* of *Pocaſſet* hath ſubmitted himſelf with fourty *Indians* more, to the Governour of *Plymouth*.[3] So that there is of late

[1] From the time Capt. Church returned to Plymouth from Rhode Iſland, in the early part of June, to the cloſe of the War, any other account of his almoſt unexampled operations againſt, and in the midſt of the enemy, than his own truthful Narrative, it would be uſeleſs to attempt. His original work, publiſhed in 1716, in a thin quarto, is never now for ſale, owing to its exceſſive rarity; but later, and tolerably correct copies are eaſily obtained.

[2] The ſurpriſe and capture of 'Tiaſhq's family is related by Church in his *Hiſtory*, p. 36. The Chief's name in that work is *Tyaſks*. The place where theſe priſoners were taken was probably in ſome part of what is ſince Rocheſter.

[3] The Records of Plymouth do not indicate the name of this Pocaſſet Chief with certainty; but we infer it to be Succanowaſſuck. On the 28th of June the Governor of

such a strange *turn of providence* (especially in *Plimouth* Colony, since the Churches in that Colony (being thereunto provoked by the godly advice and Recommendation of the civil Authority in that Jurisdiction) did solemnly *renew their Covenant with God and one another*, as the like hath rarely been heard of in any age. Whereas formerly almost every week did conclude with sad tydings, now the Lord sends us good news weekly. Without doubt, there are in the World who have been praying for us, and God hath heard them. If our poor prayers may be a means to obtain mercy for them also, who have prayed for us, how shall we re[43]joyce, when we meet together before Jesus Christ at the last great day?

But the principal actions whereof Plymouth was now the stage, must be done by the hand of that worthy man, *Capt. Church*, whose very *name*, now, might suggest unto the miserable salvage, *what*, they must be undone by fighting against; and whose *lot* it was to be employ'd by the providence of Heaven at the time and place of the catastrophe, now waiting for a generation ripe for desolation.

This gentleman made havock among the salvages, like another Scanderberg; he went out with a small party of about eighteen English, and twenty two friend Indians, and in one week he had four several engagements with the enemy, wherein he took and slew seventy nine of them, without losing one of his own;

Plymouth was informed by other Indians that he was at Seconet, and that "he was the first man that stirred up the Indians to join with Philip to fight against the English." See *Plym. Col. Records*, v, 202.

July 25. Thirty and six *English-men* who went out of *Medfield* and *Dedham*, having nine of the *Praying Indians* with them, purſued and overtook a party of the Enemy, killed and took alive fifty of them, without the loſs of any of ours. The nine *Indians* ſtored themſelves with plunder when this exploit was done: For beſides Kettles, there was about half a Buſhhel of *Wampampeag*, which the Enemy loſt, and twelve pound of Powder, which the Captives ſay they had received from *Albany*, but two dayes before. At this time another of the *Narraganſet Sachims* was killed, whoſe name was *Pomham*, and his Son was taken alive, and brought Priſoner to *Boſton*.[1] This *Pomham* after he was wounded ſo as that he could not ſtand upon his legs, and was thought to have been dead, made a ſhift (as the Souldiers were purſuing others) to

and by a particular *policy* he ſtill made his captives to find out their fellows for him, and *ſet a thief to catch a thief*, which facilitated his enterpriſes wonderfully. Nevertheleſs this hindered not others from doing their part in exterminating the rabid animals, which by a moſt unaccountable *Syderation* from Heaven, had now neither ſtrength or ſenſe left 'em to do anything for their own defence.

[1] The fate of this ſon of Pumham will be read with horror. Hubbard has preſerved it. "Among the reſt of the captives at that time, was one of the ſaid Pumham's ſons, a very likely youth, and one whoſe countenance would have beſpoke favor for him, had he not belonged to ſo bloody and barbarous an Indian as his father was." *Narrative*, 100. In another account of this expedition, it is ſaid, "there was about twenty pounds of Indian money found in the baſkets of the captured Indians, which was given to our friends the Indians." *Chronicle*, 137.

crawl a little out of the way, but was found again, and when an *Englifh-man* drew near to him, though he could not ftand, he did (like a dying Beaft) in rage and revenge, get hold on that Souldiers head, and had like to have killed him, had not another come in to his help, and refcued him out of the inraged dying hands of that bloody *Barbarian*, who had been a great promoter of the *Narraganfet War*.

July 27. One of the *Nipmuck Sachims* (called Sagamore *John*) came to *Bofton*, and fubmitted himfelf to the mercy of the *Englifh*, bringing in about *an hundred and fourfcore Indians* with him. And that fo he might ingratiate himfelf with the *Englifh*, he apprehended *Matoonas* and his Son, and brought them with him to *Bofton*, which *Matoonas* was the beginnner of the *War* in this Colony of *Maffachufets*, for it was he that committed the murders which were done at *Mendam*, *July* 14, 1675. Being thus taken and examined before the Council, he had little to plead for himfelf, and therefore was condemned to immediate death. Sagamore *John* was defirous that he and his men

On July 25, thirty fix Englifhmen from Dedham, and Medfield, with ninety Chriftian Indians, purfued, overtook, and captivated fifty of the enemy, without lofing a man; and among thefe was *Pomham*, a great Sachim of the Narraganfets, who, after he was wounded fo that he could not ftand, but was left a confiderable while for dead; yet when an Englifhman came near him, the *dying beaft*, with a *Belluine Rage*, got fuch hold on his head, that he had killed him if there had not come in help to refcue him.

might be the Executioners; wherefore *Matoonas* was carried out into the Common at *Boston*, and there being tied to a Tree, the *Sachim* who had now submitted himself, with several of his men, shot him to death.¹ Thus did the Lord (a year after) retaliate upon him the innocent blood which he had shed, as he had done so God hath requited him: And inasmuch as *Matoonas* who began the War and Mischiefs which have followed thereon, in this Colony of *Massachusets* is taken, and Justice glorified upon him, it seems to be a good *Omen*, that ere long *Philip* who began the *War* in the other Colony, shall likewise be delivered up unto Justice. In due time his foot shall slide, and the things which shall come upon him seem to make haste.

[44] *July* 31. A small party of Souldiers, whose hearts God had touched, marched out of *Bridgewater*, in order to pursuing the Enemy. And (about

On July 27, *Sagamore John* submitted himself to the English mercy, with an hundred and fourscore Nipmuk Indians; and [54] that he might ingratiate himself with the English, he brought in *Matoonas* with his son, who had begun the war in the Massachuset colony, a little above a year ago; whereupon we ordered this very sagamore to shoot him to death.

¹ "When he was brought before the Council, and asked what he had to say for himself, confessed that he had rightly deserved death, and could expect no other; adding withal, that if he had followed their counsel he had not come to this: for he had often seemed to favor the Praying Indians, and the Christian religion, but like Simon Magus, by his after practice, discovered quickly, that he had no part nor portion in that matter." Hubbard, *Narrative*, 101.

3 h. p. m.) not far from *Tetignot River*, they unexpectedly to themselves, and undiscerned by the Enemy, came upon a company of *Indians*, amongst whom *Philip* was, though his being there was not known to our men, until the engagement was over. They shot down ten *Indians*, they were well armed, and at first snapped their Guns at the *English*, but not one of them took fire, wherefore, the terrour of God fell upon the *Indians*, that fifteen of them threw down their Guns, and submitted themselves to the *English*, the rest fled; *Philip* himself escaped very narrowly with his life. He threw away his stock of Powder into the Bushes, that he might hasten his escape, albeit some of his men the next day found it again. Our Souldiers took above twenty pound of Bullets, and Lead, and seven Guns, five of which were loaden and primed: yea they took the chief of *Philips Treasure*, not being able to carry away all their plunder that day, for they found much English goods which *Philip* had stolen. *Philip* made his escape with three men, one of which was killed. And although he himself got clear, yet his Uncle whose name was *Uncompoen*, [1] being one of his chief Councellors was slain, and

---

[1] Capt. Church calls him *Akkompoin*, and relates that Philip, finding the east side of Tehticut river "too hot for him, designed to return to the other side; and coming to the river with his company, felled a great tree across it to pass over on; and just as Philip's old uncle, Akkompoin, and some other of his Chiefs were passing over the tree, some brisk Bridgewater lads had ambushed them, fired upon them, and killed the old man, and several others." *Entertaining Hist.*, 38. He is the same called in another place *Woonkaponehunt*.

*Philip*s own sister was taken Prisoner;[1] not so much as one *English man* received any hurt at this time. Thus did God own *Bridgewater*, after the People therein had subscribed with their hands, and solemnly renewed their holy Covenant with God and one another, that they would reform those evils which were amongst them, and endeavour for the future to walk more according to the will of God in Jesus Christ.

August 1. Capt. *Church* with thirty *English-men*, and twenty *Indians*, following *Philip* and those with him, by their track, took twenty and three *Indians*. The next morning they came upon *Philip*s head quarters, killed and took about an hundred and thirty *Indians*, with the loss of but one *English-man*. In probability many of the English-Souldiers had

On July 31, an handful of soldiers issuing out of Bridgewater, unexpectedly stumbled upon a company of the enemy, who being well armed, snapped their guns at the English; but, which was a marvellous accident, not one of them took fire; whereat a *pannick terror* fell upon them, so that we took fifteen, we slew ten, the rest fled, of whom *Philip* himself was one, who left the chief of his treasure behind him. Not one of the English was hurt at this time. This was the success of a people that had just before solemnly renewed the consent of their souls to the *covenant of grace*, and applied it unto the holy purposes of reformation among them.

[1] Our Author is, I believe, the only writer who mentions the capture of Philip's sister. There can, nevertheless, be no doubt of the fact, though Judge Davis thinks it strange that he alone should record it. It is not stranger than that the names of many others are not mentioned.

been cut off at this time, but that an *Indian* called *Matthias*, who fought for the *English*, when they were come very near the Enemy, called to them in their own language, with much vehemency, telling them they were all dead men if they did but fire a Gun, which did so amuse and amaze the *Indians* that they lost a great advantage against the *English*. *Philip* hardly escaped with his life this day also.[1] He fled and left his *Peag* behind him, also his *Squaw and his Son were taken Captives*, and are now Prisoners in *Plimouth*.[2] Thus hath God brought that grand Enemy into great

---

[1] Church's account of all transactions wherein he was concerned, should be read. Church with his company lodged in Bridgewater the night following the skirmish in which Akkompoin was killed. Early the next morning he started in pursuit of Philip with his force augmented "by many of Bridgwater; and by their piloting soon came to the top of the great tree which the enemy had fallen across the river. The Captain spied an Indian sitting on the stump of it on the other side, and clapped his gun up, and had doubtless dispatched him, but one of his own Indians called hastily to him, not to fire, for he believed it was one of their own men. Upon which the Indian upon the stump, looked about, and Capt. Church's Indian seeing his face, perceived his mistake, for he knew him to be Philip, clapped up his gun and fired; but it was too late; for Philip immediately threw himself off the stump, leaped down a bank and made his escape." *Entertaining Hist.*, 38.

[2] The important capture of Philip's wife and son Church thus relates: "As soon as possible he got over the river and scattered in quest of Philip and his company; but the enemy scattered and fled every way; yet he picked up a considerable many of their women and children, among which were Philip's wife, and son of about nine years old." *Ibid.* This son of Philip caused much debate among the English rulers. Some were for putting him to death, some for selling him into slavery, while others doubted what they could lawfully do. Thus the matter rested several months. At length, in the following March he was sold into slavery, but to what place or country is not mentioned. See Davis's Morton's *Memorial*, 453-5.

misery before he quite destroy him. It must needs be bitter as death to him, to loose his Wife and only Son (for the *Indians* are marvellous fond and affectionate towards their [45] Children) besides other Relations, and almost all his Subjects and Country too.

August 3. This day the Lord smiled upon this Land with signal favour, in another respect which concerns not the present War. For whereas in the month of *July*, there had been a sore Drought, which did greatly threaten the Indian Harvest, God opened the bottles of Heaven and caused it to rain all this night, and the day after, so as that the Indian corn is recovered to admiration; the English Harvest being already gathered in, and more plentiful then in some former years, insomuch that this which was expected to be a year of Famine, is turned to be a year of plenty as to provision.

Whilst I am writing this, good information is brought to me, that in some parts of *Connecticut* Colony, the Drought was sorer then in this Colony, inasmuch as the Trees began to languish, and the *Indians* to despair of an harvest, wherefore *Unkas*

On August 1, *Capt Church* again, with about thirty English and twenty friend Indians, took twenty three of the enemy; and the next morning he came upon *Philip's* head quarters, where they took and slew about an hundred and thirty of the enemy, with the loss of but *one* of their own: *Philip* himself now also hardly escaping, but leaving his *peag*, and *wife* and *son* behind him, which was no small torment unto him.

(for although he be a friend to the *English*, yet he and all his men continue *Pagans* ſtill) ſet his *Powaws* on work to ſee if they could by powawing (*i.e.* conjuring) procure rain, but all in vain; He therefore ſent Weſtward to a noted *Powaw*, to try his ſkill, but neither could that Wizzard by all his hideous and diabolical howlings, obtain Showers. Whereupon he (*i. e. Uncas*) applyed himſelf to Mr. *Fitch* (the faithfull and able Teacher of the Church in *Norwich*) deſiring that he would pray to God for rain. Mr. *Fitch* replyed to him, that if he ſhould do ſo, and God ſhould hear him, as long as their *Powaws* were at work, they would aſcribe the rain to them, and think that the Devill whome the *Indians* worſhip, and not God had ſent that rain, and therefore he would not ſet himſelf to pray for it, until they had done with their vanities and witcheries. *Uncas* and his Son *Oweneco* declared that they had left off *Powawing*, deſpairing to obtain what they deſired. Mr. *Fitch* therefore called his Church together, and they ſet themſelves by Faſting and Prayer, to aſk of the Lord Rain in the time of the latter Rain, and behold! that very night, and the next day, He that ſaith to the ſmall rain, and to the great rain of his Strength, be thou upon the earth, gave moſt plentifull ſhowers, inaſmuch as the Heathen were affected therewith, acknowledging that God whom we ſerve is a great God, and there is none like unto him.[1]

[1] Mr. Hubbard has a letter from the Rev. Mr. Fitch concerning this great drouth, printed in his *Narrative*, 113-15. The Rev. gentleman

August 6. An *Indian* that deserted his Fellows, informed the inhabitants of *Taunton* that a party of *Indians* who might be easily surprised, were not very far off, and promised to conduct any that had a mind to apprehend those *Indians* in the right way towards them, whereupon about twenty Souldiers marched out of *Taunton*, and they took all those *Indians*, being in number thirty and six, only the *Squaw-Sachem of Pocasset*, who was next [46] unto *Philip* in respect to the mischief that hath been done, and the blood that hath been shed in this Warr, escaped alone; but not long after some of *Taunton* finding an *Indian Squaw* in *Metapoiset* newly dead, cut off her head, and it hapned to be *Weetamoo*, i. e. *Squaw-Sachem* her *head*. When it was set upon a pole in *Taunton*, the *Indians* who were prisoners there knew it presently, and made a most horrid and diabolical Lamentation, crying out that it was their Queens head. Now here it is to be observed, that God himself by his own hand brought this enemy to destruction. For in that place, where the last year, she furnished *Philip*

(Mr. Fitch) got out of his dilemma about as well as did another minister, who was settled on the condition that he would cause it to rain when rain was wanted. A drouth at length came. Some of his parishoners called upon him to pray for rain, as it was much needed; but rain did not come. Some began to grow dissatisfied; several called upon him together prepared to charge him with breach of contract. After hearing them patiently, he said they must all be of one mind in desiring rain, otherwise praying would be of no use; besides he knew there were some who were not ready for it. The Parson was not further troubled. It would probably have been quite difficult for Uncas to satisfy the good Minister of Norwich that the Indians had ceased powwowing, had not rain followed his prayers.

with Canooes for his men, she her self could not meet with a Canoo, but venturing over the River upon a Raft, that brake under her, so that she was drowned, just before the *English* found her.¹ Surely *Philips* turn will be next.

August 10. Whereas *Potock* a chief Counsellor to the old Squaw-Sachem of *Narraganset*, was by some of Road-Island brought into *Boston*, and found

On August 6, an Indian deserter informing the inhabitants of Taunton where they might surprise more of the enemy, twenty men of *ours* immediately brought in thirty six of *them*. The *Squaw-Sachem* of *Pocasset* flying from this *broil upon the coast*, now in that very place, where she had furnished *Philip* with canoos for his men a year ago, she herself could not find a canoo, but venturing over the river upon a raft, which broke under her, she was drowned: and some of the English not knowing who she was when they found her, stuck her head upon a pole in Taunton, which when the Indians that knew her, saw, they fell into such hideous and howling lamentations as can scarce be imitated.

¹ The fate of Weetamoo has been celebrated by the poets. See *Yamoyden*, Cant. 5. She had been the wife of Alexander, Philip's elder brother. After his death she was the wife of Petananuet until the war with Philip began. She was well enough inclined towards the English, and John Easton has told us by what mischance she was lost to their interest. Having been hurried off with the followers of Philip, she became the wife of the famous Narraganset chief Quinnapin. This chief was at the sacking of Lancaster, and Mrs. Rowlandson became his prisoner. She gives some account of him in her *Narrative*, and also of Weetamoo, whom she called "a severe and proud dame, bestowing every day in dressing herself near as much time as any of the gentry of the land." For what has been found of her and her husband see the *Book of the Indians*, p. 240-241. See her *Narrative*, p. 73-75.

guilty of promoting the War againſt the *Engliſh*, he was this day ſhot to death in the Common at *Boſton*. As he was going to his execution, ſome told him that now he muſt dy, he had as good ſpeak the truth, and ſay how many *Indians* were killed at the Fort-Fight laſt winter. He replyed, that the *Engliſh* did that day kill above ſeven hundred fighting men, and that three hundred who were wounded, dyed quickly after, and that as to old men, women and Children, they had loſt no body could tell how many; and that there were above three thouſand *Indians* in the Fort, when our Forces aſſaulted them, and made that notable ſlaughter amongſt them.[1]

Auguſt 12. This is the memorable day wherein *Philip*, the perfidious and bloudy Author of the War and wofull miſeryes that have thence enſued, was taken and ſlain. And God brought it to paſs, chiefly by *Indians* themſelves. For one of *Philips*

But now, reader, prepare to make a juſt reflection upon that ancient and famous paſſage of ſacred ſcripture, *Wo to thee that ſpoileſt and thou waſt not ſpoiled, and dealeſt treacherouſly, and they dealt not treacherouſly with thee; when thou ſhalt ceaſe to ſpoil, thou ſhalt be ſpoiled, and when thou ſhalt make an end to deal treacherouſly, they ſhall deal treacherouſly with thee!*[2]

[1] Concerning the dreaded chief Potock, ſome additional information will be found, gleaned from MSS. of a late cotemporary with him, in the *Book of the Indians*. Mr. Hubbard is not ſo circumſtantial as Mather.

[2] A moſt extraordinary paſſage to be cited in this connexion. No one can deny but that it ſpeaks as much for the virtues of the Indians as it does for their enemies. *Audi alteram partem.*

men (being difgufted at him, for killing an *Indian* who had propounded an expedient for peace with the *Englifh*) ran away from him, and coming to Road Ifland, informed that *Philip* was now returned again to *Mount-Hope*, and undertook to bring them to the Swamp where he hid himfelf. Divine Providence fo difpofed, as that Capt. *Church* of *Plymouth* was then in Road-Ifland, in order to recruiting his Souldiers, who had been wearied with a tedious march that week. But immediately upon this Intelligence, he fet forth again, with a fmall company of *Englifh* and *Indians*. It feemeth that night *Philip* (like the man, in the Hoft of *Midian*) dreamed that he was fallen into the hands of the *Englifh*, and juft as he was faying to thofe that were with him, that they muft fly for their lives that day, left the *Indian* that was gone from him fhould difcover where he was. Our Souldiers came upon him and furrounded the *Swamp* (where he with [47] feven of his men abfconded) Thereupon he betook himfelf to flight; but as he was coming out of the Swamp, an *Englifh-man* and an *Indian* endeavoured to fire at him, the *Englifh-man* miffed of his aime, but the *Indian* fhot him through the heart, fo as that he fell down dead. The *Indian* who thus killed *Philip*, did formerly belong to Squaw-Sachim of *Pocaffet*, being known by the name of *Alderman*. In the beginning of the war, he came to the Governour of *Plymouth*, manifefting his defire to be at peace with the *Englifh*, and immediately withdrew to an Ifland not having engaged againft the

Englifh nor for them, before this time. Thus when *Philip* had made an end to deal treacheroufly, his own Subjects dealt treacheroufly with him. This Wo was brought upon him that fpoyled when he was not fpoyled. And in that very place where he firft contrived and began his mifchief, was he taken and deftroyed, and there was he (like as Agag was hewed in pieces before the Lord) cut into four quarters, and is now hanged up as a monument of revenging Juftice, his head being cut off and carried away to *Plymouth*, his Hands were brought to *Bofton*. *So let all thine Enemies perifh, O Lord!* When *Philip* was thus flain, five of his men were killed with him, one of which was his chief Captains fon, being (as the *Indians* teftifie) that very *Indian* who fhot the firft gun at the *Englifh*, when the War began. So that we may hope that the War in thofe parts will dye with *Philip*.[1]

One thing which emboldened *King Philip* in all his outrages, was an affurance which his magicians, confulting their oracles gave him, that *no Englifhman fhould ever kill him;* and indeed if any Englifhman might have had the honour of killing him, he muft have had a good meafure of grace to have repreffed the *vanity of mind* whereunto he would have had fome temptations, but this will not extend the life of that *bloody* and *crafty* wretch *above half his days!* A man belonging to *Philip* himfelf, being difgufted at him for killing an Indian

---

[1] Although Hubbard and Mather are quite circumftantial in their accounts of the fall and death of Philip, every one muft recur to the *Narrative* of Church, who was not only the leader of the party which furprifed him, but an eye witnefs of all he defcribes.

A little before this, the Authority in that Colony had appointed the seventeenth of this instant to be observed as a day of *publick Thanksgiving* throughout that Jurisdiction, on the account of wonderful success against the Enemy, which the Lord hath blessed them with, *ever since they renewed their Covenant* with him; and that so they might have

who had propounded an expedient of peace with the English, ran away from him to Rhode Island, where *Capt. Church* was then recruiting his weary forces; and upon the intelligence hereof, *Capt. Church*, with a few hands of both English and Indians, immediately set forth upon a *new expedition*.

That very night *Philip* (like the man in the army of Midian) had been dreaming that he was fallen into the hands of the English; and now just as he was telling his dream, with advice unto his friends to fly for their lives, lest the knave who had newly gone from them, should shew the English how to come at them, *Capt. Church* with his company fell upon them; Philip attempted a flight out of the swamp, at which instant both an Englishman and an Indian endeavoring to fire at him, the Englishman's piece would not go off, but the Indian presently shot him through his venomous and murderous heart; and in that very place where he first contrived and commenced his mischief, this *Agag* was now cut into quarters, which were then hanged up, while his head was carried in triumph to Plymouth, where it arrived on the very day that the church there was keeping a solemn *thanksgiving* to God. God sent 'em in the head of a *leviathan* for a *thanksgiving feast*.

ἔτως ἀπόλοιτο, ὅτις τοιαῦτά γε ῥέζοι.
Sic pereat quisquis cœptatit talia posthac.

hearts raifed and enlarged in afcribing praifes to God, he delivered *Philip* into their hands a few dayes before their intended Thankfgiving. Thus did God break the head of that Leviathan, and gave it to be meat to the people inhabiting the wildernefs, and brought it to the Town of *Plimouth* the very day of their folemn Feftival: yet this alfo is to be added and confidered, that the Lord (fo great is the divine faithfulnefs) to prevent us from being lifted up with our fucceffes, that we might not become fecure, fo ordered as that not an *Englifh-man* but an *Indian* (though under *Churches* influence) muft have the honour of killing *Philip*.

It was not long before this hand which now writes, upon a certain occafion took off the jaw from the expofed fkull of that Blafphemous Leviathan; and the renowned *Samuel Lee* hath fince been a paftor to an Englifh congregation, founding and fhowing the praifes of Heaven, upon that very fpot of ground where *Philip* and his Indians were lately worfhiping of the Devil.

At the time when *King Philip*, the beginner of the war, was thus come to the conclufion of his life, feveral of his men accompanied him into the other world; and among the reft, that very Indian who fired the *firft gun* at the Englifh in this horrible war. But our *Lebbæus, Capt. Church*, irrefiftably ftill purfued his victories at fuch a rate, that in a few weeks there were, by his means, at leaft feven hundred of the enemy fubjugated; and fome of his atchievements were truly fo magnanimous and extraordinary, that my reader will fufpect me to be tranfcribing the filly old romances, where the knights do conquer fo many giants, if I fhould proceed unto the particular commemoration of

And the day before this, was attended with a doleful Tragedy in the Eastern parts of this Country, viz. at *Falmouth* in *Casco-bay*, where some of those treacherous and bloody *Indians* who had lately submitted themselves, and promised Fidelity to

them. Albeit I must also say, there were many other commanders, whom if we should measure by *conduct* rather than by success, the fame of Capt. Church ought by no means to bring an eclipse upon *theirs;* and though it be an envious phrase at sea, that the vessel which by any advantage outsails another, does wrong her; I pray let not that phrase get ashore, to make it interpreted as a wrong to any other valiant and prudent commander, that any *one* has had *particular* successes attending of him.

In our wars there were captains engaged, upon whose graves there may be engraved the character given by *Sir Samuel Morland* of *Capt. Jahir*, who lost his life in the wars of the poor Waldenses. *They were persons worthy to be renowned unto all posterity for their zeal for* [55] *the service of God, and the preservation of his poor afflicted church, persons whom all the terrors of death could never affright; bold as lions in their enterprises, but meek as lambs in the midst of all their victories.*[1] *Always lifting up their hands towards heaven from whence deliverance came; and reciting sweet passages of scripture, wherein they were versed unto admiration, to the great encouragement of all their followers.*

---

[1] This reminds us of one who, while he was speaking to another with words of kindness, concealed the dagger with which he had just murdered his kindred and nearest friends. Alas what depravity it required to quote such a passage! How many of the poor Indians had just been killed barely to rid the country of them, to say nothing of those sold into slavery! Such is the blindness of man to his prejudices.

the *English*, killed and took Captive above thirty Souls.[1] The chief Author of this mifchief, was an *Indian* called *Simon*, who was once in the hands of the *English*, and then [48] known to have been active in former Murders, having bragged and boafted of the mifchief and murders done by him: we may fear, that God, who fo awfully threatened *Ahab*, when he had let go out of his hand a Blafphemous, Murderous Heathen, whom the Lord had devoted to deftruction, was not well pleafed with the *English* for [in-?] concluding this, and other bloody Murderers, in the late Eaftern peace. What the iffue of this new flame thus breaking forth, fhall be, or how

---

[1] The war in the eaftern parts is fingularly flighted by our author. The fufferings in that quarter, were, if poffible, more fevere among its fcattered inhabitants than in Maffachufetts. Mr. Hubbard has given an elegant narrative of it, and with furprifing particularity, confidering the time at which he wrote. But a vaft amount of facts have fince been brought to light, and perhaps a ftill larger amount yet lie flumbering in old court papers, letters, &c. Few at this day have any idea of the number of families broken up, and of people driven off and killed in thofe parts during Philip's war. Probably near twenty families were fettled about Mufcongus, Damarifcotta, Sheepfcut and Pemaquid ; all of whom were obliged to fly for their lives. Some of their names were as follows: *John Brown, John Pearce, Richard Pierce, Thomas Elbridge, Richard Fulford, William Brifcoe, James Stilfon, Walter Phillips, Alexander Gould, John Taylor, Robt. Scott, Thomas Gents, Silvanus Davis, Mark Parfons, Thomas Meffer, James Smith, Edward Euin, John Curtis, Abraham Shurte, —— Phipps, Henry Jocelyn*, &c., &c. A letter of Thaddeus Clarke, dated Cafco Bay, Auguft 16th, 1676, and printed in the *Book of the Indians*, p. 700, will reprefent the condition of the Englifh in that region at that time.

Some of the above perfons may not have been heads of families, but moft of them we know were. *Abraham Shurte* may have been dead, as he was, if living in 1676, 93 years of age, though Mr. Williamfon fays he was very active at this time in his endeavors to conciliate the Indians, that he died in 1690, and that in 1686 he was town clerk of Pemaquid. This may have been a fon of the firft Abraham Shurte.

far it shall proceed, is with him whose wisdome is infinite; and who doeth all things well:[1] inasmuch as it is too evident that a *French* Coal hath kindled this unhappy fire (blood and fire being the Elements which they delight to swim in) it is not like to be extinguished in one day. But we must leave it to God and time, fully to discover what hath been, and what shall be.

While those parts of New England, which had the glory of Evangelical churches in them, for a *defence* to be *created* upon, were thus tempestuated by a terrible war; there were other parts lying in the north-east of New England of a less evangelical temper, which felt a furious *euroclydon* also beating upon them. The designs of *lumber* and *fishing*, but especially of the *beaver trade* with the Indians, which last was very scandalously managed, had produced many fine settlements in the Province of Main, and the County of Cornwall,[2] and the brave regions lying beyond Piscataqua; but a great part of the English there grew too like the Indians, among whom they lived in their unchristian way of living; and instead of erecting churches among themselves, they neither christianized the pagans, nor by avoiding of the vices which they rather taught the pagans, did they take a due course to preserve themselves from losing of christianity in paganism.

Within twenty days after that *Philip* had began the war at Mount Hope, in the year 1675, the Indians, two hundred and fifty miles distant from him to the northward, began the same game upon the remotest of

[1] The remainder of this paragraph is omitted in the London edition.

[2] The Duke of York's patent was so denominated. It extended from the Sagadahock to Novascotia, and Pemaquid was the seat of government.

Thus have we a brief, plain, and true Story of the *War* with the *Indians* in *New-England*, how it began, and how it hath made its progress, and what present hopes there are of a comfortable closure and conclusion of this trouble, which hath been continued for a whole year and more. Designing only a *Breviary of the History of this war*, I have not enlarged upon the circumstances of things, but shall leave that to others who have advantages and leasure to go on with such an undertaking.

Magna dabit, qui magna potest, mihi parva potenti,
Parvaque poscenti, parva dedisse sat est.

these plantations. Misunderstandings happened between the English and the Indians upon very odd occasions; and many rude, wild, ungovernable English did, unto the extream dissatisfaction of the wiser sort, rashly add unto the occasions which the Indians also took to grow ungovernable. Their little swaggering at one another, advanced into scuffling, and scuffling into fighting; so that at length there was open war between them; and there were many little encounters in the first three or four months, wherein the English lost fifty, and the Indians about ninety of their people; but at last it came to very cruel depredations.

I am not willing to tire my reader with another long walk into the woods after these ravening salvages, or to enumerate the many successive destructions with which the Indians at length broke up all the English settlements to the northward of Wells; and if I should particularly relate how barbarously they murdered my dear friend, that exemplary good man, *Capt. Thomas Lake*, with many more at Arowsick island in Kennebeck river, on August 14, 1676, I should but unto my

There is one thing admirable to confider; I mean the providence of God in keeping one of thefe three *United Colonies,* in a manner untouched all

felf, *Infandum renovare dolorem.* Inafmuch as I am writing a Church Hiftory, I may be excufed, though I do not concern my felf any farther with provinces, where they made it fo little of their own concern to gather any churches; it fhall fuffice for me to write thus much; that one of the firft notable outrages done by the Indians was at the houfe of one *Wakely* of Cafco, whom with his wife, and fon, and daughter-in-law (with child) and a couple of grand-children, whom they barbaroufly butchered, and carried away three children into captivity. Now this honeft old man was one who would often fay with tears, *that he believed God was difpleafed at him, inafmuch as albeit he came into New England for the fake of the gofpel, yet he had left another place in the country, where he had enjoyed the gofpel in the communion of a gathered church, and now had lived many years in a plantation where there was no church at all, nor the ordinances and inftitutions of the Lord Jefus Chrift.*

The Maffachufet colony fent our forces under the command of *Capt. Hawthorn,* and *Capt. Syll,* and others, for the fubduing of thofe Indians, and the fuccefs of attempts againft them was very various. But the ftunningeft wound of all given to them, was, when by a contrivance of the Englifh, near four hundred of them were, on Sept. 6, 1676, furprifed at the houfe of *Maj.* Waldern in Quechecho; whereof one half which were found acceffories to the late rebellion were fold for flaves; the reft were difmiffed unto their own places; and at laft, when both fides were weary, about the latter end of the year, a fort of peace was clapp'd up for the whole;. fo *the land had reft from war.*

this while: For *Connecticut Colony* hath not been assaulted by this Enemy, only a few houses in one deserted Plantation were burnt; and it is possible that one *Indian* alone might do that.[1] Whether God intends another tryal for them, or for what reason he hath hitherto spared them, no one may as yet determine. Christ said unto *Peter, What I do thou knowest not now, but thou shalt know hereafter:* even so, although we do not at present fully perceive the meaning of this providence, yet hereafter it will be manifest. And albeit the same sins and provocations have been found with them that are to be charged upon others; nevertheless, it must needs be acknowledged (for why should not that which is praise-worthy in Brethren be owned, that so God may have the glory of his grace towards and in his Servants?) they have in the management of this affair, acquitted themselves like men, and like Christians. It was prudently done of them, not to make the *Indians* who lived amongst them their Enemies, and the Lord hath made to be as a Wall to them, and also made use of them to do great service against the common Enemies of the *English*. The Churches there have also given proof of their charity and Christianity, by a liberal Contribution towards [49] the necessity of the Saints impoverished by this *War* in the other two Colonies, having collected and transported above a thousand Bushels of

---

[1] The Author was not well informed as to what Connecticut had suffered, as will appear by an examination of its *Colonial Records*, published in 1850-1859. See a curious paper relative to this matter in vol. II, of that work, p. 471-2.

Corn, for the relief and comfort of those that have lost all through the Calamity of War; God will remember and reward that pleasant fruit. Nor have some of the Churches in this Colony (especially in *Boston*, which the Grace of Christ hath alwayes made exemplary in works of that nature) been unwilling to consider their poor Brethren according to their Ability.

To *Conclude* this *History*, it is evident by the things which have been expressed, that our deliverance is not as yet perfected; for the *Nipmuck Indians* are not yet wholly subdued: Moreover, it will be a difficult thing, either to subdue, or to come at the *River Indians*, who have many of them withdrawn themselves and are gone far westward, and whilst they and others that have been in hostility against us, remain unconquered, we cannot enjoy such perfect peace as in the years which are past. And there seems to be a dark Cloud rising from the East, in respect of *Indians* in those parts, yea a Cloud which streameth forth blood. But that which is the saddest thought of all, is, that of late some unhappy scandals have been, which are enough to stop the current of mercy, which hath been flowing in upon us, and to provoke the Lord to let loose more Enemies upon us, so as that the second error shall be worse then the first. Only God doth deliver for his own Names sake: the Lord will not forsake his people for his great Names sake; because it hath pleased the Lord to make us his people. And we have reason to conclude that *Salvation is begun,* and in a gracious meafure carried on towards us. For fince laft *March* there are two or 3000 *Indians* who have been either killed, or taken, or fubmitted themfelves to the *Englifh*. And thofe *Indians* which have been taken Captive & others alfo, inform that the *Narraganfets* are in a manner ruined, there being (as they fay) not above an hundred men left of them, who the laft year were the greateft body of *Indians* in *New-England,* and the moft formidable Enemy which hath appeared againft us. But God hath confumed them by the Sword, and by Famine and by Sicknefs, it being no unufual thing for thofe that traverfe the woods to find dead *Indians* up and down, whom either Famine, or ficknefs, hath caufed to dy, and there hath been none to bury them. And *Philip* who was the *Sheba,* that began and headed the Rebellion, his head is thrown over the wall, therefore have we good reafon to hope that this *Day of Trouble,* is near to an end, if our fins doe not undoe all that hath been wrought for us. And indeed there is one fad confideration which may caufe humble tremblings to think of it, namely, in that the *Reformation* which God expects from us is not fo [50] hearty and fo perfect as it ought to be, Divines obferve, that whereas upon *Samuels Exhortation,* the people did make but imperfect work of it, as to the *Reformation* of provoking evils, therefore God did only begin their deliverance by *Samuel,* but left fcattered *Philiftines* unfubdued, who afterwards made head and proved a fore fcourge to the Children of Irael, untill *Davids* time, in whose Reign there was a full Reformation, and then did the Lord give unto his people full deliverance. Neverthelefs a sad *Cataftrophe* will attend those that shall magnifie themselves against the people, of the Lord of Hosts. It hath been observed by many, that never any (whether *Indians* or others) did set themselves to do hurt to *New-England,* but they have come to lamentable ends at last. *New-England* hath been a burthensome stone, all that have burthened themselves with it, have been cut in pieces. The experience of the present day, doth greatly confirm that observation, and give us ground to hope, that as for remaining enemies, they shall fare as others that have gone before them, have done. Yet this further must needs be acknowledged, that as to *Victoryes* obtained, we have no cause to glory in any thing that we have done, but rather to be ashamed and confounded for our own wayes. The Lord hath thus far been our Saviour for his Names sake, that it might not be profaned among the Heathen whither he hath brought us. And God hath let us see that he could easily have destroyed us, by such a contemptible enemy as the Indians have been in our eyes, yea, he hath convinced us that we our selves could not subdue them. They have advantages that we have not, knowing where to find us, but we know not where to find them, who neverthelefs are always at home, and have in a manner nothing but their lives and souls (which they think not of) to loose, every Swamp is a Castle to them, and they can live comfortably on that which would ſtarve *Engliſh-men*. So that *we have no cauſe to glory*, for it is God which hath thus ſaved us, and not we our ſelves. If we conſider the time when the enemy hath fallen, we muſt needs own that the Lord hath done it For we expected (and could in reaſon expect no other) that when the Summer was come on, and the buſhes and leaves of trees come forth, the enemy would do ten times more miſchief than in the winter feaſon; whereas ſince that, the Lord hath appeared againſt them, that they have done but little hurt comparatively. Had there not been, Θεφ 'από μχχανῆς a divine hand beyond all expectation manifeſted, we had been in a ſtate moſt miſerable this day. Alſo if we keep in mind the means and way whereby our deliverance hath thus been accompliſhed, we muſt needs own the Lord in all. For it hath not been brought to paſs by our numbers, or ſkill, or valour, *we have not got the Land in poſſeſſion by our own Sword, neither did [51] our own arm ſave us*. But God hath waſted the Heathen, by ſending the deſtroying Angell amongſt them, ſince this War began; and (which ſhould alwayes be an humbling conſideration unto us) much hath been done towards the ſubduing of the enemy, by the *Indians* who have fought for us, ſometimes more than by the *Engliſh*. And no doubt but that a great reaſon why many of them have, of late been deſirous to ſubmit themſelves to the *Engliſh*, hath been becauſe they were afraid of the *Mohawgs* who have a long time been a Terror to the other *Indians*. I have received it from one who was returned out of Captivity this Summer, that the *Indians* where he was, would not suffer any fires to be made in the night, for fear left the *Mohawgs* should thereby discern where they were, and cut them off.

Now, as the Lord, who doth redeem Israel out of all his troubles, hath graciously and gloriously begun our Salvation, so let him perfect it, in such a way, as that no honour at all may come unto us, but that great glory may be to his own blessed Name for ever. Let him bring health and cure unto this *Jerusalem*, and reveal the abundance of peace and truth: And it shall be unto him a Name of joy, a praise and an honour before all the Nations of the earth, which shall hear all the good that he will doe unto us, and they shall fear and tremble for all the goodness, and for all the prosperity that he will procure. If wee hearken to his voice in these his solemn Dispensations, it surely shall be so. *Not unto us O Lord; not unto us, but unto thy Name give Glory for thy mercy and for thy Truths sake.* Amen!

It is observable that several of those nations which refused the gospel, quickly afterwards were so *Devil driven* as to begin an unjust and bloody war upon the English, which issued in their speedy and utter extirpation from the face of Gods earth. It was particularly remarked in *Philip* the ringleader of the most calamitous war that ever they made upon us; our *Eliot* made a tender of the everlafting Salvation to that king; but the monfter entertained it with contempt and anger, and after the Indian mode of joining figns with words, he took a button upon the coat of the reverend man, adding, *That he cared for his gofpel juft as much as he cared for that button.* The world has heard what a terrible ruine foon came upon that monarch, and upon all his people.

POSTSCRIPT.

SINCE I wrote the preceding Narrative, I hear that there are who make a scruple of using the word *Army*, when applied to such inconsiderable *Forces*, as those which have been raised and sent forth by us, in the late War. I pretend not to any skill or accuracy of speaking as to modern platforms of *Military Discipline*; but sure I am that of old a few *Cohorts* being under the command of a chief Captain, though in all there were not above four or five hundred souldiers, this was called ςεγ]ευμα an *Army*, Acts, 23. 27. Yea those three hundred Souldiers who were under *Gideon* as their *General*, are styled an *Army*, Judg. 8. 6. The Hebrew word there used cometh from צבא which signifies *turmatim congregare ad militandum*, when Troopes are assembled together, this did the Hebrews call an *Host* or an *Army*. There are small *Armies* as well as great ones, 2 Cron. 24. 24. חיל which is the word used in that place signifies, *Forces:* that Term have I commonly chosen, though the other being of the most frequent use, and aptly enough expressing what is meant by it, I have not wholly declined it. For amongst us

——— *Sic volet usus*
Quem penes Arbitrium est et jus et Norma loquendi.

And Reason saith, that those *Forces* may pass for *Armies* in one part of the world, that will not do so in another. But my design in this *Postscript* is not to Criticize or Apologize about the use of a Term. There is another matter of greater importance, &c. *That which doth concern the Grounds of this Warr, and the justness of it on our part:* concerning which I shall here adde a few words. It is known to every one, that the *Warr* began not amongst us in *Matachusets* Colony; nor do the *Indians* (so far as I am informed) pretend that we have done them wrong. And therefore the cause on our part is most clear, and unquestionable: For if we should have suffered our Confederates, and those that were ready to be slain, to be drawn to death, & not have endeavoured to deliver them, when they sent unto us for that end, the Lord would have been displeased; nor should we have acted like the Children of Abraham, Gen. 14. 14. Yea, all the world would justly have condemned us. And as for our Brethren in that Colony, where these tumults first hapned, [2] it is evident that the *Indians* did most unrighteously begin a Quarrel, and take up the Sword against them.

'Tis true the European campaigns for the numbers of men appearing in them, compared with the little numbers that appear in these American actions, may tempt the reader to make a very diminutive business of our whole *Indian war;* but we who felt ourselves assaulted by unknown numbers of *devils in flesh* on every side of us, and knew that our minute numbers employ'd

Postscript.

I said at the beginning, I would not inlarge upon that Argument, which concerns the *Grounds of the Warr*, neither will I, becaufe that would make the *Hiftory* too voluminous, contrary to my defign. Neverthelefs, inafmuch as fome are diffatisfied thereabouts, fo as to receive impreffions and prejudices in their minds, concerning our Brethren in *Plymouth* Colony (as it is natural for men in trouble to lay blame upon every body but themfelves) fuppofing that they have without juft caufe engaged themfelves and all thefe united Colonies in an unhappy *War*. Yea and that the *Indians* were provoked to do what they did, whenas (whatever may be faid of fome private perfons, of whofe injurious dealings no complaint was made and proved) it feems very manifeft to impartial Judges, that the *Government* in that Colony is *innocent* as to any *wrongs* that have been *done* to the Heathen, by thofe *where the Warr began*. And therefore for their vindication, and for the fatisfaction of thofe amongft our felves, (or elfe where) who are cordially defirous to

in the fervice againft them, were proportionably more to *us* than mighty legions are to nations that have exifted as many *centuries* as our colonies have *years* in the world, can fcarce forbear taking the colours in the fixth book of Milton to defcribe our ftory: And fpeaking of our Indians in as high terms as *Virgil* of his *pifmires: It nigrum campis Agmen!* At leaft we think our ftory as confiderable as that filly bufinefs of the invading and conquering of Florida by the Spaniards under *Fernando de Soto;* and yet that ftory the world has thought worthy to be read in divers languages.

have things cleared, respecting *the Grounds of the Warr*, I shall here subjoyn a Letter, which I received from *Generall Winslow* (whose integrity, and peculiar capacity, (as being *Governour* of *Plymouth* Colony) to give information in this affair is well known) together with a *Narrative of the beginning of these Troubles* as it was presented to the *Commissioners* of the *united Colonyes*, in September last, for the satisfaction of confederate Brethren.

 Reverend Sir,

THE many Testimonyes you have given, not
' only of your good respects to my unworthy
' self personally, but also to this whole Colony,
' manifested in your endeavours to vindicate us
' from undeserved aspersions, that some ignorant or
' worse then uncharitable persons would lay upon
' us, respecting the Grounds of these troubles, calls
' for a greater Retribution then a bare acknowledg-
' ment. But Sir, my present design is only to give
' you further trouble, by enabling you to say some-
' thing more particularly on our behalfe; to that
' end I have sent you the enclosed Paper which is
' an exact *Narrative*[1] given in by Mr. *Hinkly* and
' my self to the first Sessions of the *Commissioners* of
' the *Confederate Colonyes,* September last; from
' which the Commissioners and the *Councill* of your
' Colony, and afterwards your *General Court,* took

---

[1] That Narrative follows this letter of Gov. Winslow. It is no doubt as faithful a record as the writers could obtain; yet all such records are imperfect, and in this case the Plymouth people had little means of getting information on the other side of the country then.

'full satisfaction, as you see by their subsequent acts
'and actions. Yet much more we can truly say in
'our Vindication, (viz) that we have endeavoured
'to carry it justly and faithfully towards them at
'all times, and friendly beyond their deserts. I
'think I can clearly say, that before these present
'troubles broke out, *the English did not possess* [3] *one*
'*foot of Land in this Colony, but what was fairly*
'*obtained by honest purchase of the Indian Proprietors:*
'Nay, because some of our people are of a cove-
'tous disposition, and the *Indians* are in their Streits
'easily prevailed with to part with their Lands, we
'first *made a Law that none should purchase or re-*
'*ceive of gift of any Land of the Indians, without the*
'*knowledge and allowance of our Court*, and penalty
'of a fine, five pound per Acre, for all that should
'be so bought or obtained. And lest yet they
'should be streightned, we ordered that *Mount-*
'*Hope, Pocasset* & several other Necks of the best
'Land in the Colony, (because most suitable and
'convenient for them) should never be bought out
'of their hands, or else they would have sold them
'long since. And our neighbours at *Rehoboth* and
'*Swanzy*, although they bought their Lands fairly
'of this *Philip*, and his Father and Brother, yet
'because of their vicinity, that they might not tres-
'pass upon the *Indians*, did at their own cost set
'up a very substantial fence quite across that great
'Neck between the *English* and the *Indians*, and
'*payed due damage if at any time any unruly horse*
'*or other beasts broke in and trespassed.* And for

'diverse years last past (that all occasion of offence in that respect might be prevented) the *English* agreed with *Philip* and his, for a certain Sum yearly to maintain the said Fence, and secure themselves. And *if at any time they have brought complaints before us, they have had justice impartial and speedily, so that our own people* have frequently complained, that *we erred on the other hand in shewing them overmuch favour.* Much more I might mention, but I would not burden your patience; yet we must own that God is just and hath punished us far less than our iniquityes have deserved; yea just in using as a Rod, whose enlightning and Conversion we have not endeavoured as we might & should have done, but on the contrary have taught them new sins that they knew not. The Lord *Humble* us and *Reform* us, that he may also save and deliver us, as in his own time I trust he will. Sir, I have nothing of Intelligence worthy your knowledge. The Colds are very general amongst us and some very afflictive. The Lord rebuke the mortal Distemper that prevailes so much in your Town, and sanctifie all his Visitations to us.

'Thus craving the benefit of your Prayers, in this day of Gods Visitation, I rest
   Your obliged friend to serve you,

Jos. Winslow.

Marshfield May 1.
 1 6 7 6.

Postscript.

A brief Narrative of the beginning and progress of the present Troubles between us and the *Indians*, taking rise in the Colony of *New-Plimouth June* 1675. Given by the Commissioners of that Colony, for the satisfaction of their Confederate Brethren, and others.

NOT to look back further then the Troubles that
'were between the Colony of *New-Plimouth*,
'and *Philip*, Sachem of *Mount-Hope*, in the Year
'1671. It may be remembered, that the settle-
'ment and issue of that controversie was obtained
'and made (principally) by the mediation and in-
'terposed advice, and counsel of the other two
'confederate Colonies, who upon a careful enquiry
'and search into the grounds of that trouble, found
'that the said *Sachems* Pretences of wrongs and
'injuries from that Colony were groundless and
'false, and that he (although first in Arms) was the
'peccant offending party, and that *Plimouth* had
'just cause to take up Arms against him: and it
'was then agreed that he should pay that Colony
'a certain summe of Mony, in part of their Damage
'and Charge by him occasioned, and he then not
'only renewed his ancient Covenant of Friendship
'with them, but made himself and his People ab-
'solute Subjects to our Soveraign Lord King *Charles*
'the II. and to that his Colony of *New-Plimouth*,
'since which time, we know not that the *English*
'of that or any other of the Colonies have been
'injurious to him or his, that might justly provoke

'them to take up Arms against us: But sometime
'last winter, the Governour of *Plimouth* was in-
'formed by *Sausaman* a faithful *Indian*, that the
'said *Philip* was undoubtedly endeavouring to raise
'new troubles, and to engage all the Sachems round
'about in War against us. Some of the *English*
'also that lived near the said Sachem, communi-
'cated their fears and jealousies concurrent with
'what the *Indian* had informed: About a week
'after *John Sausaman* had given his Informa-
'tion, he was barbarously Murdered by some *In-
'dians*, for his faithfulness (as we have cause to
'believe) to the Interest of God, and of the *English*.
'Sometime after *Sausamans* death, *Philip* having
'heard that the Governour of *Plimouth* had re-
'ceived some information against him, and pur-
'posed to send to him to appear at the next Court,
'that they might enquire into those Reports, came
'down of his own accord to *Plimouth*, a little be-
'fore the Court, in the beginning of *March* last,
'at which time the Councill of that Colony, upon
'a large debate with him, had great reason to be-
'lieve that the information against him might be
'in substance true: But not having proof thereof,
'and hoping that very discovery of it so far would
'cause him to desist, they dismist him friendly,
'giving him only to understand, that if they heard
'further concerning that matter, they might see
'reason to demand his Arms to be delivered up for
'their security, [5] (which was according to former
'agreement between him and them) and he en-

' gaged on their demand they should be surrendred
' to them or their order. At that Court we had
' many *Indians* in Examination concerning the
' Murder of *John Sausaman,* but had not then tes-
' timony in the case, but not long after an *Indian*
' appearing to testifie, we apprehended three by him
' charged to be the Murderers, and secured them,
' to a tryal at our next Court holden in *June,*
' at which time, and a little before the Court,
' *Philip* began to keep his men in Arms about him.
' and to gather Strangers to him, and to march
' about in Arms towards the upper end of the Neck
' in which he lived, and near to the English houses,
' who began thereby to be something disquieted,
' but took as yet no further notice, but only to set a
' Military Watch in the next Towns of *Swanzy* and
' *Rehoboth.* Some hints we had that *Indians* were
' in *Arms,* whilst our Court was sitting, but we
' hoped it might arise from a guilty fear in *Philip,*
' that we would send for him, and bring him to
' tryal with the other Murderers, and that if he saw
' the Court broke up, and he not sent for, the cloud
' might blow over. And indeed our Innocence
' made us very secure, and confident it would not
' have broke into a *War.* But no sooner was our
' Court dissolved, but we had intelligence from
' Lieut. *John Brown* of *Swanzy* that *Philip* and his
' men continued constantly in *Arms,* many strange
' *Indians* from several places flocked in to him, that
' they sent away their Wives to *Narraganset,* and
' were giving our people frequent Alarums by

'Drums and Guns in the night, and had guarded
'the paſſages towards *Plimouth*, and that their
'young *Indians* were earneſt for a War. On the
'ſeventh of *June*, Mr. *Benjamin Church* being on
'Rhode-Iſland, *Weetamoe* (the *Squaw-Sachim* of
'*Pocaſſet*) and ſome of her chief men told him
'that *Philip* intended a War ſpeedily with the *Eng-
'liſh*; ſome of them ſaying, that they would help
'him, and that he had already given them leave to
'kill *Engliſh-mens* Cattle, and rob their Houſes.
'About the 14 and 15*th* of *June*, Mr. *James Brown*
'went twice to *Philip* to perſwade him to be quiet,
'but at both times found his Men in Arms, and
'*Philip* very high and not perſwadable to peace.
'On the 14*th* of *June*, our Council writ an ami-
'cable, friendly Letter to him, ſhewing our diſlike
'of his practiſes, and adviſing him to diſmiſs his
'ſtrange *Indians*, and command his own men to
'fall quietly to their buſineſs, that our people might
'alſo be quiet, and not to ſuffer himſelf to be abuſed
'by reports concerning us, who intended no hurt
'towards him; but Mr. *Brown* could not obtain
'any Anſwer from him. On the 17*th* of *June*,
'Mr. *Pain* of *Rehoboth*, and ſeveral *Engliſh* going
'unarmed to *Mount-hope* to ſeek their Horſes, at
'*Philips* requeſt; the *Indians* came and preſented
'their Guns at them, and carried it very inſolently,
'though no way provoked by them. On the 18, or
'19*th* of *June*, [6] *Job Winſlow's*[1] Houſe was broke

[1] He was ſon of Kenelm Winſlow. His reſidence was in nephew of the firſt Gov. Edward what was afterwards Freetown.

'open at *Swanzy*, and rifled by *Philips* men. *June*
'20, being Sabbath day, the People of *Swanzy*
'were Alarmed by the *Indians*, two of our Inhab-
'itants turned out of their Houses, and their Houses
'rifled, and the *Indians* were marching up (as they
'judged) to assault the Town, and therefore intreated
'speedy help from us. We thereupon, the 21*st* of
'*June*, sent up some to relieve that Town, and
'dispatched more with speed. On Wednesday 23*d*
'of *June*, twelve more of their Houses at *Swanzy*
'were rifled. On the 24*th*, [*Thomas*] *Layton*[1] was
'slain at the *Fall River* near *Pocasset*. On the 25*th*
'of *June*, divers of our people at *Swanzy* were
'slain, and many Houses burned : until which time,
'and for several dayes after, though we had a con-
'siderable force there, both of our own. and of the
'*Massachusets* (to our grief and shame) they took
'no revenge on the Enemy. Thus slow were we
'and unwilling to engage our selves and Neigh-
'bours in a *War*,[2] having many insolencies, almost

[1] Mr. Savage, not looking beyond what Farmer left, says "one Laighton was k. by the Ind. near Swanzey, on the first hour of outbreak of Philip's war, 24 June, 1675." The original of this *Narrative* was long ago printed by Hazard, and reprinted by Mr. Pulsifer in quite time enough for Mr. Savage to have given the Christian name of Layton. His nicety as to the time of Layton's death, is very remarkable. Mr. Hubbard places the event on the 25th of June, and says "Layton Archer and his son were slain, which three belonged to Rhode Island." This, though quite particular, may be erroneous. I am however of the opinion that two men were killed, whose names were Thomas Layton and John Archer, and a son of the latter.

[2] It does not appear that it was from any tenderness on the part of the English towards the Indians, that they did not attack them ; but that the suddenness of the outbreak partially paralyzed them.

'intollerable, from them, at whofe hands we had
'deferved better;

       Jofiah Winflow.
       Thomas Hinckley.[1]

At a Meeting of the Commiffioners of the United Colonies held at *Bofton September 9th,* 1675.

WE having received from the Commiffioners 'of *Plimouth*, a Narrative, fhewing the 'rife and feveral fteps of that Colony, as to the pre-'fent *War* with the *Indians*, which had its begin-'ning there, and its progrefs into the *Maffachufets*, 'by their infolencies, and outrages, Murthering 'many perfons, and burning their Houfes in fundry 'Plantations in both Colonies. And having duly 'confidered the fame; do Declare, That the faid '*War* doth appear to be both juft and neceffary, 'and its firft rife only a *Defenfive War*. And there-'fore we do agree and conclude, that it ought now 'to be joyntly profecuted by all the United Colo-'nies; and the charges thereof to be born and paid 'as is agreed in the Articles of Confederation

 John Winthrop.   *Thomas Danforth.*
 James Richards.   *William Stoughton.*
         Jofiah VVinflow.
         Thomas Hinckley.

---

[1] Againft thefe fignatures, on the left, is this record in the original: "The fubftance of what is here declared doth clearly more particu-larly appear in the records and let-ters related unto of the feveral dates above mentioned." It is needlefs to fay that no letters or other vouch-

Postscript. 223

[7] The above expressed Letter and Narrative will (I hope) tend to remove Prejudices out of the spirits of dissatisfyed persons, touching the grounds of the present *Warr*. Some have thought that if *Philip* (the Ring-leader of all the mischief & misery which hath hapned by this *War*) his solemn ingagement to the *English*, above four years before these Troubles began, were published, it would farther clear the justice of the Warr on our part, and the more, in that he doth desire, that that Covenant might testifie against him to the world, if ever he should prove unfaithful therein. I shall therefore here subjoyn what was by him together with his Council subscribed, (in the presence of sundry appertaining to this Jurisdiction) and doth still remain with their Names to it, in the publick Records of the Colonyes.

It is that which followeth.

Taunton, Apr. 10*th,* 1671.

WHEREAS my Father, my Brother and my self have formerly *submitted our selves and our people unto the Kings Majesty of England, and to this Colony of New-Plymouth,* by solemn Covenant under our Hand, but I having of late through my indiscretion, and the naughtiness of my heart violated and broken this my Covenant with my friends by *taking up Armes,* with evill intent against

---

ers are printed with our Colonial Records; thus rendering their publication, a worse than useless affair, inasmuch as no proper publication of them can be expected in this age. See *Hist. Gen. Reg.*, xii, 358-60.

them, and that *groundlefly*; I being now deeply fenfible of my unfaithfulnefs and folly, do defire at this time folemnly to renew my Covenant with my ancient Friends, and my Fathers friends above mentioned; and doe defire this may teftifie to the world againft me, *if ever I fhall again fail* in my faithfullnefs towards them (*that I have now and at all times found fo kind to me*) *or any other of the Englifh Colonyes*; and as a reall Pledge of my true Intentions, for the future to be faithfull and friendly, I doe freely ingage to refign up unto the Government of *New-Plymouth*, all my Englifh Armes to be kept by them for their fecurity, fo long as they fhall fee reafon. For true performance of the Premifes I have hereunto fet my hand together with the reft of my Council.

In the prefence of
William Davis.
William Hudfon.
Thomas Brattle.

The Mark of   *Philip*
    chief Sachem of *Pocanoket*.
The Mark of   *Tavofer*.
The Mark of   Capt. *Wifpofke*.
The Mark of   *VVoonkaponehunt*.
The Mark of   *Nimrod*.

[8] By all thefe things it is evident, that we may truly fay of *Philip*, and the *Indians*, who have fought to difpoffefs us, of the Land, which the Lord our God hath given to us, as fometimes *Jepthah*, and the Children of *Ifrael* faid to the King of *Ammon*,

Postscript.

I have not sinned against thee, but thou dost me wrong to war against me; the Lord the Judge, be Judge this day between the Children of Israel, and the Children of Ammon. And as *Iehoshaphat* said, when the Heathen in those dayes, combined to destroy the Lords People; *And now behold the Children of Ammon, and Moab and Mount Seir, whom thou wouldest not let Israel invade when they came out of the Land of Egypt, but they turned from them, and destroyed them not, behold how they reward us, to come to cast us out of thy Possession, which thou hast given us to inherit, O our God wilt thou not judge them?* Even so, when *Philip* was in the hands of the *English* in former years, and disarmed by them, they could easily but would not destroy him and his men. The Governours of that Colony have been as careful to prevent injuries to him as unto any others: yea, they kept his Land not *from* him but *for* him, who otherwise would have sold himself out of all; and the Gospel was freely offered to him, and to his Subjects, but they despised it; And now behold how they reward us! will not our God Judge them? yea he hath and will do so.

F I N I S.

APPENDIX.

A. Page 65.

1675.

Letter of Capt. Nathaniel Thomas.

Mounthope, Augt the 10th, 1675.

Augt. 1.

AN account of the Fight with the Indians, Auguſt 1ſt, 1675.

On the 20th day of July, General Cudworth marched toward Dartmouth with 112 men, left 20 with me in the Garriſon of Mount Hope, and on the 30th day I went to Rehoboth, and at Mr. Newmans I heard the news, that Taunton poſt brought thither of Philip's flight, and with advice from Lieut. Hunt and his town council, haſtened back again to our garriſon to go to Capt. Henchman, and in the way met with Mr. James Brown, who at my requeſt, went back with me to Capt. Henchman to deſire him with what force he could to come to Rehoboth to join with their forces in purſuit of the enemy. We came to him at Pocaſſet, about two hours after ſunſet, who readily embraced the motion, cauſed an alarm to be made to bring his ſoldiers together, and next morning early, being the laſt of July, in Mr. Almy's boat, with ſix files of Engliſh and 16 Indians, wafted toward Rehoboth. Mr. Brown and myſelf immediately returned to Mount-hope, where I, on the ſaid laſt of July, early in the morning, marched with 11 from our garriſon,

1675. and one from Mr. Miles garrison, being twelve in all, in pursuit of the enemy. Lieut. Brown with 12 men of Swanzey marched with me. At Rehoboth I sent to Capt. Henchman by some Providence men, which were there, to waft to Providence and march from thence, who did so. There were marched from Rehoboth, just before us, 30 of Stoninton men, 40 or more of Uncas his Indians, and about 30 of Providence men, whom we overtook about sunset, joined with them, called a council of war, sent out some Indians first, and after some English and Indians as scouts, who made some discovery of the enemy, by hearing them cut wood, and we left our horses there upon a plain, with some to keep them, and in the night marched on foot about 3 miles to an Indian field belonging to Philip's men, called Nipsachick,[1] and at dawning of the day marched forward, about 40 rods, making a stand to consult in what form to surprise the enemy, without danger to one another, and in the interim, while it was so dark as we could not see a man 50 rods, within 30 rods of us, there came up towards us five Indians from Witamoes camp, (we suppose to fetch beans, &c. from the said field) perceiving nothing of us, at whom we were constrained to fire, slew two of them, the others fled, whereby Wittamas and Philip's Camp were alarmed. Wittama's camp then being within about an 100 rod of us, whom we had undoubtedly surprised, while they were most of them asleep and secure, had it not been for the said alarm; who immediately fled and dispersed, whom we pursued, slew some of them, but while we were in pursuit of them, Philip's fighting men showed themselves upon a hill unto us, who were retreated from their camp near half a mile to

---

[1] About 20 miles to the northward of the west from Rehoboth.

1675. fight us. Philip's camp was pitched about 3 quarters of a mile beyond Witamas. Philip's men upon our running towards them, difperfed themfelves for fhelter in fighting, and fo in like manner did we, the ground being a hilly plain, with fome fmall fwamps between us, as advantageous for us, as for them, where we fought until about 9 of the clock, flain divers of them, whom the Monhegins ftript and fkinned their heads; alfo one of them being fhot, was taken alive and examined, who made the following relation, vid^{t.} that Wittama, that night before had pitched her camp, as I faid before and about three quarters of a mile further. Philip, with Tokomona,[1] and, as I think, the Black Sachem alfo, had pitched their camp. I afked him concerning Awafunks; he faid fhe went to Narraganfet when the wars began. I afked what ftore of provifions the Indians had; he faid they had very little powder, but fhot enough; and it feemeth true, for the firft Indian which was fhot down, (being a ftout fellow, and one of them which fhot old Tifdell at Taunton, and them with him, and had his gun) although he had his horn by his fide, had no more powder but that in his gun; and Nimrod being there flain, had but 3 or 4 charges of powder. The reft found flain was as badly provided. Near the iffue of that engagement, Mr. James Brown, Mr. Newman and others came to us with provifions. One of Providence men and two of our garrifon foldiers that marched out with us, namely, Serjeant John Parker and Wm. Porey, were wounded, and about ten of the clock Capt. Henchman with his fix files and 16 Indians came to us, who went to the Monhegins and fhowed them an order in a letter from Captain Gugins [Gookin] that he was to take the care and command

---

[1] Tockamona was Awafhonk's brother. Vide Church, 63.

1675. of them, so that we expected his vigorous prosecution of the pursuit of the enemy, whose fighting men were just then fled. Providence men returned to carry home their wounded men, and myself and the rest with me, returned to Providence to carry our wounded men, not questioning but Capt. Henchman and ensign Smith and the rest would have pursued the enemy, we promising them to be with them with all speed, with a new supply of more provisions and ammunition. We got to Providence that night about 12 or one of the clock. I sent the wounded men that were with me to Road Island to Capt. Fuller, that night, next morning returned with 5 men, and in company with 12 Provi-

Augt. 2. dence men, carrying ammunition and provisions, after Capt. Henchman, marched that day, being the 2d of

3. August, lay in the woods that night, marched early the next morning after the track, and met with Ensign Smith and Lieut. Brown coming home, leaving Capt. Henchman with the Monhegins marching after the enemy: Rehoboth men blaming Capt. Henchman for his neglect to pursue the enemy, the first day we fought them, giving them a day's march before them. Lieut. Brown who was going home with Rehoboth men, returned back with us with four men of Swanzey. After we had gone about 15 miles from the place where we fought the Indians, the Monhegens and Capt Henchman had left the track of Philip and his, on the right hand, and went the west way to a fort in the Neepmug country, and that night, being Tuesday the 3d instant, we overtook Capt. Henchman at the 2d fort in the Nepmug country, called by the Indians, Wapososhequash, which is a very good inland country, well watered with rivers and brooks, special good land, great quantities of special good corn and beans, and stately wigwams, as I never saw the like, but not one Indian to

1675. be seen. Our Indians told us they judged they were all gone to Squabauge to another Indian fort and plantation of theirs, where is great swamps and places of security for them, unto which place the aforesaid Indian prisoner told us that the Sachems of Neepmuge had sent men to Philip to conduct him up to Squabauge and they would protect him, and that thither he was going; but I should have told that in our march after Capt. Henchman, we took notice that an Indian track, newly made, wheeled about from west to South,

Aug. 4. toward Narraganset, whereupon next day, being the 4th instant, we sent out Indian scouts, to discover the tracks, who brought word that the enemy's track was divided, one part going to Squabauge and the other turned toward Narraganset. Next morning after we came to the said 2d fort, being the 4th instant, Lieut. Brown with his 4 men, went to Norwich, being, as the Indians said, about 20 miles from us, with the intent to bring, with all speed, more supplies of men and provisions to march with us to Squabauge, being, as the Indians said, about 20 miles from us to the northward of the west, to the intent to treat those Indians, that if Philip came thither, they would deliver him up, or else to look on them as enemies. We tarried there from

7. Tuesday night till Saturday morning, being the 7th instant; and Lieut Brown came not, nor sent not to us; but I should have told before, that the Monhegins, being overloaded with Philip's plunder, went away home toward Norwich with Mr. Brown. Provisions being now spent, and no news from Lieut. Brown, on the 7th instant we sent the 12 Providence men to Norwich to signify to him or them, that Capt. Henchman returned to Mendum, whither we returned with him, and, in our march about 12 miles from the said 2d fort, we met with Capt. Mosely with 60 dragoons,

1675. march from Providence up after us, who gave us the
6. following relation, that on the 6th inst. at night he met
with an old Indian going back toward Pocasset, took
him and examined him, who told him that at our fight
on the first inst. we killed 23 of Philips men, 4 wherof
were Captains, and that Philip was gone to Squabauge
and Wittaman to Narraganset; he said he was a Pocasset Indian, and one of Philip's uncles, and that
Philips men had discovered some of us, as we marched
toward the fort, and that we had outgone them after
their track was left, and that he fearing we should have
charged Philip on his front, fled back to go to Pocasset.
It vexeth me to write the remainder, which is that on
the 1st inst. when we had given the enemy such a blow,
and the fighting men just fled, Capt. Henchman came
to us, took the command of the Monhegins and of
the pursuit. Before he came we all agreed together as
one, and when he came we all agreed he should command, all expecting his vigorous pursuit of the enemy,
who as the said old man told Capt. Mosely, was all
that day in a swamp, which is not 3 quarters of a mile
from the place where we fought them, and expecting
every minute when they should be surprised, they being ready to deliver themselves up. Had not Capt.
Henchman come in we had undoubtedly taken them
before now, and when he came we doubted not of his
pursuit, but instead thereof as soon as we that were
necessitated to carry off our wounded men, were gone,
the pursuit ceased, and the Monhegins and Mattachu-
set Indians went to plundering, of which there was
store, for as soon as the alarm was given, the enemy
fled in such haste, as they left their kettles, coats, meat
dressed and undressed, some ammunition, as lead and
slugs, and other goods, so that, as was judged by some
English then present, the plunder then taken was worth

near an 100 pounds;[1] and the Indians being then suffered so to do, their days work was done; but what shall I say, however was the neglect of man, the Lord is to be looked at in the matter. But to return to our retreat. Capt. Henchman and Mosely's Lieutenant both returned to Mendum, leaving the army in the woods, at sunset, about 12 miles above Mendum, in order the next day to come to Mendum, I and those with me, went in the night with them to Mendum; next morning, being the 8th inst. Capt. Henchman and Lieut. Keat went to Boston, and I to Rehoboth. At Mendum we heard the unwelcome news of Capt. Hutchinson and Capt. Wheeler. N. T.

[The above is from a copy in the hand writing of the late Judge John Davis. I received it of Mr. GEORGE LIVERMORE May 1st, 1855. The notes I suppose are by Davis, though there is no other indication of their authorship than the notes themselves. He has rendered it in modern orthography. On the paper he has made this endorsement: "Original found among J. Winslow's papers at Marshfield, at ye family seat (1792.) The signature N. T. indicates William [?] Thomas, a Capt. in ye expedition to Mt Hope. It gives a full detail of ye purs^t of Philip after his escape from Pocasset, July 29th, 1675. These occurrences are not mentioned by Church. Vid. Hubb^d 27-30."

Why Mr. Davis should blunder about the Christian name of Thomas is remarkable. I have no doubt *Nathaniel* Thomas is the meaning of the initials. He probably withheld his name in full having made such grave charges against Capt. Henchman. This may have been the cause of the Captain's resigning his place not

---

[1] Besides many guns taken from the slain.

long after, though his refignation was not accepted by the Government.

This copy of Capt. Thomas's Letter no doubt came into Mr. Davis's hands after he had publifhed his edition of Morton's Memorial, or he would not have omitted fo extraordinarily valuable document.]

B. Page 69.

Letter of Colonel John Pynchon.

SPRINGFIELD, Aug. 4th, 75.

HONORED Sirs: Our Indians have now brought me news of a fight between Englifh and Indians 2 days agoe at Quabaug and about 11 Englifh killed, fome houfes burnt and all ye Englifh got to one houfe &c: and juft now about 4 of ye clock in ye afternoon Judah Trumble who went laft night in ye night to Quabaug is returned; he went within 40 Rod of the houfes and difcerned Cops houfe and barne burnt and faw 2 houfes more burnt: faw one Indian with a gun but noe Englifhman: at this difmall fight he returned and his horfe Tyring came in a foote very much fpent. We are very Raw and our People of this Towne extreamely fcattered fo y^t our owne Place needs all and how foone thefe Indians may be upon this Towne we know not. We earneftly requeft y^t you would Pleafe to fend what force you may judge needfull either to releife ye Englifh yet left If any be alive at Quabaug: or to purfue thefe Indians: Speedy fuccor is neceffary, fome trufty Indians alfo to be [employed] may be good: but noe delay prefent chafe to be given to thofe Indians is abfolutely neceffary and foe it may be to long to ftay for Indians unlefs 2 or 3 or 4.

Appendix. 235

If it were pofible to have your forces here to morrow morning Mr. Glover thinks at leaft 50 foldiers needfull leaft having to few a furprifall be made of y^m. I fhall not add but beg your fpeedynefs ye good Lord guide and undertake for us:

yor Lo Hr & Servt
JOHN PYNCHON.

The Indian difcovered Trumble and hid himfelfe in ye bufhes as Trumble fays.

Mufkets are beft and not Piftols fo y^t horfe in way of dragoons is moft to be defyred.

[Addreffed outfide]
{
Thefe
For ye Honorable Govr and Magiftrates or to ye Firft Magiftr^s in Conecte- cott Colony: at Windfor or Hartford.
Poft haft
For fpeciall fervice without delay.
}

SPRINGFIELD, Aug. 7th, 1675.

HONORED Sir: I have juft now Intelligence brought mee by our Indians That an Indian from Wabaquaffick brings certaine Intelligence that Philip with 40 of his men is now at a Place called Afhquoack a litle on this fide of Quabaug fomewhat to ye fouthward of our way thither, and not much being but a litle of ye way: and I fuppofe not above 23 miles off this Towne: and thereabouts he refolves to fettle If he be not difturbed: becaufe as is a Place of food: ye Englifh of Quabaug their Corne being hard by: and the Indians have another great Corne feild hard by on ye fouthward fide and not far fouthward are more Indian Cornefeilds, he came 2 days agoe to this Place and there Pitches. It is not far from Memenimiffee which is a litle to ye Norweft of Quabaug where Philip's brother¹ is, and Mattoloos² with 200 foldiers and upward, our Indians judge that either Philip will goe to them at Memenimiffe,³ or that they will come to Philip at Afquoach which ye Indians think is rather ye more convenient Place, and fo they make 250 foldiers.

<small>This news the Wabquaffet Indians had of one of Philip's men whom they had [fpeech] with.</small> Our Indians doubt yt our forces gon forth will be to weake, and urge ye fending more prefently after to fecure them: They fay ye tyme that Philip left his fwamp was 7 days agoe and that being purfued he had 10 of his men killed:⁴ That 300 of his women and children and fome men ye hufbands of thofe women adventured themfelves upon the Narriganfet, though they dyed there, concluding yt they muft perifh if they went further.

Thefe 40 men who are fled with Philip, have but 30 guns, and the other 10 Bows and Arrows, are now weake and weary and may be eafyly delt with, whereas if we let them alone (fay ye Indians) they will burne

---

¹ Perhaps his *brother-in-law*, Quinnapin.

² Matoonus, no doubt.

³ In Brookfield, near Wickabaug Pond where Captains Hutchinfon and Wheeler were furprifed, Auguft 1ft. The name is fpelt diverfely; Mominimiffet, Whitney, *Hift. Worcefter County*, 64; Menimimiffet, Allen's *Hift. Northboro'*, p. 61; Menimeffeg, Willard's *Note to Mrs. Rowlandfon's Captivity*, p. 91. That thefe all refer to the fame fpot I have no queftion, though Mr. Willard, ibid., fays "the locality of Menimeffeg has never been afcertained."

⁴ This refers to the fight at Rehoboth Plain, before mentioned.

our houses and kill us all by stealth: I commend it to
ye serious and most judicious consideration whether it
be not best and securest for yours and us and absolutely
necessary to send out some more forces after those
already gon and so to fall upon Philips and by the
blessing of God destroy them. I hope you will consider it so seriously as to send 50 or 60 men up without
delay, If it may be to morrow: I think it may tend
exceedingly to ye Peace and Quiet of all ye English
Collonys to lay hold of this opportunity to destroy
Philip, it being very capable to be easyly effected if
speedyly it be attended: I could be heartily glad if we
were able to spare some men, but this last parsell being
nine men out of this Towne hath been with difficulty
and makes a great gap and now that Philip is neerer
us I suppose if I were to speake with your selves you
would not advise to it, and indeed some doe think we
had need to get in some more strength to secure our
selves against Invasions that may be made upon us
which we may justly feare every houre, but I hope in
God we shall be able to secure our selves if we send
none out.

Just as I am writing yours p Tho Mirick is come
to hand whereby I perceive a frustration of our expect
of ye Pequet Indians which methinks speakes so much
ye more earnestly for your sending some further forces
after those gon to Brookfield, we being as it were your
frontiers and a security to you being now next ye enymy,
you may safely doe that we cannot, and Indeed our
people are so extreamely frighted that in ye very heart
of ye Towne People remove from their owne houses
to any next that they Judge more strong, as this very
night 3 famylys are come into my house more than
were there before, all our people being in fear of a sudden surprisall at hom I may not adventure ye sending

forces abroad so that I am forced to leave yᵉ matter with you.

Be pleased Gentlemen, That your men which you send may bring bread with them, our mill having bin out of order renders it extreame difficult here. As to your querys about yᵉ state of Quabaug I am not able to resolve, yᵉ Indian that came was not permitted by the Bloody Indians to go neere our English there and had only what yᵉ Indians told him, but confirmed the 9 men killed which yᵉ first spake off: and how far yᵉ 10 Travellers knew anything of yᵉ state of yᵉ Brookfield English I cannot Learne, suppose they returned before they could speake with yᵉ English, neither can I Learne what house yᵉ English are in, suppose it is Aires for Cops is burnt downe as is said: I hope we shall heare fro our forces gon thither spedyly to Resolve all: I have herd nothing of that meeting of Indians at Hoyottanick[1] which I suppose is neere Stratford; shall write to Albany when opportunity presents which is Rare: I suppose it will be of good use to conveigh some Intelligence to Capt. Hincksman That Philip is at Quabaug, and to order yᵉ Pequet Indians to pursue them thither. If yᵉ Pequet Indians and Moheags would now pursue Philip while he is faint and weary it would be the best service and so likewise for our army: for yᵉ Indians say he hath left his Country wholly; so that it is to noe Purpose to be there, neither is there any need of feare about Norwich. If Philip moves further it will be toward yᵉ French, by us and Hadley: but I doe most sadly feare he will first doe some greate mischeife upon us if he be let rest: I pray by all ways possible Informe our army and yᵉ Pequets where he is and be pleased to give Intelligence to Boston of it: now Philip hath left his Country it may be,

[1] Housatonick.

Appendix. 239

Paſſage may be yᵉ Lower way fro you or by water I requeſt yᵉ ſending yᵉ Incloſed to our Governour by yᵒ firſt and moſt ſpedy Conveyance. I have bin but Breife in my account to our Governour becauſe it is late and hope you may doe it more at large. I ſhall as I have any Intelligence fro our and your forces acquaint you ſpedyly and doe much deſire to acquaint you with this news I have, but know not how, our Indians are all gon with them except old men. I may not longer detaine you, but conclude with my due reſpects and ſervice commending you to yᵉ ſweete direction of our gracious God and am

Your ready ſervant,

JOHN PYNCHON.

Whether will not our forces gon to Brookfield be in to great danger If we doe not ſend ſome more after yᵐ

I pray Sir ſend me word ſpedyly by this Poſt what you doe : and be pleaſed to give me advice and communicate thoughts to me who am all alone and gretly need help.

[Addreſſed outſide]
    Theſe
  For yᵉ Honorable John
  Winthrop Eſqʳ Govʳ of
  Conecticut
     in
    Hartford.

C. Page 71.

Capt. Samuel Mosley to Governor Leverett.[1]

From Nashowah Allies, LANKESTOR
16th Aug. 1675.

HONORED Sir: Yesterday I spayred Capt. Beeres 26 of our men to March with him to Sprinkefeilld, and it was with Major Willord orders, and I have allso, according to my orders from Major Genorall Denison, sent to Dunstable for to Inlarge there gard, 18 men, and to Groatton, 12 men, and to Chelmsford, 12 men, out of those y^t ware under Capt. Hinkssmans, and of those y^t came with me; also, last nightt, aboutt seaven A Clock, we martched into Nashowah, wheare we are Att Presentt; butt shall as soone as the Constable Haith Prest Vs a dozen Hoasses [horses] proseed for Groatton, and so to Chemeford; according to the orders Major Willord gaue me yesttorday Att Quoahbawge. The day before I came from Quoahbaugh, I martched in Company with Capt. Beeres and Capt. Laytrop, to the Swap, wheare they left me; and tooke there Martch to Sprinkfilld; and asoone as they ware gon I tooke my Martch into the Woods about 8 mills beyond the Swape where Capt. Huttchenson and the rest ware that were wounded and killed, and so Returned to follow the Enemy as aboue saide; also we did find a pesell of Wigwomes beyond the Swamp, aboutt 20, which we burntt, &c. Our Major haueing a seartayne Intelligence of a considerable Party of Indians y^t haue gathered tooegather a littell aboue Chensford, which I hope wee shalbe vp with this Nightt, or to Morrough at furthest; and if it pleese God I come

---

[1] Mosley married a niece of the Governor, namely, Anne, daughter of Isaac Adington, by Anne, daughter of Elder Thomas Leverett.

vp with them, God affifting me, I will cloofely ingadge with them; and, God fpearing my life, I fhall as opportunity gives leave, acquaintt your honor off my Actions. I haue with me butt 60 Men at prefent; So defioring your profperity, and that it may pleefe God to prefearve your Honour in good Health, and Humbly befeach your prayor to God for my good Suckfes, in this my Vndertaking, with my Humbell Searvis, &c. In all deuttyfullnefs, I Subfcribe my felfe your Refpectiue Kinfman and Humble Searvantt,
SAMUEL MOSLEY.

My Coffon Leverett prefents his
Devty to your Honour and my Antt.

Mafs. Archives, Bk. 67, fol. 239.

D. Page 81.

SPRINGFIELD, Sept. 8th, 1675.
8 or 9 of clock at Night.

HONORED Sir: I received juft now ye enclofed from Hartford to the Commiffioners which they defire me to fend forward, and as to that they propound about fending to Gov. *Andros*,[1] I think it may be of good ufe that your felves doe act fomething that way and as ftrongly and fpeedily as may be, and the rather alfo from a letter I received from Gov. *Andros* but this day, and Hartford yet know nothing of it (it came by an Indian) though its dated 24 Auguft. I have fent inclofed ye originall letter from *Andros* to me for you to pvfe [perufe] and I haue alfo fent you [to] Hartford, letter to myfelf: *Butler* was he that caryed

---

[1] Then Governor of New York; into which place he came the year before (1674). A portrait of Andros has been difcovered in England.

Maj. *Talcots* and my letter to Albany, we knowing nothing of *Andros* being there it was sent to yͤ Comiſſary there and not directed to *Andros*, who was but occaſionally there, and *Butler* brought noe returne bec[auſe] he went downe to yͤ ſopus [Eſopus] and from thence to New York before *Andros* and that round way he went hom to Hartford and not this direct way overland. I have the more ground to beleeve *Andros* his reality bec[auſe] Indians that have come from Albany doe ſay that they will not ſell pouder &c. to any Indians that are in wars with yͤ Engliſh and that vpon that account alſo they tell their Naighbors yͤ Mohegan Indians that they will try them a while, and they ſhall haue powder at yͤ fall of yͤ leafe when they hunt, and not now becauſe they will firſt ſee and know who are at war with yͤ Engliſh here.

That project of imploying Indians that are our profeſſed ffriends, I have formerly hinted and I would hope yͤ Commiſſioners would doe ſome thing to effect that way: and none in my opinion like *vncas* who hath of old had a grudge againſt yͤ vp River Indians and yͤ Pequets I would hope might joine with them, theſe I ſuppoſe may be well employed, but yͤ Narriganſets are not ſo likely, haueing formerly held more correſpondence with theſe vp River Indians.

You cannot be enough ſenſible how theſe Indians here doe rage, and if forces be not out to give check (however chargable) it is to be feared they will qvickly (vnleſs yͤ Lord prevent) be buſy in fyring all our towns and we ſhall not be like to hold it without a ſtrong garriſon. We have at preſent 16 here ſent yeſterday from Hartford, which may be called off this day or two.

The Lord effectually humble vs, the little ſucceſs of our forces ſpeake we are not yet truly humbled: and that our forces and Conecticut forces returne ag[ain] in such a manner as if they were afraid when the Indians were there, and yet doe nothing. What shall we say [?] is the Lord about to ruine vs and to leaue vs to be destroyed [?] It is matter of Lamentation some of our people speake of breaking vp and will be gone and discouragements enough are on all. The Lord turn vs to himse[lf] you will haue (I know) all matters by Major *Willard*, with whom I had Labouring to have come but yet I am obstructed of all hands, and yet I am fit for nothing. I run a venture in sending this after Major *Willard* fear it is hasardous and doubt [not] all passage ther way will be stopt. I pray God we may haue all our dependance vpon himselfe. With my due respects I take leaue and am Sir

    Your Humble servant,

       JOHN PYNCHON.

  Although I may not for ye breaking vp ye garrison at Quabaug yet it being done and all ye corne destroyed there whether ye settling it agane will countervaile ye charge may be considered.

[Superscribed]

  These
ffor ye Honorable John
 Leverett Esqr Governour:
    at
      Boston.

hast Post
hast.

       Copied from the Original.

Letter from Col. John Pynchon to the Rev. John Russell, on the day of the burning of Springfield.[1]

SPRINGFIELD, October 5, 1675.

REVEREND Sir: The Lord will have us lie in the dust before him; we that were full are emptyed. But it is the Lord and blessed be his holy name. We came to a lamentable and woful sight—the town in flames, not a house and barn standing, except old Goodman [William] Branche's, while we came to my house; and then Mr. Glover's, John Hitchcock's, and Goodman [John] Stewart's burnt down with barns, corn and all they had. A few standing above the meetinghouse, and then Goodman [Thomas] Merrick's downward, all burnt to two Garrison houses at the lower end of the Town. My Grist-mill and Corn-mill burnt down, with some other houses and barns I had let out to tenants. All Mr. Glover's Library burnt, with all his corn, so that he hath none to live on as well as myself and many more, that have not for subsistence.

They tell me thirty two houses and the barns belonging to them, are burnt, and all the livelihood of their owners, and what more may meet with the same strokes the Lord only knows. Many more had their estates burnt in these houses, so that I believe forty families are utterly destitute of subsistence—the Lord show mercy to us. I see not how it is possible for us to live here this winter, and if so, the sooner we were holpen off the better.

[1] This and the following letter are from copies from the originals and printed in the *Springfield Gazette* some fifteen years ago. They were probably communicated to that print by Judge Morris.

Postscript.

Sir, I pray you acquaint your Honored Governor with this dispensation of God. I know not how to write, neither can I be able to attend any public service. The Lord in mercy speak to my heart and to all our hearts is the real desire of

Yours to serve you

JOHN PYNCHON.

I pray you send down by the post my doublet coat, linen, &c. I left there, and pray.

[According to Mr. Pynchon's request, Mr. Russell enclosed his letter to Gov. Leverett, and accompanied it by the following letter:]

RIGHT Worshipful: The light of another day hath turned our yesterday fears into certainties and bitter lamentations, for the calamities and distresses of our brethren and friends at Springfield: whose habitations are now become an heap. Such increase of judgements, shows the great increase of wrath that is kindled against us, and the greatness of the provocations that have caused it. We have nothing to say but that the Lord is righteous, and we have rebelled, greatly rebelled against him. The enclosed from the honored Major, will give you such account of it as it is with us to make. We have little more to add only that the houses standing are about thirteen. Two men and one woman slain, viz. Lieut. [Thomas] Cooper, who was going towards the [Indian] fort [on Long Hill] to treat with the Indians that the day before pretended great friendship, being with three or four more at about a quarter of a mile out of town [near the Mill River], was shot so as he fell off his horse, but got up again and rode to the end of the town, where he was shot again and died. The other was one

[Thomas] Miller, of Springfield, [the ancestor of the Millers of West Springfield and Ludlow.] There appeared not (according to their estimate) above 100 Indians, of whom their own was the chief. Their old Sachem *Wequogan* (in whom as much confidence was put as in any of their Indians, was ringleader in word and deed. Another of their principal men cried out to them and told them he was one that burnt Quabog, and now would make them like to it. They were gone ere Major Pynchon came in with his forces, which was about two or three of the clock. They signified their sense of his approach by their whoops or watchwords, and were presently gone. Major Treate was got adown some hours sooner on the west side of the river, whose coming being perceived, five men went out of town, and although pursued by twenty Indians, carried over a boat which was filled with men, but the Indians standing on the river's bank, shot at them, and shot one through the neck (who is not like to recover) they durst not adventure to pass the river till Maj. Pynchon was come in and the Indians gone.

It was but the day before, viz., on the 4th of October, that the garrison soldiers, about 45 in number, left them, to their mutual sorrow: as looking they should quickly after be in hazard of that ruin which is now come upon them. Our army had prepared all things in readiness to go forth on Monday, (which was the occasion of calling forth those from Springfield) against a considerable party discovered about five or six miles from Hadley; but the three alarms we met with, and the tidings from Springfield, wholly disappointed it.

The men in those towns, who before trembled at the order, that none should be left in garrison when the army went out are now much more distressed at the thoughts of it as looking at themselves thereby expofed to inevitable ruin upon their enemy's affault, which we might then expect, efpecially the town of Hadley is now like to drink next, (if mercy prevent not) of the fame bitter cup. We are but about fifty families and now left folitary. The neareft town now left upon the river on this fide being, (as I guefs) about 70 miles diftant, and thofe on the other fide of the river being fo unable to come to us with any help had they it to afford. Experience fhows us that an hundred men on the other fide the river, can lend little relief.

Your Worfhip's humbly in all fervice
JOHN RUSSELL.

Our wounded men are greatly diftreffed for want of medicines. Thofe by fea not yet come at us, thofe expected by Capt. Waite laft at Roxbury.

E. Page 103.

To the Honored Gouernor And Councill now Sitting In Bofton.

SEUERALL propofalls humbly made to your honors by feuerall of the Commiffion officers of the Army in this prefent expedition.

Firft. Whether each Commiffion officer fhall haue a horfs Alowed them on the Countrys Charge.

The Aut[es] [Authorities] the Counfel Allowes to each Company three horfes to be difpofed by the Captain.

Secondly. If this be Alowed how many your honors will Alow to each Company for Cariage of Lugage and tranfporting fouldiers ouer Riuers on ocafion.

Thirdly. Whether your honors will Alow a trumpet

to each Company and if Alowed defire power from your honours to Imprefs them.

The Court Allows one to each Company [ ] E. R. S.

Fourthly. Whether your honors will Alow to Eury offifer and Souldier in the Army theire prouifion powder and fhott out of the publick ftock of the Country.

In Anfwer to this they muft Attend their order.
E. R. S.

Fifthly. Whether your honours will be pleafed forthwith to giue an order for the Impreffing of foe many horfes as your honors fhall be pleafed to Alow either to the officers or Souldiers. Anfr Yes. E. R. S.

Sixthly. Whether your honors will be pleafed to Alow to each Company a Quarter mafter. And If foe then whether you will give them Comiffions.

One quarter mafter only Allowed, to be Appointed by Major Apleton. E. R. S.

All which we leave to your honors Confideration, Humbly begging your prayers for Vs who fubfcribe your honors Seruants.

4 December 75.

JAMES OLIVER
ISAAC JOHNSON
NATH DAVENPORT.
EPHRAIM TURNER.
PHYNEHES VPHAM.
EDWARD TYNG.

Mafs. Archives, Bk. 68, p. 87.

F. Page 105.

To the Honored General Court now assembled at Boston. The Humble petition Peter Freeman, Indian

HUMBLY showeth that whereas your poor petitioner hath in these Indian Wars, though but in some small measure been serviceable therein yet as an encouragement unto faithfulness to the English was in the day thereof promised by the Honorable General Josiah Winslow Esquire my freedom and also the freedom of my wife who was given me at Narraganset by the General and his Council as may appear under the Honored Generals own hand. But my wife being detained from me by Capt. Samuel Mosely or his order, makes me bold to supplicate your honors for Relief herein and a Grant of my wife to be at her Liberty and to my own proper use as besides what the honored General hath signified under his own hand I can prove by sufficient witness to be granted me by the honored General and his Council at Narraganset, wherein your honors will engage your poor petitioner unto further faithful service for yourselves and this whole country.

> It is ordered that Peter have his wife delivered him and that the Treasurer make Capt. Mosely due and rational satisfaction for what he hath been out for her. The magistrates have past this. Their brethren their deputies hereto consenting.   EDWD RAWSON Sec.

14 May, 1676.

> The Deputies Consent not hereto
> WILLIAM TORREY Clerk.

Orig. Petition, MS.

An Order to supply Peter Freeman, an Indian guide, with clothing and money.

PETER Freeman, Indian of Narraganſet, having been a guide to the Engliſh army for the Colonies, under the command of the late General Winſlow, having done good ſervice to the country, and whilſt his doing that ſervice his daughter was taken and made a ſlave; the Court judgeth it meet to order the Treaſurer to give him two Engliſh coats, two pair of ſtockings, and two pair of ſhoes, one for himſelf and one for his wife, a white ſhirt, four ſhillings in money to carry him home, having ſpent much time both now and formerly to obtain his recompence. And it is left to the Major General to inform himſelf where his ſaid daughter is in captivity, and with whom; and to endeavor for her repriſal and freedom, that ſhe may return to her father. Voted by the whole Court, 30th of May, 1685.

Ordered, that the Secretary write to Captain Prentice.   EDWARD RAWSON, Sec.

The Court being informed that the girl being taken by the army, the General of the Army and ſeveral other Captains as the ſaid Peter affirmed, promiſed him that his daughter ſhould be releaſed, and free, in caſe he proved a faithful guide to the army, which ſeveral chief officers in that army yet living, teſtified in Court on their certain knowledge: the ſaid Peter Freeman did faithfully perform the ſervice of a faithful guide to the ſaid army. The Court ordered that the Secretary write to Captain Thomas Prentice, and inform him of the order that ſaid Peter's daughter being diſpoſed [of] by him not only for three or four years ſervice, as the other gentlemen promiſed, and no longer; it now being altogether ten years since, and that he take care for her freedom and release.

E. R., Secy.

Mass. Archives.

G. Page 125.

ON the 12th of June, 1676, several Indians, a part whereof were sent in by Major Bradford, with others sent in by a small party of ours that issued out as scouts, were convented before the Council, such of them as were accused of working insufferable mischief upon some of ours.

The first of them was named Wotuchpo, alias Tuchpo. It was demanded of him, 1. Why he fled out of his confines, which he was injoyned to keep on pain of death; to which he made little answer to purpose. 2. Why he abused our Governor by fraud and falsehood, endeavoring to persuade him that there would be no need to send forth an army, as Philip's men had deserted him, having few left with him except old men and boys; to which he could say nothing. 3. Why he continued with our bloody enemies all the time of the wars hitherto; neither could he defend this.

At the same time three other Indians appeared before the Council, whose names were Woodcocke, Quanapawhan, and one called John Num. The two former were accused by a squaw of being present and actors in that bloody murder of Mistris Sarah Clarke, on the 12th of March before the date hereof; and these two accused John Num of the same fact, and they all, upon examination, confessed they were present at the committing of that horrid murder and outrage. John Num owned also, that he was of that company that murdered Jacob Mitchell and his wife and John Pope; and so sentence of death was pronounced against them, which was accordingly immediately executed. These three, a little time before their sentence, accused Keweenam, an Indian sometimes living about Sandwich, that he was the first instigator of Tatoson, to commit the aforesaid murder; namely, that he went to him and certified him that he had lately been at the house of William Clarke, at the Eel River, and that his house was slightly fortified, and that it was well furnished with necessaries, and that his way would be to repair thither now; and that, on the Lords day, the folks of the house being but three, the most of them would be gone to meeting, and they, being there, might discerne it; and in case they left a man at home or so, they might soon dispatch him, and then they would meet with no opposition, but might do as they pleased; on which information, the night following, (this being the last day of the week,) the said Tatoson went towards Plymouth, and on the morrow following, in the morning, about nine or ten of the clock, he with his company did this cruel villany.

On the 21st of July (1676,) Keweenam was brought before the Council and examined. He did not fully own said accusation; only he owned that he was at William Clarkes house a little before the fact was committed, and that he was in company with Tatoson the day before, which was Saturday, and the said fact being committed on the Lord's day following. He further confessed that he held correspondency with Tatoson, one of the most notorious of our enemies, and had given him information of the weakness of the house, and yet gave no information to the English, that they might prevent the intended mischief. Upon this he was required to speak, if he had aught to say for himself; but he said little or nothing to any purpose. Whereupon the Council, considering that their three positive testimonies who witnessed as above said, and with all divers concurring circumstances, which have a tendency to the clearing up of the case, do judge that the said Keweenam is worthy to die; and so received the sentence of death, which was that his head should be severed from his body, which was immediately accordingly executed.

The names of those Indians who were copartners in the outrage committed at William Clarkes house at the Eel River, in the township of New Plymouth, on the 12th of March, 1676.

Imp^r TATOSON, WAPANPOWETT, TOM PIANT, UTTSOOWEEST, MUSHQUASH, TOM, TATASON'S, SANBALLETT, WOONASHENAH, brother's son.

Plymouth Col. Records.

H. Page 129.

HADLEY, March 28th, 1676.

ON the 26th inst., at night, we had advice from Springfield that eight Indians assaulted 16 or 18 men, besides women and children, as they were going to meeting, from a place they call Long Meadow, and killed a man and a maid, wounded two men, and carried away captive two women and two children. They sent some after them, which did return that night without discovering of them. In the night, having advice from Major Pinchon which way the Indians with their captives were marcht, I sent out 16 horse in pursuit of them, who met with some that were sent from Springfield, and overtook the Indians with the captives, who, as soon as they saw the English they killed the two children, and sorely wounded the women in the heads with their hatchets; and so ran away into a swamp where they could not follow them. The scouts brought back both the women and the children. One of the women remains still senseless, by reason of her wounds; the other is very sensible and rational, and doth say that the Indians were very free in their speech to them that night they were with them, and told them that they should go to Deerfield where the Nashua [Lancaster] captives were, and told them that there was 3000 Indians at Deerfield, and that they did not want for powder; they could have enough from the Dutch, and that there was two Dutchmen with them, that had brought four bushels of powder, and went from them but two days since: the names of them, as they told her, was one *Jerrard*, and the other *Jacob*, that lived with Major Pinchon, who are dwellers at Fort Albany; and two Dutchmen more. They say also that there is 300 [Indians] at Squakheage, and that they have built 300 [wigwams?] above Deerfield, and that some French were lately with them, who persuades them not to burn and destroy the houses, but to make what slaughter they can of the people, because they intend to come and inhabit them. She says also, that the Dutch bring their powder on horses, and that they intend to come again with another supply within a few days; and that they do intend to fall on those towns shortly; and that they were very inquisitive to know the number of our men, which the women did inform them as near as they could, and that Connecticut forces were gone. The woman says that the Indians told her that Capt. Tom of Natick, and the rest of them Indians with him, were come last week to Deerfield, and that they do intend to make that their head-quarters; and that the Mohaugs had killed some of their Indians, but that they had made peace with them again.

THOMAS SAVAGE.

Mass. Archives.

Appendix.

I. Page 30.

1676.
May 18.

A WRITER in the *Chronicle* says, that "but for Philip and one Sachem more, the Indians, after the Fall Fight, would gladly have yielded to any terms of peace." This "one Sachem more" was probably Pumham. To him, perhaps, more than to any other, was owing the rally and effectual onset made by the Indians; causing the rout and loss of many of their assailants. But there was another great chief, a conspicuous actor there. He was neither a Wampanaog nor a Narraganset, but an Eastern Chief, of the region of the Kennebeck. His name was Megunnaway, who, Mr. Hubbard informs us, "was a notorious rogue, that had been in arms at Connecticut last June, at the falls, and saw that brave and resolute Capt. Turner, when he was slain about Green River, and helped to kill Thomas Bracket at Casco, August last."

Very little of personal narrative has come down to these days, even of the whites, and almost nothing of that of the Indians, concerning those who were engaged in the most important enterprises. There were two of the survivors of the Fall Fight, among the English, who have left some memoirs of their participation in it. One of these was Jonathan Wells of Hatfield, "then a youth in his 17th year," as Mr. Taylor styles him. The same author says "he was afterwards a gentleman improved in public life, and sustained a worthy character." The other was the Rev. Mr. [Hope] Atherton, minister of the gospel in Hatfield."

Mr. Taylor informs us that "the following Narrative is the substance of an attested copy of an account taken from Mr. Wells' own mouth."

"He was one of the 20 men, who were under a necessity of disputing the ground for the purpose of

1675.
May 18.

recovering their horses. Soon after he had mounted, being in the rear, three of the enemy fired upon him; one of their balls brushed his hair, another wounded his horse, and a third struck his thigh in a place where it had before been broken with a cart wheel. The ball did not wholly break his thigh anew, but fractured the end of one of the bones, which was a little projected over the other, it having been badly set. Upon receiving the wound, it was with difficulty that he kept in his saddle. The Indians perceiving they had wounded him, pressed hard upon him. Mr. Wells recovering a little from the first shock, and perceiving the enemy almost upon him, presented his gun, which gave them a check, and whilst they were charging, he made his escape, and reached the company. He represented to Capt. Turner the danger to which the people in the rear were exposed, and urged him to return to their relief, or halt till they might come up; but he answered, *It is better to lose some, than all.* The army was now divided into several companies, one pilot crying, *If you will save your lives, follow me;* and another, *If your regard your safety, follow me.* Mr. Wells was now following a company, whose course was towards a swamp; but perceiving that a body of the enemy were there, he left that company, who were all lost, and joined a small party who were taking a different route; but his horse soon failing by reason of his wound, and himself being much weakened by loss of blood, he was left by this party, having only one Jones, a wounded man, to accompany him. They had no path to guide them, and were both unacquainted with the woods. They had not travelled far before Mr. W. was separated from Jones, and finding himself faint, ate a nutmeg which he had in his pocket, upon which he revived. After having wandered in the woods for some time, he

1676.
May 18.
came upon Green River, and he followed the courſe of it up, till he came to a place called the *Country Farms*. Having paſſed the river he attempted to aſcend a mountain on the weſt ſide, but fainted and fell from his horſe. How long he lay in this condition he knew not, but when he recovered he found his horſe ſtanding by him, and his bridle hanging on his hand. He aroſe, tied his horſe, and again laid himſelf down; but upon reflection, finding himſelf already ſo weak as to be unable to mount, concluded he ſhould have no further uſe for his horſe, and being unwilling he ſhould die at the tree, diſmiſſed him; but unhappily forgot to take any proviſion from his portmanteau, although it contained a plenty. Towards night, being troubled with muſquetoes, he ſtruck up a fire; but this almoſt proved his deſtruction. It aroſe and ſpread with ſuch fury among the leaves and bruſh, that it was with difficulty, in his faint condition, he eſcaped periſhing in the flames. After he was out of danger from the fire, he again laid himſelf down to reſt; but now new fears aroſe; he imagined that the fire would direct the enemy where to find him, and ſerve to betray him into their hands. Unwilling the enemy ſhould be benefitted by his ammunition, he caſt it to as great a diſtance as he could, reſerving only a round or two for their uſe, ſhould he fall into their hands. After ſome time, finding his fire had ſpread conſiderably, he took courage, put ſome tow into his wounds, bound them up with his handkerchief, and compoſed himſelf to ſleep. In his ſleep he dreamed that his grand-father came to him, and told him he was loſt, and muſt turn and go down that river, till he ſhould come to the end of a mountain, where he would find a plain upon which he muſt travel, in order to find his way home. When he awoke he found himſelf refreſhed, his bleeding ſtopped, and

Hh

1676.
Iay 18.

his strength recruited, and with the help of his gun as a staff, he was able to walk, though but slowly. The rising of the sun convinced him he was lost, and that the course he intended to pursue was wrong. He had now wandered several miles farther from home, than when he set out from the place of action. And though at first he paid no attention to his dream, now he determined to follow the directions of it. Accordingly he travelled down the river, found the end of the mountain, and soon came to the plain; all of which agreed to the representation in his dream. Soon after he entered upon the plain, he found a foot path which led him to the road in which the main body of the army returned. When he came to Deerfield river he met with much difficulty in crossing; the stream carrying his lame leg across the other; so that several of his first attempts were without effect. Finally, however, with the help of his gun, with much difficulty he reached the opposite shore. When he had ascended the bank, being greatly fatigued, he laid himself down under a walnut bush and fell asleep. When he awoke, the first object that presented, was an Indian in a canoe, coming directly towards him. Mr. Wells now found himself in a very unhappy condition; being so disabled by his wounds that he could not make his escape, and his gun being so filled with gravel and sand in crossing the river, that he could not fight. As soon, however, as he perceived the Indian had discovered him, he presented his gun, which so affrighted him, that he leaped out of the canoe, leaving his own gun, and made his escape. Mr. Wells concluding that he would inform the whole tribe, who were only a few rods distant, went into a neighboring swamp, and finding two logs lying near each other, and covered with rubbish, he crept between them. He soon heard the noise

1676. of Indians, but was not curious to look out after
May 18. them. When the noise had ceased, he ventured to
proceed forward. In Deerfield meadow he found some
horses bones, from which he scraped some matter,
which served for food. He also found two or three
rotten beans, where the Indians had threshed, and also
two blue bird's eggs, which was all the sustenance he
had till he reached home. He came to Deerfield town
plat on Saturday night about dark, but as there were
no inhabitants present, the town having a little before
been burnt, he continued his course in the evening.
He was often under great discouragements, and frequently laid himself down to die, expecting to rise no
more. He reached no farther than Muddy Brook as
the sun rose on Sabbath morning. Here seeing a
human head, which had been dug up by wild beasts,
notwithstanding his distressed condition, Mr. Wells
stopped to find the grave, which having found, he laid
the head to the body, and covered it with billets of
wood, to defend it from the ravenous beasts of the
wilderness. After he had left the brook and entered
upon the plain, he grew faint and very thirsty, but
could obtain no water for a considerable time; he was,
however, often refreshed, by holding his face in the
smoke of burning knots of pine, which he frequently
met with, as the woods were on fire. Mr. Wells arrived at Hatfield on the Sabbath, between meetings,
and was received with inexpressible joy, as one having
risen from the dead. He endured indescribable pain
and distress with his wound, being confined several
times to his bed, for six months together; and it was
upwards of four years before he was found."

Here closes our account of the narrative of Mr.
Jonathan Wells. Mr. Taylor has added a very sensible note to that part of it where the author speaks of

1676.
May 18.

being directed by his grandfather in a dream. "I doubt, he says, whether in this dream there was anything supernatural, as some may be ready to suppose. Mr. Wells having wandered in the woods six or seven miles, must necessarily have had some doubts whether his course was right; and his mind when asleep would more naturally employ itself on this subject, than any other; because to find the way home must have been his great object when awake. His dreaming that his grand father appeared to him was nothing strange; and his local situation at this time was such, that he could not be entirely unacquainted with the natural make of the ground; and his thoughts running as they did in this dream, would be natural. The river was near him, the plain was before him, and the end of the mountain, near the side of the plain, if he had not previously seen it, would naturally be supposed."

Mr. Taylor closes his account of the Fall Fight with the following short narrative of the Rev. Mr. Atherton, before mentioned.

"In this action was also the Rev. Mr. Atherton, minister of the gospel in Hatfield. The following is the substance of a paragraph which he delivered to his people the sabbath after his return:

"In the hurry and confusion of the retreat," says Mr. Atherton, "I was separated from the army. The night following I wandered up and down among the dwelling places of the enemy, but none of them discovered me. The next day I tendered myself to them a prisoner, for no way of escape appeared, and I had been a long time without food; but notwithstanding I offered myself to them, yet they accepted not the offer; when I spake to them, they answered not; and when I moved toward them they fled. Finding they would not accept of me as a prisoner, I determined to take the courfe of the river, and if poffible, find the way home; and after feveral days of hunger, fatigue, and danger, I reached Hatfield."

To this account Mr. Taylor appends a note as follows: "There were various conjectures at the time, relative to this ftrange conduct of the Indians [in avoiding Mr. Atherton]. The moft probable one was that it arofe from fome of their religious fuperftitions. They fuppofed he was the Englifhman's God."

"Deerfield, October 10th, 1793." This was the time Mr. Taylor drew up the preceding account of the Fall Fight.

To this Appendix may be appropriately added a lift of thofe weftern men who ferved under Captain Turner; it not having been before printed, that I am aware of. Thofe from the eaftern part of the country have been printed in the *Hiftory and Antiquities of Bofton*.

A Lift off Souldiers vnd^r the Comand off Capt Willm Torner.

Hadly Souldiers Fro the 7th of Aprill, 1676.

Capt William Turner	David Hartfhorne
Serg^t John Throppe	Benjamin Poole
Serg^t John Newman	John Uppum [Upham]
Corp^{ll} Jofeph Hartfhorne	Simon Grover
Corp^{ll} Robert Sympfon	Stephen Grover
William Armes	John Pratt
John Strowbridge [Trow-	Thomas Briant
Samuel Sybly bridge?]	Triall Newbury
Thomas Jones	Jofuah Phillips
Robert Coates	Benjamin Chamberlin

Jonathan Chamberlin
John Luddon
John Preſſon [Preſton]
John Bill
William Chubbe
Moſes Morgan
Roger Jones
John Wiſeman
Phellip Jeſſop
Joſeph Griffin
Joſiah Man

Thomas Chard
John Sheapheard
Ephraim Roper
Nicholas Duerell
Phellip Cattline
Joſeph Chamberlin
Richard Snodin
Joſeph Smith
Joſeph Bodman
Drumer John Chapple
William Torner

Souldiers ſent to the Mill.

Robert Seares
Samuell Rawlins
John Sawdy
Jonathan Duninge
Samuell Davies

John Fiſher
Thomas Cobbett
Thomas Sympkins
Richard Lever.

Hampton Souldiers.

Serg^t Eſaiah Toy
Corp^{ll} John Wilde
John Smith
John Babſon
John Whiterage
John Aſhdowne
John Roleſtone
John Langbury
John Foſter
John Wattſon
John Chaplin
John Belcher
John Stukely
John Boyd
John Walker

John Roberts
Martin Smith
Abraham Shaw
Thomas Roberts
Richard Hudſon
Samuell Ransford
Joſeph Fowler
Solomon Lowde
William Jaques
Jacob Burton
William Smith
Nicholas Maſon
Phellip Matoone
Samuell Soutch
Thomas Lyon

Appendix.

Robert Price
Thomas Poore
Peter Bufhrodde
Samuell Phefy [Vefey?]
William Willis
Thomas Harris
George Bewly
William Howard
Phellip Lewes

William Hopkins
William Hunt
Samuell Tyly
James Burrell
William Hartford
Ephraim Beeres
Richard Bever
John Fifke *Left wounded by Capt. Lathroppe.*

Hatfielde Souldiers.

Robert Bardwell
Samuell Laine
Benjamin Barrett
Hugh Goliko
Anthony Baker
John Largin [Larkin?]
Richard Staines
Nicholas Gray
John Allen
Richard Smith
William Elliott
John Wilkins
John Jones
Thomas Staines
Gilbert Forfith
Benjamin Lathroppe
Robert Dawes
Hugh Pike
Daniell Stearlin
John Verin
Jonathan Nicholds
James Verin
John Downinge

Jofeph Moringe
John Cooke
John Hix
John Salter
Jeremiah Cloather
John Arnold
Simon Williams
Daniell Clow
Edward Byfhoppe
Henery Raynor
Samuell Neale
Jeffery Jeffers
Hugh Price
Archebold Forreft
Jabefh Duncan
John Hughes
William Batt
Walter Hixson
Jabefh Mufgroue
Matthew Groves
Anthony Ravenfcraft
James Molt.

Sent to Springefielde.

Serg.^t Roger Proffer
Ely Crow
William Briggs
Jeremiah Norcroffe
William Mitchell

Timothy Froglie
Onesepherus Stanly
William Crane
Henery Willis.

RICHARD FRANCIS, Clerk.

Mass. Archives, Bk. 68, fol. 212.

NOTE.—Some of the Christian names in the preceding list are much abbreviated in the original MS. That of Joⁿ I have rendered John. Where *Jonathan* occurs it was spelled out in full in the old list. The long list of *Johns* on page 262, are all spelled out in the original, and so in most cases.

INDEX.

ABBOT, George, 133.
    Joseph, killed, 133.
    Timothy, taken, 133.
Acts and Monuments, 100.
Adams, Henry, killed, 119.
Addington, Isaac, 240.
Aieres, ———, house burned, 238.
Akkompoin—see UNCOMPOEN.
Albany, news from, 238, 242.
    Fort, 254.
Alderman, kills Philip, 194.
Alexander, brother of Philip, 192.
Allen, Bozoune, tanner, 120.
    John, 263.
Alvis, Roger, wounded, 152.
America known to the Ancients, 24.
Anabaptists, tenets, 161.
Andover, attacked, 132-3.
Andrews, Henry, killed, 144.
Andros, Edmund, Sir, 168, 174, 177, 241-2.
Anecdotes, of praying for rain, 191; of a German Prince, 171; of Eliot and Philip, 208-9.
Annawon's Rock, 180.
Antinomians, 161.
Apparel, proud excesses in, 98.
Apparitions, 158-9.
Appendix, 227.
Appleton, Samuel, Capt., at Hatfield, 101; narrow escape, 102, 110.
Archer, John, killed, 221.
Arms, William, 261.
Army, what constitutes, 166, 211.
Arnold, S. G., Hist. R. Island, 106, 109.
Arnold, John, 263.
Arowsick Island attacked, 201.

Ashdowne, John, 262.
Ashquoack, 235.
Atherton, Hope, 255, 260.
Awashonks, sues for peace, 170; flies to Narraganset, 229.

BABIT, Leonard, killed, 144.
    Babson, John, 262.
Baker, Anthony, 262.
    Joseph, killed, 122.
Baldwin, Stephen, 156.
Barbour, George, 121.
Bardwell, Robert, 263.
Barrett, Benjamin, 263.
Barron, Peter, killed, 85.
Barrow, Sam (Ind.), 124.
Barney, James, killed, 92.
Bartlett, J. R., R. I. Records, 105-6.
Batt, William, 263.
Beers, Ephraim, 263.
    Richard, Capt., sent against Philip, 70-73; Indians attack, 76; cut off and slain, 77-8; barbarities on his slain, 80; at Lancaster, 240.
Beer's Mountain, 79.
Belcher, Andrew, Capt., 113.
    Corporal, wounded, 58.
    John, 156, 262.
Bell, James, killed, 144.
Bennet, George, killed, 71.
Bever, Richard, 263.
Bewley, George, 263.
Bill, John, 262.
Bible, Indian, 172.
Billerica, attacked, 133.
Bishop, Edward, 263.
Black-Point, attacked, 91.

Black-Sachem, 229.
Bloghead, Ruth, 160.
Bloody-Brook, 86.
Blue-Point, attacked, 91.
Bodman, Joseph, 262.
Bonython, Richard, 90.
Book of the Indians, 11.
Boston taverns, 83; great mortality, 153; Indians alarm, 121.
Bottes, Isaac, killed, 92.
Bowers, John, killed, 120.
Boyde, John, 262.
Boyle, Robert, Hon , 173.
Bracket, Thomas, 255.
Bradford, attacked, 142.
    William, Maj., wounded, 109; expeditions, 170-2; 179, 251.
Bradstreet, Simon, 141.
Braintree, mischief at, 139.
Branch, William, 264.
Brattle, Thomas, Capt., 150, 179, 224.
Breevort, J. Carson, 68.
Briant, Thomas, 261.
Bridgewater, burnt, 143; fortunate, 187.
Briggs, William, 264.
Brinsmade, William, 127.
Briscoe, William, 199.
Brocklebank, Samuel, Capt., 136, 138.
Brook, Henry, 160.
Brookfield, destroyed, 67-70; 238.
Broughton, George, 87.
Brown, James, 220, 227, 229.
    John, 199, 219.
        Lieut., 219, 228, 230.
Brownlow, W. G., 105.
Bulkley, Gershom, wounded, 121 174.
Bull, Jireh, garrison destroyed, 105-7.
Bulling, Samuel, 121.

Burrell, James, 263.
Burton, Jacob, 262.
Bushrod, Peter, 263.
Butler, ———, 241-2.

CANDLESTICKS, removed, 25, 114, 125, 127.
Canonchet (Quanonchet), 140.
Cape Indians—see PRAYING I.
Captives, return of, 145, 165, 167.
Carter, John, 160.
Casco, destroyed, 89, 90, 198-9.
Cattline, Philip, 262.
Chamberlin, Benjamin, 261.
    John, 261.
    Joseph, 262.
Chaplin, John, 262.
Chapple, John, 262.
Chard, Thomas, 262.
Charles Second, 217.
Cheever, Ezekiel, 86.
Chelmsford, attacked, 132, 240.
Chenary, John, killed, 79.
Chickon, a Chief, killed, 140.
Child, Ephraim, killed, 79.
Christian Indians—see PRAYING IN.
Chubbe, William, 262.
Chubbuck, Nathaniel, 135.
Church, Benj., Capt., expedition, 60; exploit at Pocasset, 61; on the Long March, 115; fight with Totoson, 124; makes captures, 181-2; expedition, 187-8; surprises Philip, 196; meets Weetamoe, 220; injustice to, 170.
Churches—see MEETINGHOUSES.
Clark, Daniel, killed, 120.
Clark, Samuel, Examples, 161.
Clark, Sarah, Mrs. killed, 251.
Clark, Thomas, counsellor, 93, 141.
Clarke, Samuel, killed, 102.
Clarke, Thaddeus, 199.
Clarke, William, family murdered, 123, 252-3; 175.

Index. 267

Cloather, Jeremiah, 263.
Clow, Daniel, 263.
Cluff, William, killed, 72.
Coates, Robert, 261.
Cobbett, Thomas, 262.
Cochickawick (Andover), 133.
Cole, Isaac, 160.
Coleborn, Edward, killed, 74.
Collins, Nathaniel, killed, 101.
Commissioners declare war, 222.
Conjurers, Indian, 190.
Connecticut, its services in the war, 140, 147, 151-2, 154-5, 162-3, 165, 173; slightly injured, 203.
Cooke, John, 263.
Cooper, John, killed, 120, 245.
  Thomas, killed, 97-8.
Copp, —, house burned, 234, 238.
Cotton, John, 22, 38, 128.
Coweset (Wading River), 51.
Coy, John, killed, 75.
Crackbone, Benjamin, killed, 79.
Cranberry, Nathaniel, killed, 72.
Crane, William, 264.
Cromwell, Oliver, 22, 55.
Crossman (Indian), 177.
Crow, Ely, 264.
Cudworth, James, Gen., 57, 59, 227.
Curtis, John, 199.
  Nathaniel, killed, 78.

DAMARISCOTTA, desolated, 199.
Danforth, Thomas, Counsellor, 93, 141, 222.
Dartmouth, people killed, 61.
Dating, ancient mode of, 126
Davenport, Nathaniel, Capt., killed, 109-10, 248.
Davies, Samuel, 262.
Davis, John, Hon., 233-4.
  Sylvanus, Capt., 87, 199.
  William, 224.

Dawes, Robert, 263.
Deerfield, attacked, 72; burnt, 80; letters concerning, 234-9.
Denison, Daniel, Gen., 93, 141, 240.
Denison, George, Capt., expeditions, 137, 140, 174
Devil, Dr. C. Mather's views regarding, 27; appears to an Indian, 90; large family of children, 138; worshipped by the Indians, 190, 197; Indians Devil driven, 208.
Dickinson, Azariah, killed, 72.
Dickinson, Joseph, killed, 79.
Dogs, used against Indians, 101.
Dorchester, indifferent to the memory of a founder, 17.
Dover, inhabitants killed, 96.
Downing, John, 263.
Drew, Mrs., a captive, 119, 167.
Drouth, severe one, 189-90.
Dublet, Tom, exploit, 154.
Dudley, Joseph, Assistant, 141.
Duncan, Jabesh, 263.
Dunning, Jonathan, 262.
Durell, Nicholas, 262.
Dunstable, a guard stationed there, 140.
Dutch, accused of selling arms and ammunition to Philip's warriors, 129.
Dwight, Timothy, killed, 120.
Dyer, William, 161.

EAGLESTON, James, killed, 72.
Eastman, Philip, killed, 142.
Easton, John, Gov., Narrative of the beginning of Philip's War, 35.
Eclipse of the moon, portentous, 57.
Eel-River massacre, 252-3. See PLYMOUTH.
Elbridge, Thomas, 199.
Elice, John, Medfield, 121.

Eliot, John, Indian Bible, 172; interview with Philip, 208-9.
Elliott, William, 263.
England and the Southern Rebellion, 14, 20.
Euin, Edward, 199.
Everett, Edward, Hon., at Muddy Brook, 86.
Eyres, John, killed, 75.

FAGG, William, killed, 71.
Fall Fight, 148-9, 255, 260.
Fall-River, men killed, 221.
Falmouth, desolated, 87, 90.
Farley, Timothy, killed, 74.
Farrar, Jacob, killed, 71.
Fasts, 95, 96, 121, 123, 136, 144, 163, 166
Fellows, Richard, killed, 72.
Fisher, John, 262.
Fiske, John, wounded, 262.
Fitch, James, Chaplain, 174; anecdote, 190-1.
Forrest, Archebold, 263.
Forsith, Gilbert, 263.
Fort Albany, 254.
Fort-Fight, Narraganset, 106-111; number of Indians then killed, 108, 193.
Foster, John, at Fall Fight, 262.
John, printer, 6.
Fowler, Joseph, at Fall Fight, 262.
Fox, John, Martyrologist, 83, Acts and Monuments, 100.
Francis Richard, 264.
Froglie, Timothy, 264.
Freeman, Peter (Indian), guide, 106; Petition, 249-51.
French, John, wounded, 75.
Fulford, Richard, 199.
Fuller, Matthew, Capt., 60, 290.
Fusell, John, killed, 120.

GALLOP, John, killed, 109-10.
Gardner, Joseph, Capt., killed, 109-10.
Gatchell, John, killed, 79.
Gents, Thomas, 199.
Gilbert, John, Jr., wounded, 120.
John, a captive, 146-7.
Gill [John?], 58.
Glover, Pelatiah, house destroyed, 97; had a brave library, 98; library burnt, 235, 244.
Goliko, Hugh, 263.
Gookin, Daniel, Gen., his Histories, 39, 117; Maj., 172; Capt., 229.
Gorham, John, Capt., died, 110.
Gould, Alexander, 199.
Grafton, Joseph, 86.
Graves, Thomas, of Groton, 127.
Gray, Nicholas, at Fall Fight, 263.
Green, Bartholomew, printer, 172.
Green-River, 257.
Griffen, Joseph, 262.
Groton attacked, 123, 125; guard at, 240.
Grover, Simon, 261.
Stephen, 261.
Groves, Matthew, 263.

HADLEY, fight near, 79; critical state, 146; assaulted, 155.
Hair, proud excesses in long, 98.
Hall, Richard killed, 152.
Hammond, William, killed, 58.
Harrison, Isaac, killed, 156.
Hartford, William, 263.
Harris, Thomas, 263.
Hartshorne, David, 261.
Joseph, 261.
Hatfield, threatened 76; attacked, 84; troops at, 100-1; assaulted, 150-1.
Hathorne, William, Counsellor, 93, 141; Capt., 202.

Index. 269

Haverhill, attacked, 142; captives return, 145.
Henchman, Daniel, Capt., march against Philip, 56, 227-9; censured, 230-3, 238, 240.
Hinckley, Thomas, Gov., 222.
Hingham, Indians attack, 135.
Historical Collections by Prince, Sewall, Hubbard, Mathers, 15-16.
Hitchcock, John, 244.
Hix, John, 263.
Hixon, Walter, 263.
Hobart, Israel, house burned, 135.
Holyoke, Samuel, Capt., 148.
Hoosick-River, fight, 168.
Hopgood, Sydrack, killed, 75.
Hopkins, William, 263.
Housatonick, near Stratford, 238.
Howard, William, 263.
Hubbard, William, Indian Wars, 6; its merits, 8; editions, 9; his Collections, 16; copied without credit, 29.
Hudson, Richard, 263.
    William, 51, 224.
Hughes, John, 263.
Hunt [Edmund ?] Lieut., 227.
    William, 263.
Hutchinson, Edward, expedition and death, 65-6.
Hutchinson, Elisha, 66.
    Thomas, Gov., 18; misguided, 20; carries off valuable papers, 22; his volume of Original Papers, 23.
Hutchinson, William, 66.

INDIANS, numbers at the time of Philip's War, 30; subordination a "rope of sand," ib; arms, ib; early threats against the English, 31; boastings, ib; former state, 47; grounds of the War, ib, 217-21; Eastern, hostile, 87-90; debauched by traders, 99; one torn by dogs, 101; taunt the English, 125; barbarity to dead enemies, 61, 80; to animals, 133; Pequots fight for the English, 140; distress of the Eastern, ib; cause of hostility, 141; sickness, 145; some surprised near Lancaster, 154; in Narraganset, 155; request liquors be not sold them, 175-6; fond of their children, 189; worship the Devil, 190; "Devil Driven," 208; no complaint against Massachusetts, 212; Devils in flesh, ib; favored by Plymouth, 215.
Ireland, charity to N. England, 65.
Irons, Thomas, Boston, 156.

JACKSON, Edward, killed, 120.
    Jacob, John, Capt., 120; killed, 135.
Jacob, Richard, Lieut., exploit, 131.
James-the-printer, 172-3.
Jeans, Ebenezer, killed, 78.
    Jonathan, killed, 78.
Jeffers, Jeffery, 263.
Jaques, William, 262.
Jerrard, ——, of Albany, 254.
Jessop, Philip, 262.
Jocelin, Henry, 199; Mrs., 167.
Johnson, Edward, Capt., 37.
    Isaac, Capt., killed, 109-10, 248; Mrs., 160.
Jones, ——, wounded, 256.
    John, 263.
    Joseph, house burned, 135.
    Roger, 262.
    Thomas, 261.

KEAT, ——, Lieut., 233.
Kendall, Lydia, 160.
Kendall, Mary, 160.
Kennebeck, Indians, 91.

Keweenam executed, 252-3.
Kimball, Thomas, killed, 142, 145.
Kingſbury, Ephraim, killed, 142.
Kittery, people killed, 91.

LAINE, Samuel, 263.
Lake, Thomas, killed, 201-2.
Lancaſter, attacked, 70; deſtroyed, 117, 192.
Langbury, John, 262.
Largin [Larkin?], John, 263.
Lathrop, Benjamin, 263.
Layton, Thomas, killed, 221.
Lee, Samuel, renowned, 197.
Leet, William, Governor, 141.
L'Eſtrange, Roger, 34.
Lever, Richard, 262.
Leverett, Anne (Moſely), 24.
Leverett, John, Gov., 93, 141.
Lewes, Phillip, 263.
Lewis, James, killed, 72.
Winſlow, M. D., 3.
Littlefield, John, letter, 87.
Livermore, George, Eſq., 233.
Long March, 114, 115.
Long Meadow, 253.
Lothrop, Thomas, Capt., ſent againſt Philip, 70-71, attacked, 76; ſlain, 84-5; family, 86; defeat deſcribed, 85, 88, 96, 240.
Lowde, Solomon, 262.
Luddon, John, 262.
Lyon, Thomas, 262.
Lyra, George, killed, 79.

McLEOD, Mordecai, killed, 71.
Magnalia, the, 9, 10, 28.
Magnus (Squaw-Sachem), killed, 174, 176.
Magus, Simon (Matoonas), 185.
Malden, prodigies ſeen at, 159.
Mann, Joſiah, 262.
Mansfield [Moſes], Capt., 174.
Marbury, Edward, 66.

Markham, William, killed, 79.
Marlborough burnt, 126-8, 135.
Marſhall, Samuel, killed, 109-10.
Maſon, John, 141.
Nicholas, 262.
Samuel, killed, 72, 122.
Thomas, killed, 120.
Zechariah, killed, 120.
Mather, Cotton, his account of Philip's War, 9, 27-8; as a novel writer, 27; Wonders of the Inviſible World, 28.
Mather, Increaſe, account of his "Brief Hiſtory," 5-7; a hurried performance, 6; his materials, 16.
Mather, Nathaniel, 165.
Richard, 16, 17.
Samuel, 16, 17; neglected by biographers, 18; his ſon, 19; his library, 23; "laſt of the Mathers," 24.
Matoonas, taken and killed, 184-5, 236.
Matoone, Phillip, 262.
Matthews, Pentecoſt, killed, 98.
Matthias, ſervices of, 188.
Medfield aſſaulted, 119.
Meetinghouſes, Indians ſpare, 25, 96; Candleſticks, 114.
Megunnaway, Eaſtern Chief, 255.
Mekins, Thomas, killed, 101.
Memenimiſſee, 236.
Mendham, attacked, 63; a hiſtory propoſed, ib; burnt, 113, 118, 233.
Merrick, Thomas, 237, 244.
Meſſer, Thomas, 199.
Metacomet (Philip), 33.
Middle-Ages of N. England, 15.
Middleborough, attacked, 61.
Miller, James, killed, 79.
Thomas, killed, 98, 206.
Mitchel, Jacob, killed, 252.
William, 264.

Index. 271

Mohegans in the war, 71, 116, 231-2, 229-30, 238, 242.
Mohawks, attack Philip's men, 145, 157, 168-9, 178, 207-8, 254.
Molt, James, 263.
Monoco, a noted Nipmuck, 120.
Monster, one born, 161, 179.
Morgan, Moses, 262.
Morland, Samuel, Sir, 198.
Morse, Samuel, bravery, 121.
Moringe, Joseph, 263.
Mosely, Samuel, Capt., marches against Philip, 57, 71; at Hadley, 82; fights the enemy, 85, 88; letter from Hatfield, 100-1; at Narraganset fight, 110; in Plymouth Colony, 179; pursuit of Philip, 231-2; at Mendon, 233; Lancaster letter, 240.
Muddy-Brook, 259.
Muscongus, settlement broken up, 199.
Musgrove Jabesh, 263.
Musketequid (Concord), 120.
Mushquash (Indian), 253.

NAHAUTON, William, "a godly Indian," 48.
Namasket, burnt, 146.
Nanunttenoo (Canonchet), killed, 134.
Narragansets, jealousies concerning, 46; expedition against, 59; ill reports of, 103; an army to be sent against them, 104; Swamp Fight, 106-11; Indians retreat from, 114, 205, 240.
Narraganset towns burnt, 126.
Naticks, join against Philip, 71; one releases a captive, 80.
Neale, Samuel, 263.
Negro, saves Taunton, 177-8.
Nehemiah (Ch. Ind.), 172.
Newbury, Benjamin, Capt., 152, 174.

Newbury, Triall, 261.
New England, its condition at the time of Philip's War, 13, 29; *Middle Ages* of its literature, 14; population in 1675, 29; loss in the war, 30; history of desired, 37; " Goings down of the Sun ;" " Ends of the Earth," 46; a New Jerusalem, *ib ;* second generation of English less godly, 47; its degenerate state 92.
Newman, Noah, on Pierce's defeat, 128, 229. Serg' John, 261.
Nichols, Robert, killed, 91. Jonathan, 263.
Nimrod—see WOONASHUM, 224; killed, 229.
Ninnigret, old crafty Sachem, 106, 108, 134, 140.
Nipmucks, rise in the war, 62-3; receive Philip, 204; not subdued, 204.
Nipsuckhooke, 173, 174, 228.
Nixon, Capt., lines on, 129.
Norcross, Jeremiah, 264.
Northampton, attacked, 122; affairs, 146; prodigies seen, 158.
Northfield, battle near, 79.
Norton, Freegrace, killed, 102.
Nowel, Samuel, Chaplain, 111.
Num, John (Indian), 251.
Numphow, Sam (Indian), 133.

OAKES, [Edward], Lieut., exploit, 58-9.
Oates, John, killed, 85.
Old Indian Chronicle, 35.
Oliver, James, Capt., 110, 248.
Olverton, William, killed, 102.
Omens, 157.
One-eyed-John, destroys Medfield, 120.
Oneco, son of Uncas, 190.
Ordinaries, order concerning, 99.
Owaneco—see ONECO.

PACOMPTUCK (Deerfield), 72; soldier killed at, 78.
Paine, Elizabeth, killed, 120.
——— [Stephen ?], insulted, 220.
Parker, John, wounded, 229.
Parsons, Ebenezer, killed, 78.
——— Joseph, killed, 72.
——— Mark, 199.
Patuckson, a Wampanoag, 50.
Pearce, John, 199.
Pease-field, battle, 60.
Peck, John, killed, 78.
Pecowsick (in Springfield), 129.
Pegypscot (Brunswick), 89.
Pemmaquid, destroyed, 199, 200.
Pendleton, Brian, letter, 87.
Pepper, Robert, wounded, 79.
Pequots, serve against Philip, 140, 237-8.
Petananuet (Wampanaog), 192.
Peter Indian—see FREEMAN, PETER.
Pettequamscot (S. Kingston), 106.
Petts, John, killed, 102.
Phesy, Samuel— see VESEY, S.
Philip, alias Metacomet, 33; Sachem of Mount-Hope, 47; disturbs Plymouth, 52; Indians flock to, 53; begins war, 54; hides in a swamp, 61; escapes, 64-5; fights at Rehoboth Plain, 65; raises the Western Indians, 68; attacks Medfield, 120; in great straits, 167; Mohawks upon him, 168; returns to Mount-Hope, 169-171; flies to Dartmouth, 180; to Squannaconk, *ib*; another escape, 186; another, 187-8; killed, 194; capture of his sister, 187; his wife and son, 188; an uncle taken, 232; his head and hands cut off and exhibited, 195; a Leviathan, 197; origin of trouble with, 217-18; arms his men, 219; hostile acts, 220; signed a submission, 223-4; at Ashquoack, 235; a brother, 236.
Phillips, Henry, killed, 144.
——— Joshua, 261.
——— Walter, 199.
——— William, house burnt, 90.
——— Zechariah, killed, 74.
Phips, ———, 199.
Piant, Tom (Indian), 253.
Pierce, Michael, Capt., killed, 127.
——— Richard, 199.
Pike, Hugh, 263.
Pitman, Mark, killed, 72.
Plaisted, Roger, 87; killed, 92.
Plummer, John, killed, 72.
Plymouth, trouble with Philip, 52; invades him, 54; order about ammunition, 99; attacked, 123-4; buildings burnt, 138, 145; ancient limits, 146; a prodigy seen at, 157; vindicated, 213; just cause of war, 217.
Pocassets, join Philip, 58-9.
Pokanoket (Mount-Hope) 47.
Polock, John, killed, 102.
Poole, Benjamin, 261.
——— Jonathan, Capt., 101,
Pomham—see PUMHAM.
Poore, Thomas, 263.
Pope, John, 252.
Population, of New England, 29.
Porey, William, wounded, 229.
Post, Richard, killed. 63.
Potowmut (Warwick), 126.
Potock, taken and executed, 192-3.
Pratt, John, 261.
———, Sergt. killed, 135.
Praying Indians, six churches of, 39; services in the war, 117, 146, 170, 183.
Prentice, Thomas, Capt., 56, 250.
Presson [Preston], John, 262.

Price, Hugh, 263.
Robert, 263.
Prince, Thomas, Rev., 16.
Pritchard, Joseph, killed, 75.
Prodigies, at Plymouth, 52; at Malden, *ib;* Hadley and Northampton, 157-8.
Proffer, Roger, Lieut., 264.
Providence, buildings burnt, 132.
Pulsifer, David, 99, 221.
Pumham, on the Fall-Fight, 149; killed, 183, 255, a grandson killed, 140.
Pumham's Town, 116.
Purchase, Thomas, 89.
Pynchon, John, Maj., Letters, 68, 234-9, 243, 246, 253-4; Counsellor, 93; buildings burned by Indians, 98; Assistant, 114.

QUABAOG (in Brookfield), 66-7, 116, 231, 234-5, 238, 240, 243, 246.
Quakers, idolatrous, 99.
Quanapawhan, 251.
Quanonchet, taken, 134; executed, *ib;* "mighty Sachem," 137, 164.
Quaqualh, great Sachem, 116.
Quiddington, Abraham, killed, 102.
Quinnapin, brother-in-law to Philip, 192, 236.
Quonsickamuck (Worcester), 104.

RANSFORD, Samuel, 262.
Ravenscroft, Anthony, 263.
Rawlins, Samuel, 262.
Rawson, Edward, 95, 248-9, 250-1.
Raynham men killed, 144.
Raynor, Henry, 263.
Rea, Joshua, 86.
Rebellion, the Southern, similar to Philip's War, 14, 15; both waged in the cause of barbarism, 14;

that of the Indians less atrocious, 14, 20.
Rehoboth Plain, fight there, 65, 227; burnt, 131; fight near, 150; military watch, 219; Indians killed in the Plain-Fight, 232.
Religion, what it was in the time of Philip's War, 26; a caution to those of this age respecting, 27.
Richards, James, Worshipful Mr., 165, 222.
River Indians, 117.
Roberts, John, killed, 123, 262.
Thomas, 262.
Robinson, John, 27.
Rolestone, John, 262.
Roper, Ephraim, 264.
Rowlandson, Joseph, 117.
Mary, captivity, 118-19; released, 142, 167, 192.
Russell, John, of Hadley, 72; letter of, 73-7, 98, 244-7.
Russell, Richard, Counsellor, 93, 141; dies, 153.

SACO, attacked, 87, 90.
Saconesset (Wood's Hole), 179.
Sagamore John, submits, 184.
Salmon, Thomas, killed, 123.
Salter, John, 263.
Sanballett, a murderer, 253.
Sausaman, John, discloses Philip's designs, 47; found murdered, 48; a translator of the Bible, 49; Secretary to Philip, *ib;* real name, 51; his case stated, 218-19.
Savage, Thomas, Maj., marches against the enemy, 121-2; letter from him at Hadley, 253-4.
Saway, John, soldier, 262.
Scales, Matthew, killed, 72.
Scalps, Indian, 59; English, 61.

Kk

Scamman, Richard, 89.
Scanderberg [Geo. Caſtriot], 182.
Scarborough, deſtroyed, 87.
Scituate, burnt, 138; prodigy ſeen there, 159.
Scott, Robert, 199.
    Thomas, killed, 78.
Seares, Robert, 262.
Seily, Robert, Capt. killed, 109.
Selleck [Jonathan], Capt., 174.
Sewall, Samuel, Hon., 16, 109.
Shackſpeer, Uzacaby, 122.
Sharp, John, killed, 136.
Shaw, Abraham, 262.
Shepherd, John, 262.
    Thomas, 165.
Sherman, William, 58.
Shurte, Abraham, 199.
Simon, michievous Indian, 142, 199.
Simſbury burnt, 165.
Small Pox, 166.
Smedley, Samuel, killed, 74.
Smith, Elizabeth, killed, 120.
    Enſign, 230.
    Jobama, killed, 151, 152.
    James, 199.
    John, 262.
    Joſeph, 262.
    Martin, 262.
    Richard, 105, 113, 263.
    William, 156, 262.
    Zachary, murdered, 56.
Snodin, Richard, 262.
Soutch, Samuel, 262.
Southern Rebellion, 14, 20.
Sprague, Anthony, 135.
Springfield, Indian treachery, 81; burnt, 97; people killed, 128-9; troubles, 234-9, 241-7.
Squabauge—ſee QUABAOG.
Squakheag (Northfield), 78-9.
Squanakonk, deſcribed, 180.
Squando, deſtroys Saco, 90.
Squaumaug, Sachem of Maſs., 51.

Squawbetty, in Middleboro', 144.
Staines, Richard, 263.
    Thomas, 263.
Standley [John], Capt., 174.
Stanley, Oneſepherus, 264.
Stearlin, Daniel, 263.
Stebbins, Edward, captive, 146.
Stewart, John, 244.
Stilſon, James, 199.
Stone, Richard, killed, 102.
Stoughton, William, 93, 141, 222.
Stowe, John, wounded, 152.
Strowbridge, John, 261.
Stukely, John, 262.
Succanowaſſuck, 181.
Sudbury, attacked, 123, 131, 136.
Sugarloaf-Hill, battle, 78.
Superſtition, univerſal, 158-9.
Swanzy, half conſumed, 61; further troubles, 162, 219, 221.
Swearers, how to be treated, 99.
Sybly, Samuel, 261.
Syll, Joſeph, Capt., 202.
Symonds, Samuel, Dep., 93, 141.
Sympkins, Thomas, 262.
Sympſon, Robert, Corp., 261.
Synagogues of God burnt, 125.

TALCOTT, John, Maj., letter, 173, 242.
Taunton, attacked, 60; people killed, 144, 177.
Taverns, in Boſton, complained of, 83; order concerning, 99.
Tavoſer, Indian warrior, 224.
Taylor, John, 199, 256-61.
Tehticut (Taunton river), 144, 186.
Thatcher [Thomas], Mr., 165.
Thankſgivings, 164, 166, 196.
Thebe, noted Chief ſlain, 59.
Thomas, Nathaniel, Capt., letter, 227-33.
Thomſon, James, 160.
Throppe, John, Sergt., 261.

Thurston, Samuel and Margaret, killed, 120.
Tiashq, escapes Church, 181.
Tift, Joshua, executed, 108.
Tisdell, John, killed, 60, 229.
Tispequin, a noted Chief, 146.
Tobias, one of the murderers of Sausamon, 48.
Tokamona, killed, 229.
Tom, Capt., of Natick, 254.
Tom, Totoson's brother's son, 253.
Torrey, William, 249.
Toy, Esaiah, Sergt., 262.
Totoson attacks Clark's garrison, 174, 252-3.
Tozer, Richard, killed, 92.
Trading-Houses, debauch the Indians, 99.
Treat, Robert, Maj., commands against Philip, 77; at Squakheag, 80; wounded, 81; relieves Mosely, 85; at Hatfield, 101; Deputy Gov., 141, 246.
Treaty with Narragansets, 59; Philip, 223; Eastern Indians, 174.
Trowbridge, John, 261.
Trumble, Judah, 234-5
Trumbull, J. H., Records of Connecticut, 106.
Tuckpoo, put to death, 176, 251.
Turner, Ephraim, Counsellor, 248.
   Praisever, killed, 122.
   William, Capt., killed, 148, 162, 255-61.
Tyley, Samuel, 263.
Tyng, Edward, Counsellor, 93, 141, 248.

UNCAS, attacks Philip, 65; son, 75; relieves Capt. Mosely, 85; pursues the Narragansets, 116; kills many, *ib*; story about powwowing, 190; men in the fight at Rehoboth Plain, 228, 242.

Uncompoen, killed, 186.
Upham, John, 261.
   Phinehas, wounded, 248.
Uttsooweest, a Wampanoag, 253.

VERIN, James, 263.
   Verin, John, 263.
Vesey, Samuel, 263.

WABAQUASSICK, 235, 236.
   Wading-River, 51.
Wadsworth, Samuel, Capt., exploit near Marlboro', 115; another, 118; killed, 136-8.
Walker, John, 262.
Wait, Richard, wounded, 98, 247.
Wakely, Thomas, killed, 89, 202.
Waldo, John, wounded, 75.
Waldron, Richard, Maj., 87, 175, 202.
Walls, Jonathan, 156.
Wampampeag, Indian money, 71, 77, 183.
Wampanoags, jealous, 46; joined by others, 59.
Wampatuck killed, 51.
Wanalancet, 142, 175.
Wapanpowett, 253.
Wapososhequash, 230.
War, the grounds of stated by Plymouth, 214-22.
Warner, Thomas, killed, 102.
Warren, Joseph, 156.
Warwick, burnt, 125-6.
Warwick-Neck, 174.
Watson, John, 262.
Watts, Thomas, Capt., 110.
Watuckpo, a murderer, 251.
Weetamoo, Queen of Pocasset, 58-9; interview with Church, 220; her men killed, 228; at Narraganset, 232; her fate, 191-2; Yaymoyden on, 192.

Index.

Weld, Thomas, a work falsely ascribed to, 161.
Wells, Jonathan, Narrative, 255-60.
Wequogan, perfidious, 246.
Weshacom Ponds, 154.
Weymouth, houses burnt, 121, 125.
Wheeler, Joseph, killed, 71.
  Thomas, Capt., wounded, 66-7.
White, John, 119.
Whiterage, John, 262.
Wickabaug-Pond, surprise, 66-7, 74.
Wilde, John, Corporal, 262.
Wilkins, John, 263.
Willard, Samuel, Rev. Mr., 125.
  Simon, relieves Brookfield, 68-70; Counsellor, 93; at Quabaug, 240, 243; dies, 153.
Willett, Hezekiah, killed, 163, 177.
  Thomas, Capt., 177.
Williams, Simon, 263.
  William, killed,
Willis, Henry, 264.
  William, 87, 263.
Willoughby, Francis, 160.
Wilson, John, Rev. Mr., 120-1.
  John, killed, 79.

Winslow, Job, house robbed, 220.
  Josiah, Gen., 104, 115; Narrative of the rise of the war, 216-22, 249-50.
Winthrop, John, author of "Rise, Reign and Ruin," 161.
Winthrop, John, Gov., 222, 239; dies, 152.
Winthrop, Wait, Capt., 106.
Wiseman, John, 262.
Wispoke, Indian Captain, 224.
Wizards, among Indians, 190.
Woburn, monster there, 160.
Wood, Jonathan killed, 120.
Woodcock, John, son killed, 139.
Woodcock (Indian), 251.
Woods Hole (Saconesset), 179.
Woonashenah, 253.
Woonashum, killed, 65.
Woonkaponehunt, 186, 224.
Woosausaman—see SAUSAMON.
Wowaus—see JAMES-THE-PRINTER.
Wright, Joseph, 160.
  Samuel, killed, 78.

YORK, Duke of, Patent, 200.

ERRATA.

To Note 1, page 81, add D.
Page 116, in first column of Note, line 13, read *qualh*.
  126, line 16 of text, read 1676.
  141, line 1 of Note 2 read rechosen.
  142, line 15 of Note 1, read Wonalancet.
  156, line 20 of Note 1, read *Mass*.
  170, last line of text, read *Squaw-Sachem* 2.
  193, line 5 of Note 2, read *Audi Alteram*, &c.

Pedigree of the Fa[mily]

John Mather w[as of an]
ancient family o[f Low-]
ton, parish of W[inwick,]
Lancashire, Engl[and.]

Thomas Mather[...]

1. Catharine, da. of Edmund = Richard, b. in Winwick, 1596, student B[r...]
Holt, of Bury, Lancashire, | minister of Toxteth, about 15 years, eje[cted, ar-]
29 Sept. 1624, d. 1655. | rived at Boston, N. England, 17 Aug., 1[...]
| 23 Aug., 1636, d. 22 April, 1669.

Samuel, b. in Wootton, = Sister of | 1. Kath- = Timothy, b. in = Elizabeth, da. | Nathaniel, b. in Toxteth,
Lancashire, 13 May, 1626, | Sir John | erine, da. | England, 1628; | Amiel Weeks, | Lancashire, 20 Mar. 1630;
H. C. 1643, freem. 1648; | Stevens, | Maj.Gen. | witnessed a re- | of Dorchester, | H. C. 1647; minister in
ret'd to England, went to | of Dub- | Humphry | quest of Wampa- | b. 18 Aug. | Barnstaple, Eng. 1656;
Scotland, thence to Ire- | lin. | Atherton. | tuck, to Dorches- | 1659, m. 20 | ejected at Restoration, suc-
land; d. in Dublin, 29 | | | ter, for lands at | Mar. 1680, d. | ceeded his bro. in Dublin;
Oct. 1671. | | | Punkapaug,1667, | 19 Feb. 1709- | d. in London, 26 July,
| | | d. at Dorch'r by | 10. | 1697. A great benefactor
Four or five ch. all d. young, except one, a dau. | a fall, 14 Jan. | | to N. Eng. in Philip's War.
| | | 1684-5. | | See *Brief Hist.* p. 165.

Samuel, b. 5 = Hannah, da. | Richard b. 22 = Elizabeth | Catharine, | Nathaniel, | Joseph, b. = S[...]
July, 1650, | Gov. Robert | Dec. 1653, m. | Wife. (1) | b. 6 Jan. | b. 2 Sept. | 25 May, | C[...]
mi. at Wind- | Treat of Ct. | 1 July, 1680, | | 1655-6, d. | 1658. | 1661, d. | 2[...]
sor, Ct. 45 | d. 8 March, | settled in | | ab. 1694. | | ab. 1691. | 1[...]
yrs., d. 18 | 1707-8, a. | Lyme, Ct., d.
Mar. 1727- | 47. See *In-* | 17 Aug. 1688.
8; H. C. | *dex.* | | | | Katherine, 5 yrs.
1671. | | | | | old in 1695.

[...]muel b. = Abigail, | Hannah, | John. | Azariah, b. 29 = ... | Ebenezer, | Nath'l, b. 30 | Timothy, b. = Sarah, | Elizabeth, | Samu[el]
[16]77, H. | d. 1 Sept. | b. Sept. | — | Aug. 1685, a | b. 3 Sept. | May 1695. | 20 March, | .... | b. 20 Nov. | 23 Ja[n.]
1698, a | 1722, a. | 1682, d. | Joseph. | min. of Say- | 1687. | — | 1681, d. 25 | d. 16 | 1682. | 1683-[...]
[ph]ysician, | 43. | 1683. | — | brook d. there | — | Benjamin, b. | July, 1755. | Aug. | | 17 Jul[y]
[...] Feb. | | — | John. | 11 Feb. 1737. | Joseph, b. | 29 Sept. | | 1756. | | 1725.
[17]46. | | Elizabeth, | | | 6 March, | 1696. | | | |
| | b. 2 Jan. | | Azariah, b. Oct. | 1689. | | B | | A
| | 1691. | | 1722, d. Oct. 1796.

1. Abigail, da. = COTTON. b. = 2. Wid. Eliz- = 3. Lydia. Maria. b. 16 Elizabeth. b. 6 Jan. Nathaniel. b. 6 July.

mily of Mather.

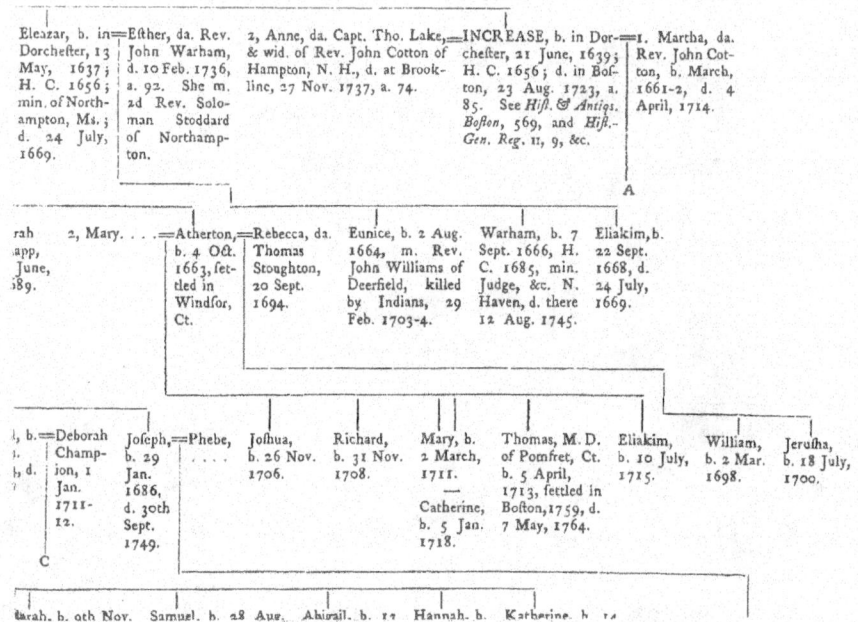

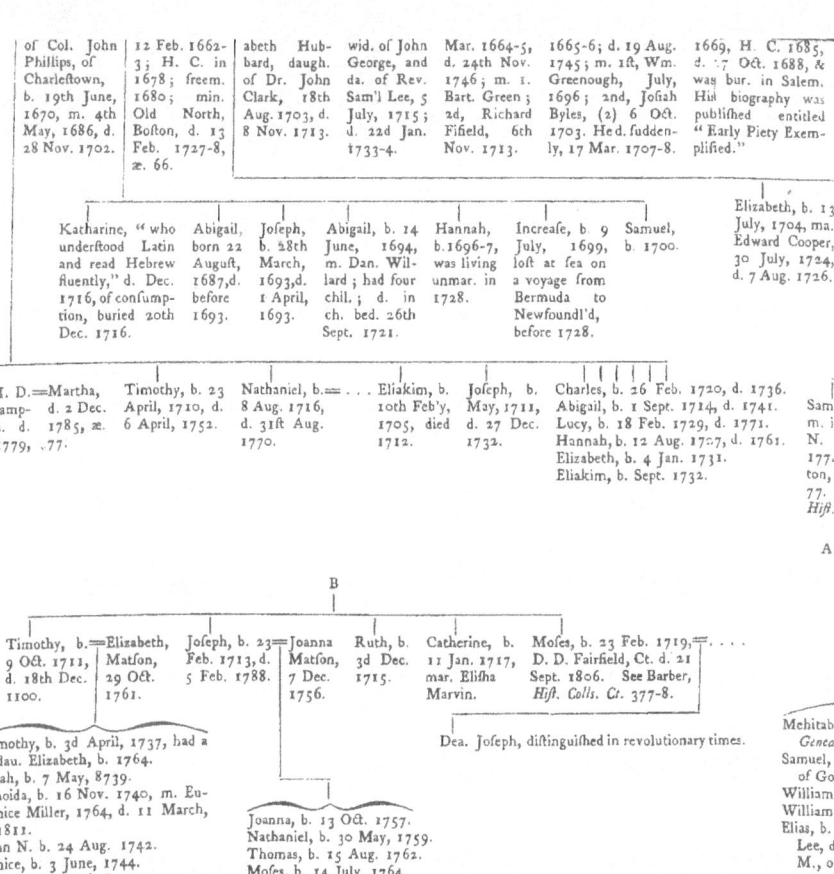

1671, d. ☙ Nov. 1746; m. Rev. Nehemiah Walter, of Roxbury, who d. 17 Sept. 1750, and was succeeded by his son, ord. 1718.	1674; H. C. 1690; minister at Witney, Oxfordshire, England, having accompanied his father there in 1688. Had 7 daus. all m. but one.	Ap. 1677, had 2 husbands, Newcomb Blake, & Rev. John White, of Gloucester, Mass.	30th May, 1680, d. 2d Dec. 1706, mar. John Oliver, 28th Jan. 1697.	Sept. 1682, d. 11 June, 1683. Jerusha, b. 16 April, 1684; m. Peter Oliver, 8 Mar. 1709-10, d. 20 Dec. 1710.	Joseph, b. 15 March, 1715. Eleazer, b. 17 Nov. 1716, m. Ann Waterman, 5 Nov. 1741. (3) Phebe, b. 15 March, 1718-19, m. Andrew Sill, 19 June, 1744. John, b. 13 July, 1721, m. Marc Higgins, 13 June, 1745. Jerusha, b. 11 Feb. 1725-6, m. Daniel Shipman. Samuel, b. 10 Nov. 1728, d. Oct. 1739. Benjamin, b. 19 Sept. 1732, set. i Whately, Mass., m. Irene Parsons, 16 Aug. 1753. Ann, b. 22 Sept. 1733. Simeon, b. 21 Feb. 1736, d. 2 Feb. 1736.

Samuel, b. 30 Oct. 1706; H. C. 1723; min. in Boston, d. 27 June, 1785, æ. 79. Had the degree of D. D., and published a life of his father, and many other works.	=Hannah, d. of Thos. Hutchinson, and sist. of Gov. Thos. Hutchinson, 23 Aug. 1733, d. 31st Aug. 1781.	Nathaniel, b. 16 May, 1707, d. 24th Nov. 1709.	Jerusha, b. April, 1711, d. November, 1713.	Eleazer, and Martha, twins, b. 1713, d. Nov. same yr.

..l, b. 1736,=Margaret, da. Benj. Hampton, H., July, d. in Boston, 1813, æ. ab. See Brief ..., 18.	and Margaret Gerrish, b. 16 April, 1748, d. Salem, 25 Feb. 1842, a. 96.	Thomas, bapt. 13 Aug. 1738, a surgeon in the army against Canada, d. at Halifax, 8 Dec. 1762.	Elizabeth, d. 30 Jun. 1788, a. 48.	Increase, at the taking of the Havana, d. there, Mar. 1763, ag'd ab. 22.	Sarah, m. Rev. W. Shaw of Marshfield, d. 30 Mar. 1788, s. p.	Abigail, d. unm. 1780.	Hannah, b. 1752, son of Rev. Josiah Taunton, Mass. and 1829, buried at Co Boston. She was au Rights of Woman, works still in MS. descendants of D Mather are in this li...

only child stillborn.

C

Richard, b. 22nd Dec. 1712.	=Deborah Ely, 18th May, 1742.	Mary, b. 14 Nov. 1715.	Deborah, b. 11 Jan. 1718, m. Benj. Marvin, 11 Nov. 1742, d. 21 Jan. 1775.	Mehitable, b. 28 Dec. 1723, d. unm. 1741.	Lucy, b. 18 Dec. 1720, m. Nathaniel Peck, 24 May, 1744, at Lyme, Ct.

..., b. 7 March, 1743, m. Gen. Samuel H. Parsons. See ...gical Register, vol. I, p. 273.
. 22 Feb. 1745, m. Lois, dau. of Thomas Griswold, son . Mathew G. She died in Lyme, 17 Nov. 1804.
b. 15 Sept. 1746, d. 24 Sept. 1746.
b. 21 Nov. 1741, m. Rhoda Marvin, 1 May, 1768.
n E. Haddam, 10 Feb. 1750, m. Lucinda, da. of Abner at Lyme, Ct. 30 Aug. 1788. His son, Capt. Andrew New London, is father of Hon. J. P. C. MATHER, of New London, in 1848.
b. 3 Oct. 1752, m. Ezra Lee.
5 Feb. 1755, d. 4 June, same year.
7 April, 1756, d. 10 Nov. 1758.
b. 1 Sept. 1758, m. Elizabeth, dau. of Richard Wait.
31 March, 1760, m. William Champlin, 13 Jan. 1780.
13 March, 1763.
b. 4 July, 1765, m. Eunice, da. of Dr. Caulkins.

(2) Josiah Byles was the father of the Rev. Mather Byles of Boston, well remembered for his wit and puns, by the last generation.

(3) This Eleazer had a son Eleazer, who, by Frances, dau. of Nathan Williams, was father of the late William Williams Mather of Columbus, O., an eminent scholar, formerly a Professor in the University of Louisiana. See *N. E. Hist. & Gen. Reg.* vol. XIII, 280.

www.ingramcontent.com/pod-product-compliance
Lightning Source LLC
Chambersburg PA
CBHW071424150426
43191CB00008B/1032